BEYOND
ACADIA

EXPLORING THE BOLD COAST
OF DOWN EAST MAINE

Rich Bard

Down East Books

Camden, Maine
Guilford, Connecticut

For Rebecca—my wife, partner, and trail guide.
I am never lost with you.

Down East Books

An imprint of The Rowman & Littlefield Publishing Group, Inc.
4501 Forbes Blvd., Ste. 200
Lanham, MD 20706
www.rowman.com

Distributed by NATIONAL BOOK NETWORK

Copyright © 2019 by Rich Bard
All photos by Rich Bard
Maps by Natalia Mariana Denkiewicz

British Library Cataloguing in Publication Information available

Library of Congress Cataloging-in-Publication Data

Names: Bard, Rich, author.
Title: Beyond Acadia : exploring the Bold Coast of Down East Maine / Rich
   Bard.
Description: Camden, Maine : Down East Books, an imprint of The Rowman &
   Littlefield Publishing Group, Inc., [2019] | Includes index.
Identifiers: LCCN 2019001292 (print) | LCCN 2019005941 (ebook) | ISBN
   9781608936724 (Electronic) | ISBN 9781608936717 (pbk. : alk. paper)
Subjects: LCSH: Maine—Description and travel. | Maine—Guidebooks. |
   Atlantic Coast (Me.)—Description and travel. | Atlantic Coast
   (Me.)—Guidebooks.
Classification: LCC F17.3 (ebook) | LCC F17.3 .B37 2019 (print) | DDC
   917.4104—dc23
LC record available at https://lccn.loc.gov/2019001292

Printed in the United States of America

The authors and Rowman & Littlefield assume no liability for accidents happening to, or injuries sustained by, readers who engage in the activities described in this book.

Contents

Introduction

Are you looking for a place to explore that has incredible natural beauty but hasn't been turned into a tourist trap? Are you wishing you could hike some trails where the animal prints outnumber the boot prints? Do you want to experience "the real Maine" without the traffic, chain stores, and expensive boutiques of most of coastal Maine? If so, you've picked up the right book. Come explore *Beyond Acadia*!

In 2002, I was among the more than two and half million visitors to Acadia National Park when I came to Maine on vacation (today that number is closer to four million). Like many, I enjoyed the majestic Mount Desert Island and the picture-postcard town of Bar Harbor. I appreciated the rugged coast, distant views, and picturesque lakes. However, I waited in traffic for hours, shared every trail with hordes of strangers, and pitched my tent in a campground that was more like an RV city. One day, spreading a map out on the hood of my car, I traced my finger from New York, where my vacation had begun, up the coast of Massachusetts, New Hampshire, and Maine to Mount Desert Island and Acadia National Park. My finger paused there and then continued along the coast toward Canada. I wondered what I might have found if I had driven that final hundred miles. If only I knew then what I have since learned so well. This roughly fifteen-hundred-square-mile area is completely unlike the rest of the New England coast, precisely because most people stop driving when they get to Acadia—as I did.

In 2004, I took a job as a wildlife biologist with the State of Maine and found myself living smack dab in the middle of the very area I had been intrigued by two years earlier. Little did I know that not only would I fall deeply in love with the wild places of the region, but over many years I would also become so intimately connected to this unique place that it would be more familiar to me than the Catskill Mountains where I was born and raised. The trees and trails, the waters and wildlife, the sounds and smells of the Bold Coast are my world, but it would be selfish to keep the beauty I discovered all to myself! I was fortunate to have so many experiences that helped me know this region like the back of my hand. For example, in my first few years as a biologist, bald eagles were still listed as an endangered species. I spent countless hours flying over every inch of this region at low altitude in a small Cessna airplane, searching the miles and miles of ocean, river, and lake shorelines for eagles' nests to count the number of eggs or chicks and track the population as it recovered. Other surveys I did over the years added to my love for and knowledge of this area. I studied shorebirds, ducks, frogs, and rare wildlife, and I even measured the depth of the snow every week of winter for eleven years.

I also got to know the people and the back roads, as every November I drove thousands of miles searching out successful deer hunters to measure and take samples from their deer. On a daily basis I pored over maps of the area, helping people who called me for anything from a nuisance skunk to concerns over major industrial

Quiet beauty is everywhere in Down East Maine.

developments. I learned quickly that people really love to talk about their favorite places to hike, birdwatch, photograph nature, and so on, and I always took the opportunity to learn something new.

It was also as a wildlife biologist that I first became involved with Cobscook Trails, a group that includes all of the conservation organizations working in Cobscook Bay and the Bold Coast. The Cobscook Trails Guide, which is now a free brochure available around the region, is a great way to get to see what all of the various organizations are working on. For me, being a member of the Steering Committee for almost fifteen years kept me up to date on any new developments of places to hike or explore.

These were beautiful times, but this wilderness paradise I had found was in danger. Over many years a number of large industrial projects have come a hair's breadth from changing the character of some of the most special places in the region, including some that are highlighted in this book. In the mid-2000s there was a flurry of proposals to build liquefied natural gas (LNG) import terminals around Cobscook Bay. Activists from a group called Save Passamaquoddy Bay tirelessly fought the proposals, dragging them out for years. I was the lead reviewer of the applications for these terminals for the Department of Inland Fisheries and Wildlife, and I did my best to ensure that, if approved, the impacts on our birds, wildlife, and scenic beauty would be minimized. Ultimately, fracking became a much more efficient way to get LNG than importing it, despite the horrible pollution that results, so the proposals were finally abandoned. These brushes with industry left me treasuring the quiet beauty of the Bold Coast all the more.

Times change, and in 2014 I accepted a position as executive director of Downeast Coastal Conservancy, the land trust that protects open space and promotes public access to nature in nearly the entire region featured in *Beyond Acadia*. Moreover, the office of Downeast Coastal Conservancy served as a de facto tourist information center. Visitors to the region often stopped in to ask us about hiking trails and ended up getting all kinds of other information that you will find in *Beyond Acadia*, including places to eat, camp, shop, and paddle. I have dished out this information hundreds of times and have been fortunate to receive feedback that my advice helped visitors have the perfect Maine experience.

While working for Downeast Coastal Conservancy, I learned how passionately people care for the natural areas that have been conserved. Each preserve, park, Wildlife Management Area, and National Wildlife Refuge has people who love and help care for it. Many of the trails that you'll walk on the Bold Coast were built by volunteers, sometimes with the help or advice of professionals, but often it was just a group of people who saw the need for a trail on a piece of land that had been conserved.

In the fifteen years since I first contemplated what was in that mysterious region beyond Acadia, there has been an explosion of local food, breweries, wineries, hiking trails, art galleries, restaurants, lodging, and tours. As the local economy shifts from one that is primarily based around extraction of natural resources to one that caters to the active and adventurous tourists who are flocking to Maine, the time is right to begin your explorations east of Ellsworth.

How to Use This Book

This book is largely the product of my own experience and knowledge of the region. As such, it has biases that reflect my own opinions and ways of appreciating the world. It certainly doesn't contain everything there is to do in the region. I could probably fill another book this size if I really dug deep and tried to include everything. Some omissions are intentional; if I felt that something wasn't significant enough compared with what is included in the book, or, for example, if a hiking trail simply can't handle more people, I chose to not mention it here. I hope you find some of these places when you're out and about, because they are some of the most special. Some omissions will be unintentional, so I offer apologies to any of my friends or neighbors whose favorite event or destination was forgotten.

Everyone will come to this book from a different place. You may be daydreaming about a someday adventure in far eastern Maine without a specific plan. You may have plans to be here, or in nearby Acadia National Park, and want to make some specific plans to make sure your experience is as rich as it can be. You may already be in Acadia National Park on vacation and, like me, want your wilderness experience to include more wild and fewer people. No worries. *Beyond Acadia* has the information you'll need to get the most from your Down East Maine adventure!

I suggest that you look at a visit to this region as just that—come to see the region rather than just one town or one event. It only takes an hour or so to get from one end to the other, so think broadly and maybe organize a day around a particular town or hiking trail, but watch for interesting things to see or do anywhere in the area.

The first few chapters of the book are introductory information to ground you in the geology, ecology, climate, and human history of the region. No visit to this special place is complete if you don't at least take in something of all of these subjects.

Following this are chapters that give more broad context, including overall information sources, nearby attractions that could bring you within striking distance of the Bold Coast, descriptions of the main villages in the region, and a list of many of the important conservation organizations that have worked tirelessly to ensure that the most amazing, most special places will be available to everyone far into the future.

The features in the chapters that follow are arranged in a general order going from the southwest of the region to the northeast, as you'd encounter them if you drove north on Route 1 (which really goes northeast and even east in this area). If you were sailing, you would be moving downwind and heading easterly—thus, Down East!

Then we get down to business with lists of things to do and places to go. I combined **Festivals and Seasonal Events** to give you a year-long summary of the weather, the natural progression of the year, and annual gatherings, many of which celebrate the natural world.

The ripening and harvest of the blueberry crop is a major annual event.

The **View!** chapter includes things to see, from beautiful destinations to lighthouses to boat tours.

Do! is for those looking to do something active other than paddling and hiking, which are the biggest draws to the region. This section includes information about the Down East Sunrise Trail, bicycling, running, swimming, all-terrain vehicles, horseback riding, and winter fun.

Paddle! includes tips and guidance for setting off on salt water, flat water (lakes), and rivers. It also includes a listing of the guides and outfitters who can take you out on the water.

Hike! is the largest section of the book and includes twenty-nine of my favorite hikes in the area. Some are classics and some are my little secrets. At the end of this section is a list of the major conservation organizations that have protected these places and keep them available for public use.

The **Camp!** chapter is a list of places to pitch your tent, park your RV, rent a glamping tent, or even stay in a rustic cabin.

The **Eat!** chapter includes a sampling of options to find local food and descriptions of just a few of the many restaurants.

Shopping is admittedly a thin section. We don't have a lot of shopping here, but it does tend to be interesting stuff you won't want to miss.

Finally, the **Culture** chapter lists live music, workshops, and continuing education that are available throughout the year.

Where to Find Information

For many of the sites described in this book, access to the Internet on a phone or computer is very useful. I've tried to provide relevant online resources wherever I could. Sometimes there is no substitute for talking with someone knowledgeable about the area or having a paper brochure or booklet to peruse. If you're driving here on Interstate 95, as most people do, you can pull in to one of several rest stops with visitor information. A number of brochures are available for features listed in this book as well as others. Don't expect the attendants at the visitor desk to have any firsthand knowledge of the Bold Coast region. For most Mainers, this area may as well be a blank spot on the map.

Once you are here, there are relatively few official visitor information sources. In Milbridge, at 19 Maine Street, the DownEast Acadia Regional Tourism office provides brochures and good firsthand experience across the region. Hours can be irregular, so call ahead if you're making a special trip to get brochures. The Machias Area Chamber of Commerce in Machias is probably the largest collection of brochures and information about the region. The Chamber is located at 11 Maine Street in the historic and newly restored train station that served Machias for more than a century. Staff are very knowledgeable about the region.

The DownEast Acadia Regional Tourism office maintains the best overall website dedicated to things to do in this region, including many not covered in this book. Visit downeastacadia.com.

About the Region

The Natural World

Whether you are a visitor or a resident of the Bold Coast, it is highly likely that the natural world is your reason for being here. The mystique of this area comes from a combination of the extreme tides (the largest in the continental United States); the dramatic cliffs that plunge into the North Atlantic; the deep, dark forest, dotted with marshes, ponds, and lakes; and the abundant wildlife and birds that live here. Despite the primeval feeling, this is actually a relatively new environment.

The coast of Maine has been a dynamic place, with massive changes occurring since being covered with at least 1.5 miles of ice twenty-five thousand years ago. The ice compressed the earth's crust, making the surface of the earth five hundred feet lower than it is today. As the glacier melted, around twenty-one thousand years ago, the Bold Coast region was flooded by the Atlantic Ocean. Eventually the earth's crust rebounded from the glacial weight and reached roughly the current level around three thousand years ago. It was only then that the geophysical features assumed their current configuration. The oldest living trees in the world are about five thousand years old, so an entire ecosystem that has developed in only three thousand years can reasonably be called young.

Many physical features of the region, both prominent and more subtle, were created by the action of the glaciers, their melting, or the shallow sea that followed them. The Maine Ice Age Trail is a wonderful information source for observing this evidence of the creation of Maine. You can find more information at iceagetrail.umaine.edu.

The immense pressures that created the bedrock are evident in the slanted, crooked, and jagged shorelines.

The soils, formed from inorganic minerals deposited by the glaciers, are highly acidic and not very fertile—factors that have a great influence on which plants thrive here and where. In places with the poorest fertility with sandy, well-drained soils, lowbush blueberry plants are able to outcompete nearly every other species, resulting in the vast blueberry barrens dotting the region. Similarly, poorly fertile regions that do not drain water well form acidic bogs with their unique plants, like the carnivorous sundews and pitcher plants that gain their nutrients from insects that they capture and digest. In places with more soil fertility, more complex forests can take root.

At this northern latitude, most ecosystems are much simpler than they are farther south. Think of a tropical rainforest that may have many hundreds of plant species on each acre of land. By comparison, the Bold Coast may have a few dozen (perhaps up to a hundred) in some places.

In the western and southern parts of the region, we find the northern fringe of the typical New England deciduous forest, also called a northern hardwood forest. This forest is dominated by maple, oak, birch, and beech, along with some areas of spruce, pine, and fir trees. As you travel east and north toward the Canadian border, the proportions of the various species reverse until you reach the boreal spruce-fir forest, which includes occasional stands of maples, oaks, and others. Wetter areas may have virtually no trees except white cedar. The colder climate favors evergreen trees that keep their needles all year long and can photosynthesize and grow at any time of year, rather than as few as five to six months for some deciduous trees.

Like nearly all of New England, vast areas of this region were once completely bare of trees, either for farmland or villages or simply because the demand for wood

The boreal spruce-fir forest often has a soft, spongy forest floor that feels like you're walking on thick carpet.

for ships, buildings, heating, and, later, paper, resulted in clear-cutting the forest. Today the Bold Coast region is a patchwork of human-dominated cleared land, forests that are heavily managed by people, forests that are slowly maturing and naturalizing, and old stands that have been unmanaged for hundreds of years. The majority of the hiking trails and other natural areas described in *Beyond Acadia* fall into the latter two categories. They may have some history of being logged or even farmed, but they are slowly returning to a fully natural state. There are some exceptions, particularly fields that are remnants from the region's agricultural past and continue to be mowed to maintain the diversity of plants and animals that they add to the region.

This mosaic of environments, from heavily disturbed to pristine, echoes the natural history of the region before European colonization. With no human intervention, purely natural disturbances include forest fires, disease, clearing by beavers, ice storms, and hurricanes, which result in patches of forest that are "set back" in their development toward an old-growth mature forest. After the disturbance, the slow but relentless march toward old growth continues. Across the landscape, areas are at various points in the timeline from cleared land to early forest to mature forest.

For most of the time that this region has been habitable by plants and animals, humans have lived here and had effects on the environment. Although the native Wabanaki people (the group of tribes that includes the local Passamaquoddy and Penobscot) are not thought to have cultivated land and grown crops, they nevertheless played an active role in shaping the environment around them.

Night Sky

Take a look at a satellite photo of North America at night and you can clearly find the major cities. Places like Boston, New York, and Los Angeles glow brightly with all of the ambient light from streetlights, cars, and businesses. You might be lucky to see a handful of stars on a clear and moonless night. Between the cities, the photos have a kind of hazy brilliance that indicate suburbs and other places that are less affected by light pollution than cities. You can see lots of stars here, and you might even feel like you can see all of them—until you arrive in a place like Down East Maine.

On the night sky maps, Washington County is essentially a dark spot with very little light pollution. There is almost no area east of the Mississippi River with so little light pollution; only the Everglades in Florida, the Outer Banks of North Carolina, and Adirondack Park in upstate New York are similar pockets of darkness. In fact, experts have calculated that 99 percent of the population of the United States and Europe are virtually unable to see the Milky Way galaxy! Fortunately, on cloudless nights in this region, the broad, white swath of densely packed stars that form the center of our galaxy arcs across the sky with a spectacular and truly humbling radiance. In our dense forest it can be hard to find a place where the sky isn't partially obstructed by trees, but taking in the full impact of the Down East Maine night sky is worth the effort. If all else fails, you can go almost anywhere on the coast for at least a 180-degree view.

When you are here and standing outside under the vivid night sky with your jaw on the ground because you don't remember ever seeing so many stars, consider the millennia that passed before electric lights and even before fire, when this view inspired people to learn to navigate by the stars and create stories that became cosmologies that became religions. Then think of what we're losing when we can't properly see the night sky.

The northern lights, or aurora borealis, are a spectacle usually associated with the Arctic, but, in fact, it is often visible in Maine. Although the phenomenon can happen at any time of year, it is much more likely to be noticed in the winter due to the simple fact that people are awake for more of the dark hours in the winter, when there are as few as nine hours of daylight. The aurora is often subtle here and requires careful observation. Stand somewhere with a clear view of the northern sky and observe with a soft focus, allowing your peripheral vision to kick in and give you a wider view. You might detect subtle changes in the sky, with a faint green, blue, or sometimes white gauzy haze that moves around slowly. This is the aurora. It can also be dramatic and unmissable, with brilliant sheets of color moving across the sky, but it is much more common to see the subtler version.

Climate

The climate of the Down East region can be hard to pin down with a span of easily more than one hundred degrees in the course of a year. Every season has its share of variation in temperatures and precipitation. As the saying goes, "If you don't like the weather, just wait a minute." The seasons in this section are divided to approximate the official solar start and end of each season. For example, winter technically begins on or near December 21. Here, I count January as the beginning of winter.

Winters here might be expected to be extraordinarily harsh given the northern latitude, but being next to the ocean tempers both the length and the severity of the occasional cold snaps. Plenty of places that are farther south than this region have consistently harsher winters. Daytime high temperatures in December are around thirty-four degrees (all data in this section are courtesy of National Oceanic and Atmospheric Administration), with a nighttime low of seventeen degrees. January is statistically the coldest month, with an average daytime high of twenty-seven degrees and a low of just nine degrees. In my experience, however, there is often a January thaw, where warm temperatures cause most of the snow to melt, and a February cold snap, when we may suffer with a week or two of below-zero temperatures for days, even dipping down to double digits below zero. So be ready for anything if you visit in the winter.

Spring comes in late April or early May, with the greening grass followed by the leaves on the trees. All the while birds are arriving from their southern wintering grounds for the warm season. High temperatures in April often reach fifty-one degrees, with a low of thirty-one degrees. By late June, highs are around seventy-one degrees and the average low is fifty-one degrees. Many Mainers consider this ideal weather—warm enough for short sleeves during the day and cold enough for extra blankets at night. It is not unheard of to have to fire up the woodstove once or twice in early to mid-June before the temperatures stabilize.

Summers in Down East Maine are known for crystal-clear, blue-sky days, interspersed with days when thick fog never lifts. With more than fifteen hours of sunlight around the summer solstice, you can pack a lot of activity into a Maine summer day, which is more than an hour longer than in Florida. July's highs average seventy-seven degrees, with a low of fifty-seven degrees, and September's average range is sixty-nine to forty-nine degrees.

Autumn begins the gradual descent into winter with temperatures in October of fifty-seven to twenty-eight degrees, and ends in December with temperatures of thirty-four to seventeen degrees. The cascade of fall colors begins by mid-September or even earlier. Fall is characterized by strings of sunny days broken up by high winds that can sometimes strip the trees of their leaves prematurely.

History and People

Any discussion of the people of the region covered by *Beyond Acadia* must begin, of course, with the people who lived here before Western colonization. The Passamaquoddy occupied most of the region, though the western fringes were likely also used by the Penobscot. The people migrated each year, spending the summers in large groups near the ocean and building up larders of fish (particularly pollack), hunting game in the forests, and gathering plants for food. As winter approached, the large bands would break up into family groups and set off to the inland forests, where they spent the winter hunting. I should note that this is not *my* history to tell and I don't presume to know enough to do it justice. For more information about Passamaquoddy people and their history, go to wabanaki.com, the website of the Pleasant Point Reservation.

After Europeans came to the area, the native people's culture and habits were disrupted by new concepts of land ownership and the wars between far-off countries that were fought on these shores, including the French and Indian War. The Passamaquoddy and Penobscot tribes survived this period and today live primarily on three small reservations or on other land that is owned by the tribes. Their names for natural features are commonly used to this day. *Machias*, *Cobscook*, and *Narraguagus*, among others, are all native words that you'll find in this book and in this region.

Europeans may have first arrived before recorded history. Relatively new evidence is giving hints that Vikings may have temporarily settled in nearby New Brunswick, Canada, so it is reasonable to assume they also explored this area. Some interesting research is planned for a site in far eastern Maine that shows some indication that it could be a Viking site.

The first modern Europeans to reach the shores of what is now Washington or Hancock County arrived in 1525. These sailors from the Spanish Empire mapped the shoreline of large areas of Maine, but they did not establish settlements. The first settlement, tragic as it was, was built in 1604, when Samuel de Champlain landed at St. Croix Island, just to the north of the region beyond Acadia. This small group was decimated when half of the people wintering on the island died of scurvy, or vitamin C deficiency, a condition easily cured by drinking tea made from pine needles, among many other remedies unknown to the settlers.

A series of wars fought by colonists from across the sea kept the region unstable enough to prevent permanent white settlements in this area. It wasn't until after the French and Indian War that a lasting peace (at least for a while, relatively speaking) allowed European pioneers to move into the region, beginning around 1760.

The first settlers, in places like Machias, Jonesboro, and Milbridge, began logging the seemingly unending forests. Transportation around the region was completely by boat, as no roads or railroads had penetrated the region. The virgin forest produced enormous tall and straight white pines, all of which were claimed by the king of England for masts for his royal navy.

Over time a very lucrative fishing industry evolved in towns like Jonesport, Lubec, and Eastport. Cod and eventually sardines were targeted and fished until the stocks were decimated. Fortunes were made building sardine canneries, only to be wiped away when the fish disappeared. The hulking carcasses of sardine canneries littered the shores of Eastport and Lubec for many years. They have virtually all been either torn down or converted to other uses. One remaining building, part of the McCurdy Smokehouse Museum in Lubec, recently floated away on the tide during a strong "'nor'easter," to the dismay of many residents who were actively trying to preserve it.

Today it is hard to imagine the bustling streets of Machias and Lubec when they were in their heyday as centers of economic activity. From a low point in the mid- to late 1900s, the economies of the area are gradually improving, led by the lobster fishing industry. As the climate is changing around us, lobsters are slowly migrating north to stay in their preferred cold water. The once-thriving lobster fishery in New York to Massachusetts has all but disappeared, leaving Maine as the primary source of the world's lobster, followed closely by New Brunswick, Canada.

Lobster is the most famous fishery these days, but it must be mentioned that a lot of people make their living harvesting all kinds of creatures from the sea. Halibut, pollack, herring, clams, crab, scallops, and urchins are probably the most well known of these.

Digging clams is a lucrative but backbreaking way to make a living.

Lobster traps that are lost can remain in the ocean for decades.

Along with the booming lobster and other fishing industries, logging has continued as a source of income for many, although technological advances now let one person do the work of a whole crew of people and a team of horses. For many locals, a year's income is still made by patching together various types of seasonal work. This leaves the worker as an independent businessperson in a largely underground economy. From digging clams and bloodworms to harvesting blueberries to making holiday wreaths and a dozen other jobs in between, someone with a strong back and good health can earn enough money to modestly support a family.

More recently, there has been a move to create a new economy, based on tourism to the area. Acadia National Park, for instance, has long been a draw for visitors who travel up the coast, making Bar Harbor a successful example of what can happen by highlighting nature-based tourism. Unfortunately, the Bold Coast seemed a little too far from the urban centers to entice visitors to venture farther Down East. In recent decades, road improvements, more comfortable and reliable cars, and more efficient engines have made the extra distance seem less daunting. Beginning in the 1960s, a group of people recognized the amazing natural beauty of the Bold Coast and worried about it all being bought up by wealthy people who would control large areas and prevent the public from accessing the coast. Today nearly 17 percent of the area of Washington County is permanently conserved in one form or another, and most of that guarantees public access. This was accomplished by a network of nonprofit land trusts and the state and federal governments (see page 261). These organizations, though they probably didn't realize it at the time, helped create the infrastructure to support a shift to a tourism-based economy. This, along with the recent explosion of entrepreneurs providing an array of services, means all the pieces are in place to allow you to create a unique adventure beyond Acadia.

It would be disingenuous to imply that everyone is on board with land conservation and the move to a tourism economy. Those with deep roots in the area, with many exceptions, tend to resent the intrusion of wealthy elites "from away" (as non-natives are referred to). The stereotype of a tourist here is someone who is loud and rude, with brightly colored synthetic clothing, driving a Subaru with a bike rack on the tailgate and a couple of expensive sea kayaks on the roof. Fortunately, over the past several years, a trickle of tourism has led to an improvement in locals' perceptions of those who come to visit or even live in the region.

For the tourist or new resident, the world of the locals is on display but can be unreachable without dedicating a very long time to build trust. Fifteen years ago it was more common than not to get a friendly wave over the steering wheel if you met an oncoming car on a side road. The assumption was that the two drivers probably knew each other, and even if they didn't, they probably had some connection since they were on the same back road together. I can only assume that the influx of strangers over the past decade or so is what led to the gradual disappearance of this quaint and welcoming practice.

As a visitor here, it is prudent to know something about the local culture and local economy, to try to blend in and not bring offense to lifelong residents. You are safe here, so be yourself and be open to experiencing a bit of the old Bold Coast.

Critters

Wildlife

The physical environment and plants that live here provide the structure for the various animals that inhabit Down East Maine, from the ocean to freshwater wetlands to forests and even alpine mountaintops. It is beyond the scope of this book to describe every animal you may see on your visit here, but a few of the iconic species are described in some detail, with a few rare animals and even some that you may never have heard of.

Lobster—Nothing, except perhaps a moose, is as emblematic of Maine as the lobster. It wasn't always this way. Down East Maine used to be the fringe of lobster habitat, but warming oceans have caused a slow march northward up the Maine coast toward Canada, leaving the formerly strong lobster fisheries in New York and southern New England behind. The lobster fishery has been a spark that reignited the economy of Down East Maine after the collapse of the sardine fishery.

One aspect of this economic boost for the region is the lack of consolidation in the lobster industry. Briefly, this means that virtually every lobster boat out on the water is being operated by its owner, who stands to gain or lose money depending not only on the success of his or her traps but also on the sustainable management of the lobster fishery. By contrast, most fisheries today are dominated by large corporations that own fleets of boats and hire the fishers. Short-term riches for corporate shareholders have always and will continue to result in the collapse of the fisheries involved.

Lobster fishers sure love "mud bugs."

One tip for summertime visitors eating lobster is to watch for "shedders," also known as soft-shell lobster. As the ocean warms in early summer, lobsters begin to molt their shells, which enables them to grow. When they emerge from their old shells, the soft shells that are exposed take a while to harden to fully protect the lobster. Lobsters that are caught in traps during this transitional period are called shedders. These lobsters can't be shipped very easily without dying in transit, so people who live outside the lobster zone aren't familiar with them. Many locals strongly prefer to eat lobster during shedder season. The meat is sweeter and tastier, and it is so much easier to crack the shells. Most people, and even children, can use their bare hands to open a shedder, whereas hard-shell lobsters require special tools similar to nut crackers. Plus, the price of shedders is lower than a hard-shell lobster, because they can't be shipped, resulting in lower demand for them. The downside of eating shedders is that because the new shell is larger than the lobster needs (to accommodate growth), you may open a nice-size lobster and find it filled with a higher percentage of water relative to the meat. Order a size larger than you would otherwise and enjoy.

You can get a taste (pun intended) of lobstering by booking a cruise aboard one of the tour boats that doubles as a lobster boat. You'll get a firsthand look at lobstering and what life is like making your living on the sea (see page 111). If this isn't possible, the next best thing is to get your lobsters right off the boat. Many towns have a lobster wharf where the boats sell lobsters to distributors, and you can buy yours right there at a much better price than you'd get ordering at a restaurant or grocery store. Of course, this means you'll have to cook the lobsters yourself, which isn't for everyone. Some grocery stores will steam your lobsters for free if you buy them live at the store. This is still a better deal than ordering from a restaurant. Although you can't beat the charm of eating a lobster dinner (including clams and corn on the cob) outside with a view of the sea and a red checkerboard tablecloth!

Whales—The best time to see whales off the Bold Coast is from April to October, when they travel north to this region to feed in the cold, rich waters. Most species tend to breed and rear their young in more southerly waters, but the food is not nearly as abundant, so they come to the North Atlantic and Bay of Fundy to pack on the pounds. Whales are not often seen from the Maine shore, though sightings do happen from time to time. Campobello Island, just across the border into Canada, frequently sees whales from the southern tip of the island (see page 296). Most people take whale-watching trips to view these intriguing species (see page 111).

The more common species that you might see on a whale-watching trip include finback, minke, pilot, and humpback whales, along with harbor porpoises and Atlantic white-sided dolphins. Right whales, sperm whales, and even orcas (killer whales) are occasionally seen out on the open water.

Weasel family—The family of species known as mustelids is one of the more diverse groups in this region, and many people may not know about most of these secretive and interesting creatures. The family includes river otters, mink, weasels, fishers (or fisher cats), marten, and skunks—all found in this region. Years ago the list would have included sea mink, a now extinct species that lived on islands and near the ocean. Other well-known mustelids are wolverines, sea otters, and badgers. Domestic ferrets are also mustelids. Other than skunks, it is quite rare to see any of these animals. I have frequently found tracks of them all while out snowshoeing in the winter, but only a handful of times have I seen a live otter, mink, or weasel, and never the other species.

River otters and mink could reasonably be called aquatic mammals. They are rarely found far from water and require it to mate and bear young. Martens seem to be among the rarest of this group in the Bold Coast, and they are more frequently seen farther north. Fishers are perhaps the most intriguing of this group, at least for me. They are a ferocious predator that is larger than a housecat. They course across the forested landscape, inspecting every hole in the ground or a tree, climbing over, under, and around every downed tree or other feature where prey could be hiding. Fishers are the only animals that routinely kill porcupines. They bite the nose of the porcupine until the porcupine flips over onto its back, exposing the stomach, the only part of its body not covered in quills. The fisher can then make quick work of the now defenseless porcupine. To avoid being pricked by quills while eating, fishers have a way of turning the porcupine's skin inside out. When I was a wildlife biologist, I had more than one phone call from someone who thought aliens had turned a porcupine inside out!

Beaver—One of the easiest animals to find is the beaver. You can't always actually see them, but their handiwork in the form of dams and lodges are everywhere around the region. Almost every freshwater lake, pond, river, and marsh will have at least one active beaver lodge, unless the area is kept free of the animals by regularly trapping them. The telltale dome-shaped lodges are easy to spot along the shores or out in the water. The lodges persist for many years even if they are abandoned, but there are clues to tell you whether the lodge is being actively used—if you can get close. Look for fresh sticks (still brown rather than dried-out gray) or mud on the dome. If you see a lot of bushy growth on the lodge, it is probably empty, as residents tend to keep the shrubs well trimmed. The lodge is separate and sometimes far away from a dam that creates the beaver pond.

If you want to see an actual beaver, you'll probably have to be around right at dusk or dawn. It is pretty easy because you know that they are in their lodges during the day, so just sit quietly (or float in a canoe or kayak) nearby and wait for a beaver to surface close to the lodge. Alternatively, you can stake out a beaver dam, knowing that one of the first things a beaver will do after leaving its lodge is check the dam for leaks. If they detect you, they'll slap their tail on the water to scare you, and then dive and swim to another location to see whether you're still there.

For a small animal, beavers have had an outsize effect on life in New England and probably everywhere they were once abundant. They are one of the only animals other than humans that creates entirely new ecosystems. Before European colonization, beavers were one of the primary disturbance factors of the northern forest, as already described. The cycle that a beaver flowage (or pond) goes through creates a variety of habitats and benefits nearly all species at one point or another.

One- or two-year-old beavers set off from their parents' lodge to find their own body of water to occupy. They will look for an empty lodge with adequate food, but in some cases they will pair with a beaver of the opposite sex and settle along a stream in the middle of the woods. These beavers are watching for some qualities that we will never quite understand—something about the lay of the land and its suitability for damming combined with enough food nearby. The beavers will set to work damming the stream and flooding the forest. They build the dam higher and wider as the water rises until it is deep enough for them to build their lodge. Once the lodge is built, they will begin to cache their food reserves for the coming winter. They harvest branches of aspen, birch, and maple trees, among others, both for food and to build their dams and lodges. Branches that don't get eaten right away get stuck into the mud at the bottom of the pond to keep it safe and preserved. When winter sets in and the pond freezes over, the beavers are safe and protected, with access to their food. The winter world of a beaver is hard for us to comprehend. If the pond freezes over completely, the family of beavers (young from the previous year generally stick around for a year or more) is limited to either the small, dark lodge interior or under water in the pond. They won't see the sky or stand on land or even breathe air outside the lodge for months if the winter is very cold.

Meanwhile, the forest that has been flooded will begin to die. Any trees that are good for food or dam building may be chopped down, but the rest will stay standing in the water. These standing trees can remain for decades, becoming a perch or nest site for a variety of birds. Beaver ponds provide homes for lots of wildlife, including otters, ducks, ospreys, eagles, and fish, and produce food for many others. When beavers were plentiful across the landscape, wildlife of all kinds thrived as a result. When the beaver population was decimated from the fur trade, deforestation, and relentless road development, thousands of ponds drained, and animals that depend on this dynamic and ever-changing ecosystem also suffered great losses as the forest reclaimed the ponds.

At some point the beavers in a particular pond will be gone. They may be trapped by humans or killed by predators (which doesn't happen often) or disease, or they may exhaust the nearby food supply and either starve or leave their home. As holes in the dam get bigger and more water escapes, the pond will eventually empty. The rich muck that accumulated on the pond floor provides fertile ground for marsh grasses and shrubs that can spring up quite quickly. For several years the old beaver flowage may exist as a wet meadow that provides food and habitat for a number of birds and mammals.

Over time small trees will become established, and eventually the area may become a young forest with a particular suite of animals that live there. Finally, a "climax" forest will develop, once again with its own group of animals that benefit.

Beaver lodge in a pond at the Bog Brook Cove Preserve.

At any point in this entire cycle, new beavers may move in, repair the dam, flood the pond, raise their young, and reset the clock on the beaver flowage.

With all of this benefit to other animals, it is a shame that beavers' instincts frequently bring them into direct conflict with humans. The sound of rushing water and a constriction in a stream channel can cause a beaver to settle and begin building a dam. Unfortunately, culverts that pass a stream under a road fit this description perfectly. Hundreds of beavers are likely trapped every year to keep roads from being flooded and washed away. Trapped beavers are killed 99 percent of the time, but even the few that are relocated may die as a result of the trauma of their capture and finding themselves in a strange place that may have other beavers already in residence. There are often alternative solutions that allow the beavers to remain, but they can be expensive and time-consuming to implement, so many beavers are lethally removed.

Moose—In Maine there should be a moose around every corner, right? Well, not so much in Down East Maine. Moose do live here in low numbers and they can be seen from time to time, but if seeing a moose is your goal, good luck. Other areas of Maine are flooded with these enormous ungulates (hoofed animals), and you can be pretty much assured that if you drive down certain roads at dusk, you're going to see one, or maybe fifteen.

Down East Maine is at the southern edge of moose range, which means that something keeps them from populating farther south. There are several factors, but one that has come to light in recent years is the winter tick. If the winter is severe enough, moose actually fare better because ticks are unable to remain active. If the winter is warm, literally tens of thousands of ticks may attach to a single moose, killing it or, at the very least, keeping it from thriving.

In my fourteen years in the Bold Coast region, including thousands of hours in the woods and on the roads, I've seen probably ten or fewer moose. One moose was a little too close for comfort when I ran into it on my way to a campsite at Cobscook Bay one May. The moose trotted away, seemingly no worse for wear, but the windshield and hood of my minivan were destroyed. This brings up an important point for visitors to understand: Even though moose are uncommon, the risk of hitting one with your car behooves you to keep a close watch for them around dusk and in the dark. The challenge is their height, for two reasons. First, their eyes tend to be above the level of your headlights, so their eyes may not glow the way a deer's or coyote's eyes will, which makes it harder to see them at night. Second, if you do hit one, most vehicles will sweep the legs out from under the moose, causing the bulk of the moose (often up to 1,500 pounds for a bull) to fall squarely on your hood and, tragically, smash through the windshield and into the car, killing the driver or passengers. The point is that moose on the road can be dangerous, so vigilance at night is well worth the extra effort.

You are much more likely to come across moose tracks or their feces in the woods than actually see a moose. If you do come across a moose, it is likely not to flee as a deer would but will ignore you unless it feels like you are a threat. Do yourself a favor and don't pose a threat to a moose by approaching too closely (such as for a photo op)—moose can and do trample people from time to time. Appreciate the moose from a safe distance and then move along. Be aware that male moose rut (or come into breeding season) around October every year. During the fall, moose can be extremely on edge and likely to threaten or harm a person, so keep a little extra distance at this time.

Just knowing that you're sharing the woods with a moose should be enough to heighten your senses and remind you that this is the wild Maine woods.

Deer—White-tailed deer are much more common than moose across the region. With that said, their population is patchy. Some densely human-populated areas seem to offer the perfect habitat for deer. Eastport and Machias, in particular, have resident deer herds that grow increasingly large and tame every year. In undeveloped or less developed areas, the population of deer is much lower. It is quite common to see their tracks or fecal pellets when you are out on the trail, or along the road.

During winter, when and if snow depths reach about two feet and/or temperatures go below about twenty degrees for an extended time, deer will migrate from their summer ranges to traditional sheltering sites that they learn from their parents or other deer. These deer yards, also known as deer wintering areas, tend to have a dense canopy of evergreen trees that block the snow from falling to the forest floor and reduce wind speeds, both of which make the snow shallower and the temperature slightly warmer within the deer yard. Because many deer band together to brave

The birth of twin fawns is not common but can happen when the doe is in excellent physical condition.

the winter, trails are formed in the snow, making travel easier, and familiarity with the trail system helps deer elude coyotes, dogs, and other predators that might otherwise take advantage of the deep snow to kill a deer.

Even with all of these advantages of deer yarding together for the winter, a severe winter will take its toll on the herd. The longer and harder the winter, the more deer will succumb to starvation, cold, or predators. Wintering deer live on a metabolic knife's edge in which every calorie spent moving around or avoiding danger is one less calorie available for finding food, warming the body, or just surviving another minute as they wait for spring's relief. We humans should do our part to avoid making this situation worse by staying out of deer yards when snow is deep enough for deer to congregate. If you are following a trail that takes you into such an area (you'll know by the deep trails through the snow that meander the forest), be as careful as you can not to spook deer. In particular, dogs should not be brought into a deer yard if you know you'll be entering one, and if you happen to find yourself in one, please leash your dog and/or consider turning back.

Deer are the number one target for hunters in the region. Unlike some places, such as the mid-Atlantic and southern states, most hunters are limited to killing a single buck per year. It is possible in some places to get a permit for an additional deer of either sex, but competition for these permits is so fierce the selection is done by lottery and the list of winners is eagerly anticipated. Some people argue that the

A pile of white hair is all that remains of a deer that succumbed the previous winter.

deer population, once a lot lower than it is now, has become unsustainably high for a specific reason. The deer tick, also known as the black-legged tick, is the vector for Lyme disease, an epidemic whose full impact has yet to be felt by the population at large. Fewer deer equals fewer deer ticks, or so the reasoning goes, but it isn't that simple. Studies have shown that the tick population is much more closely tied to the population of small mammals and birds in an area. Unless every last deer is removed, the number of deer is unlikely to have much impact on the tick population.

One oddity you may find in this region is the piebald deer, sometimes referred to as albino deer. They aren't true albinos because they aren't pure white, but they have large patches of white fur like a paint horse. I have often seen them in my yard in East Machias, but I've also heard reports of them elsewhere in the region.

Bear—In Maine, all bears are black bears, even though their coats may be many different shades of brown or black. This name separates them from grizzly or brown bears that live in the western part of the continent. Black bears eat just about anything and are considered omnivores. They will eagerly take a deer fawn or young bird when they can, or dive into carrion that they find, but they really subsist on fruit, leaves, and roots on a daily basis. One interesting fact about bears is that, unlike most other animals, they do not stop growing as they get older. A big boar (male) that weighs in at more than three hundred pounds can easily be twenty years old. Bears are hunted and trapped in Maine, typically during the month of September. Although they can be frightening to see face-to-face, there has never been a significant bear attack on a human in Maine.

Coyote—The history of coyotes in Maine, and elsewhere in New England and eastern Canada, is very interesting. Before European colonization, coyotes were strictly a western animal. Wolves dominated the woods of the Northeast and Midwest, keeping coyotes on their side of the Great Plains. After Europeans virtually eliminated wolves from at least 99 percent of their range in the Lower 48 states, coyotes began to take advantage of the opportunity to spread east. Over the course of one hundred years or more, coyotes inched eastward. Coyotes that found themselves north of the Great Lakes continued eastward but encountered wolves in Ontario. When the wolf population density is low, as it was in this case, they sometimes will interbreed with coyotes. The resulting wolf–coyote hybrids continued their march toward the Atlantic, but they were now larger, more packlike than their independent western ancestors, and more effective predators of larger animals. The coyotes that were first spotted across Maine in the 1960s, and straight through to today, are the descendants of these wolf–coyote hybrids. Genetic analysis shows that virtually every coyote in Maine has some wolf genes. Some animals have more than 50 percent wolf genes. Given this information, some researchers are advocating for a name change from coyote to coywolf, to acknowledge this history.

This adaptable predator always seeks to eat meat but supplements its diet with ripe berries and apples, along with grass and other vegetation. It also will eat human food waste of all kinds, given the chance. Their diet seems to be heavy in small

A coyote stares down the author.

mammals for most of the year, including a lot of mice and squirrels. In the winter they are much more effective at taking down weak and hungry deer or scavenging the remains of deer that die of other causes.

Some farmers recognize the value of coyotes, foxes, and other predators for their ability to control the mouse or rat populations on the farm. However, many farmers shoot first and ask questions later in an effort to protect their livestock. This practice can be counterproductive, because a stable resident coyote population can coexist with farm animals, but if you remove a cooperative coyote family, others will immediately move in. The newly settled coyotes may not have the same restraint, resulting in dead livestock, which then leads to more dead coyotes. There is much more information about coyotes and strategies for coexistence at coyotelivesinmaine.org.

It is worth stating that you are in no danger from coyotes when you are out in the woods. Although some people have been bitten, they usually lured a coyote in or otherwise put themselves in harm's way. There was one tragic case of a young woman being killed by coyotes in Canada, not so far from the US border, but this one example doesn't undermine the millions of peaceful interactions between coyotes and people. If you see a coyote, consider yourself lucky, but don't be overly afraid.

The yips and howls of a coyote family are a treat to hear. I have often been serenaded at night or in the early morning while camping. Contrary to some legends, howls are not a sign that the coyotes are hunting or killed anything. In fact, these wary predators would rather not attract attention if they just made a kill.

Wolf—"Are there wolves in Maine?" Along with the same question about cougars, this was one of the most common and interesting questions I was asked as a wildlife biologist with the Maine Department of Inland Fisheries and Wildlife. The answer is certainly not a simple one. See the section on coyotes for a description of how wolf genes are present here in Maine, even if a pure wolf doesn't haunt the forest. There is little doubt that, with these genes, coyotes have effectively filled most of the ecological role of wolves.

There are those who believe they've seen a wolf, based on the enormous size and thick fur of an animal they saw. A large coyote may weigh in at as much as fifty pounds and can look much larger depending on the context of the sighting. So what's keeping wolves from migrating in naturally from existing wolf populations? The nearest source of wolves is around Algonquin Provincial Park in Ontario, some 350 miles from northern Maine as the crow flies (or as the wolf migrates). In between here and there, however, are Montreal and the Saint Lawrence River, which drains the Great Lakes. This river used to freeze solid during extreme winters, which would allow more animals to cross, but shipping traffic today keeps the channel open. It is possible that some wolves could swim over, but this would amount to only a fraction of those who would cross through a forest or even a frozen river. Given the many miles between the Saint Lawrence River and Maine, this small number of animals is unlikely to reach Maine, though it could and eventually will happen (if it hasn't already). The final nail in the coffin of the idea of wolves naturally recolonizing Maine is one of the same reasons that reintroduction of wolves isn't a viable idea. Coyotes are widespread and densely populated. A small number of wolves who wander in or are released intentionally would have trouble finding other wolves to breed with and over time would eventually be hybridized and incorporated into the coyote population, as happened years ago when coyotes passed through wolf country on their way to the Northeast. This brings up the question of the definition of the word *species*. Most of us were taught in high school that two species are unable to interbreed; yet we have all heard of hybrids like mules (horse and donkey) and ligers (lion and tiger). The members of the canine family are similarly close enough biologically to interbreed in certain situations but generally stay apart due to differences in size, breeding seasons, or courtship behaviors. Very sparse populations sometimes overcome these barriers in their drive to reproduce, and, indeed, unlike the former examples, the resulting offspring are fertile and thus continue the blending of DNA.

The mystique of the Maine wolf remains alive, but it is unlikely that anyone alive today will see a wild wolf in Maine.

Cougar—This animal, named *Puma concolor* by science, is known by many common names across its range—cougar, mountain lion, panther, puma, catamount, and painter, among other names in native tongues. This may be the most awe-inspiring and fear-inducing animal ever to walk Maine's woods. Like wolves, they were wiped out during the colonial period when they posed a danger to farm animals and occasionally killed humans. The last native cougar known to have been in Maine was killed in 1938. Since then, I think I can safely predict that thousands of people believe they have seen one. I myself have probably spoken with more than one hundred of them. Nevertheless, hard evidence of a wild population—in the form of tracks, dead cougars, confirmed tracks in the mud or snow, feces, or cached prey animals—hasn't been found. This despite more than seventy thousand deer hunters fanning out across the Maine woods searching for animal signs.

Personally I used to believe that there were no wild cougars in Maine. Every single time someone reported seeing one, I investigated and tracked down the available clues. In every case where something could be confirmed, it turned out not to be a cougar. Dog or coyote tracks are mistaken for cougars. Sounds heard in the night end up being a porcupine (search online for audio of their screaming), fox, house cat, or something else. Photos and even video of these animals turn out to be house cats. This last mistake is possible because it is very difficult to get the proper perspective in a two-dimensional photograph or video. We would use clues in the image to re-create the photo in the real world and often would be able to show how a bush or other feature that is near the animal matches the smaller size of a house cat rather than a cougar.

My opinion changed, or at least evolved, in 2011, when a cougar was killed on a road in Connecticut. By sheer coincidence and luck, that same cougar had been genetically sampled (meaning a hair or feces or some other biological sample was collected) in South Dakota, and then later in Michigan, before meeting its demise in Connecticut. If one cougar can make that fifteen-hundred-mile trek, what's to say that others haven't done it and remain in Maine? I seriously doubt that a viable population exists here based on the same lack of evidence I described above. However, I now believe that it is completely possible that many of the people who think they have seen a cougar really did see one as it was passing through Maine or searching for a mate. My own wife has a vivid story of seeing a cougar from only feet away as it leaped across the road, several years before I met her. She was not amused to hear my scientific explanation about why it probably wasn't a cougar, and she made sure I remembered this when we heard news of the cougar killed in Connecticut!

The idea that cougars could be out there is fascinating, but it shouldn't cause anyone to stay indoors for fear of them. You're much more likely to be harmed by the following animal than a cougar.

Tick—This may be the most dangerous animal to walk the Maine woods today. The tiny tick, of which there are several species that live in Maine, spreads disease and saps the life-blood of animals as large as moose. The most infamous tick is the deer tick, also known as the black-legged tick, which is the vector for the dreaded Lyme disease. The idea of contracting this terrible disease from an animal so small that you almost can't see it is terrifying to some people and keeps them out of the woods (and even out of lawns). It is important to keep the risk in perspective, gather information about ways to stay safe outdoors, and think of the larger picture. It is within our power to modify our behavior to reduce the risk of ticks.

The following are some general guidelines for reducing your risk of tick attachment:

- Stay out of tall grass. Ticks are much less likely to find you if you stay in mowed paths through a field or stick to deeper forest with little undergrowth.
- Wear appropriate clothing. Light-colored clothes help you spot any ticks that may be on you. Long pants protect your lower legs. For extra protection, tuck your pant legs inside your socks to keep ticks from crawling up inside your pants, giving you more opportunity to spot and remove them. After coming in from the field or woods, many people put their clothes directly into a hot clothes dryer to dry out and kill any ticks that might be on them.
- Use appropriate repellents. Bug sprays containing the insecticide DEET are proven effective against ticks. There are some herbal repellents that may also repel them, but you should always use extra vigilance and other methods if you rely on nontoxic repellent, since they simply are not as effective. Finally, you can (and should if you're regularly in the woods) treat your clothing with pyrethrin. This chemical is not to be used on your skin and should be applied to clothing when it has a chance to fully dry before you wear it. Given these guidelines, pyrethrin is generally considered a safe repellent, and it will remain effective for several washes, so you can treat your entire wardrobe of hiking clothes and shoes at the beginning of the season and the protection will continue for up to weeks at a time. Note that pyrethrin is toxic to cats and it shouldn't be used where a cat can come into contact with the liquid or breathe the spray—it could be fatal.
- Do tick checks. Make it a habit to do thorough tick checks on yourself, your kids, and your pets every time you're out in the woods from April through at

least October. Some people recommend checking for the subsequent three days after every visit to the woods.

All of this might seem like a heavy cost for just going outside, but once it becomes a habit, it isn't as much of a burden as it seems. I frequently remind people that our need to get outside in nature is exactly that—a need—and not a luxury. People, and especially children, need opportunities to connect with the wild, unplug from our modern life, and, as John Muir famously said, "climb the mountains and get their glad tidings." We all risk our lives just leaving our beds each day, so keep the risks of tick-borne diseases in perspective and manage your own behavior to minimize the risk. The alternative, a life spent indoors or on pavement, is no alternative, in my opinion.

For more information about ticks, Lyme disease and other tick-borne diseases, and treatment, see the Maine Centers for Disease Control web page at maine.gov/ dhhs/mecdc/infectious-disease/epi/vector-borne/.

Atlantic salmon—It is unlikely that you'll see an Atlantic salmon in any river in the United States due to their exceedingly low numbers. I have chosen to include them in this section to highlight the tremendous work being done to restore their numbers in this region. Salmon declined due to a host of contributing factors, including dams and other manmade obstacles that prevent fish from migrating up or down the river, as well as acid rain, which acidified the rivers and affected the ability of salmon to transition from fresh water to salt water. These are anadromous fish, which means that they are born in fresh water but migrate out to sea to grow and mature before returning to the river of their birth to breed. Salmon fishing was once popular in the Down East region, but the activity dwindled as salmon grew rarer and came to a full halt by the time the fish were protected under the Endangered Species Act in 2000.

The Downeast Salmon Federation (see page 261) has been hard at work for decades studying the reasons for salmon declines and trying to find solutions. Today, momentum seems to be building with advances in hatchery rearing techniques that allow biologists to release large numbers of strong young fish into the East Machias River. Thanks to all of this work, more adult salmon are returning to the river to breed. Hopefully, this technique can be duplicated on other rivers to bring back the population, at least in the Down East region, where the rivers are still mostly wild and clean. In the past few decades, the coalition of conservation organizations has protected thousands of acres of forest to protect water quality and river habitat for Atlantic salmon, among other work being done to ensure that these fish have a healthy place to spend their first several years. You can learn more about the work of the Downeast Salmon Federation and maybe even see some young fish in the hatchery at their visitor center, called EMARC, in East Machias (see page 88).

I won't get into a detailed description of these animals, but you might also see porpoises, seals, bobcats, lynx (in the northern fringes of athe region), snowshoe hares, squirrels, and mice, among others.

Birding

Many factors come together to make the region beyond Acadia a worthy destination for birders. The diversity of forest types; regular ecological disturbances in the form of ice storms, logging, and beaver activity; and the location on the edge of the rich waters of the Bay of Fundy all provide ideal conditions for various types of resident and migratory birds. If birding is your thing, I recommend you buy a copy of *Maine Birding Trail: The Official Guide to More Than 260 Accessible Sites* by Bob Duchesne, which has many more specific places to find birds than can fit in this space. Nevertheless, here are a few recommendations for places to see some of the more popular species found in the region.

Bald eagles are heralded as one of the great success stories of the Endangered Species Act. From a low of just twenty-nine pairs in the state of Maine, and none in nearby states or Canadian provinces in 1972, the population has grown into the hundreds. One of the strongholds for eagles has always been Cobscook Bay. Careful protections of eagle nest sites there resulted in a higher rate of surviving eaglets until the Cobscook population began to spill over, repopulating the rest of Maine and beyond.

Eagles tend to return to the same nests year after year, so some nests have been used for generations of eagles. Although they usually mate for life, when one of the pair dies, the other will re-mate, effectively passing on the nest for future use. Young, newly paired eagles will search out an unoccupied territory, and if they can't find an existing nest, they'll begin work on a new one.

Bald eagles are known as fish eaters, and it is impressive to watch one catch a fish. Seemingly out of nowhere, an eagle will dive toward the water and then level out just above the surface, reaching down and plucking a fish right out of the water without so much as wetting its feathers. It is less commonly known that a large portion of an eagle's diet comes from eating carrion and waste. Outside the breeding season, when they shun all other eagles but their mate, eagles can congregate in large numbers at trash dumps, at compost facilities, and near fish-processing plants.

The best ways to view eagles depends on the season. The courting and brood-rearing season runs from February through July. Adult paired eagles will be within a couple of miles of their nest for pretty much that entire period. If you know the location of a nest, you can pretty reliably spot an eagle within a few minutes. During the earlier part of the winter, eagles tend to be fairly social and will come together over food sources or just to roost in the same tree. I have seen at least fourteen eagles sitting in the same tree near Cobscook Bay.

The population remains strong across the region, but nowhere are eagles more visible than in Lubec. In the winter, congregations of eagles are often seen on mudflats and in trees where South Lubec Road bends toward Quoddy Head State Park. During the breeding season, they can be seen almost everywhere as their nests dot Cobscook Bay. Of particular note is a nest on Pop Island that is visible from the public wharf in Lubec.

A pair of bald eagles observe the field below.

An eagle stands guard over a goose that it killed.

An osprey takes flight from its nest at the top of a dead tree.

Ospreys are often mistaken for eagles because they are large soaring birds that pluck fish from the water. Unlike eagles, which remain all year long, ospreys migrate to the area to breed each summer, so they are nowhere to be seen from around October to March. They do arrive early each year to take advantage of the runs of migratory fish that are headed up the rivers and streams to spawn. In particular, the alewife run causes a frenzy as hundreds of thousands of fish race upstream. In East Machias, this drama unfolds near the head of tide and nearby stretches of river just above. This means that a walk on the Sunrise Trail through town, a stop at the Downeast Salmon Federation facility along the river, and a pause on the Willow Street bridge (near the Salmon Federation building) and along Water Street are all a must in April. Not only ospreys but also several kinds of gulls, eagles, and seals all take part in the feast.

Other than the East Machias hot spot, ospreys are often seen around nearly any large body of water, and their nests can be very visible atop utility poles and in dead trees. Unlike eagles, which reach down into the water to grab fish as they soar along, ospreys appear to hover far above the water and then plunge straight down into the water headfirst, where they grab their fish, reemerge, and then fly to a nearby tree to eat.

Puffins are a comical-looking seabird that is considered an umbrella species. This generally refers to a charismatic species that people care about, and when you protect or restore this species, it also protects a range of other animals that have similar needs but may not be as attractive or have a compelling story that inspires people to care. Protection of puffins also ensures suitable and undisturbed habitat for birds like black guillemots, razorbills, arctic terns, and endangered roseate terns. If your response is "What are those birds?" but you've heard of puffins, then you understand the concept of an umbrella species.

Puffins and the other seabirds that nest on offshore islands were in steep decline in US waters during the 1960s and 1970s. Maine is the southern edge of their range, which makes the birds particularly sensitive to perturbation and fluctuations in food availability or temperature. North of us, in Newfoundland, Iceland, and Britain, the birds are doing well and thriving. Here in Maine the population dipped to just two nesting colonies on two islands, prompting the state to list the birds as threatened. The risk was that a freak occurrence, like an oil spill, a disease, or even the arrival on one of the islands of a mink or weasel (which can and do swim across open ocean to islands), could decimate the remaining breeding birds. The Audubon Society's Project Puffin began in 1973, with the goal of returning breeding puffins to as many historic nesting islands as possible. Project Puffin and agencies of the federal and state government have been successful in expanding seabirds to at least six islands, with work underway to attract them to more.

Despite the spread of seabird colonies to more islands, many of the birds face a perilous future due to climate change. Warming waters are causing a shift in the habits of fish that the birds need to feed their young. In a recent year there were virtually no surviving chicks on any of the Maine seabird islands. The tiny fish that the

Biologists place puffin decoys to encourage real birds to land and raise their young on these remote and rugged islands.

An arctic tern returns to the nest with a fish for its chick on a protected seabird nesting island.

young chicks need were nowhere to be found. Researchers saw many dead chicks surrounded by larger fish that the parents brought to the nest in desperation but that the chicks simply couldn't swallow. This tragedy did not repeat in the subsequent year, but it was a harbinger of things to come from climate change.

The only way to see puffins is to get out on the water during the summer. All actively used seabird nesting islands are owned by the state or federal government and are closed to public visitation during the nesting season, but you can approach the islands from the water. Experienced kayakers can make their way to Petit Manan Island, but most people will go on a boat tour (see page 111). Note that one of the islands, Machias Seal Island, is the subject of a dispute between the United States and Canada over which country the island is a part of. The extended standoff on this topic has resulted in a compromise in which the Canadian federal government manages the wildlife on the islands. As a result, this is the only seabird nesting island that the public can actually land on, and only one of the tour boat operators listed on page 111 is authorized to do so. Nevertheless, the birds are numerous in their colonies and relatively easy to view or photograph from a boat.

When it isn't breeding season and the birds aren't obligated to stay at their nests to rear their young, most of them are out at sea, perhaps never even landing on dry land in the nine months or so between breeding seasons.

Migratory shorebirds are very dependent on the region's mudflats to fuel up for their southward journey each autumn. A number of species migrate through

Thousands of tiny shorebirds dot the coastline in the late summer and fall on their way south.

each year, including various sandpipers, plovers, yellowlegs, and others. After nesting and rearing young in the Canadian arctic, the birds stop in this area for up to two weeks and may double their body weight by eating the abundant invertebrates at the water's edge. Flocks that can number into the thousands flit around on mudflats or in the wrack line (washed-up seaweed on a beach), pecking away while the tide is low. They can be difficult to see at this time, because the tiny birds disperse across sometimes expansive mudflats. When the tide comes in and water covers the feeding grounds, shorebirds take advantage of the time to congregate on rocks, islets, and isolated stretches of beach in dense clusters, where they groom, rest, and socialize for several hours until the flats are once again exposed.

Recent studies indicate that undisturbed access to the rich resources in this region are critical to the long-distance migration of the birds. Here, birds may stay about two weeks before setting off across the ocean, bound for the Caribbean Sea or South America. They may not land or stop flying for close to a week, and if they don't have the body fat to fuel the journey, the birds will die in the open ocean. In more populated areas farther south, migratory shorebirds stay for far less time, and instead of going across the ocean, they will "hopscotch" down the coast, feeding as they go. This is much more risky for the birds than the direct flight, as it puts them within reach of predators and human disturbance. The point of all of this is to say that the health of these birds requires minimal human disturbance while they are stopping in the area. Unleashed dogs and overeager birders can disrupt an entire feeding cycle, which the birds may not be able to recover from before their time to migrate.

Hot spots for shorebirds include the area around Mowry Beach (see page 90) in Lubec and the entire Lubec Channel, which creates hundreds of acres of exposed mudflat at low tide. As the tide comes in, the birds slowly follow the leading edge of the water and become much easier to spot. Flocks can also be seen adjacent to the Dike in Machias and along the stretch of Sunrise Trail from Machias to East Machias. Farther west and south, flocks can be found anywhere there are mudflats in Pleasant Bay, including Addison, Harrington, Milbridge, and Steuben.

Warblers and other songbirds are the focus of the annual Down East Spring Birding Festival. Of course, there are outings to view eagles and puffins as well, but the focus of the festival, held each April, is to catch the northward migration of the tiny passerine (songbird) species that flit through our trees on their way to the breeding grounds, and of course many will stop here to breed. This area is particularly attractive to the birds thanks in part to the sporadic human development here. In more developed areas, there are few wild core areas, and in deep wilderness, the forest tends to be more homogenous. In Down East Maine, small villages are surrounded by old farmland and managed woodlots with lots of shrub habitat, fields, and early successional habitat. Farther from the villages, the intact forest reigns. All of these habitat types multiply the number of species who will at least pause in this region to make use of its resources.

As mentioned, the *Maine Birding Trail* book has specific lists of where to go to find these birds. A hot spot that gets little attention is Dennison Point, part of the state's Cobscook Bay Wildlife Management Area located in Trescott Township. You'll find a small parking area with a sign 0.3 mile up Commissary Point Road (off Route 189, 1.8 miles from the intersection of Route 189 and Route 1 at Whiting Corner). From behind a gate adjacent to the parking area, a grassy lane heads off to

Savannah Sparrows nest in fields and marshes.

a peninsula where the forest is specifically managed for bird diversity. The old road takes you through a series of fields and former homesteads that have gone back to nature. A large part of the area was clear-cut a number of years ago to create ideal habitat for ruffed grouse and woodcock, among many other species. These areas have grown back to a dense, shrubby tangle that you won't even think about entering, but the road passes right by, so the birding can be excellent without getting twigs in your hair. The full distance to the end of the road and back is only about 1.75 miles. There is also always plenty of coyote and bear sign in this area. Abundant apple trees and berry bushes provide lots of food for the whole growing season. Look for large bear scats filled with apples in September and October. Though I always see bear sign here, I've never encountered a live bear and don't know anyone who has had a bad experience, so don't let this deter you from exploring Dennison Point.

Wintering ducks and other waterfowl fly to the coast of Maine for the winter as their retreat from the cold arctic where they breed. Although conditions can be pretty fierce here, there is plenty of food in the bays and coves of the region, so it is better for the birds to remain here and deal with winter than continue flying south to warmer climes. A diverse assemblage of scoters, mergansers, eiders, black ducks, and a few others arrive in late fall and can be found all along the coast. The dabbling ducks, primarily black ducks and mallards, keep to the shallows where they can dip their head down and find food. Scoters, mergansers, and eiders keep to slightly deeper water because they dive to find their meals.

Turkeys are numerous in the region, and there is a popular hunting season for them.

Hunting and Fishing

Hunting and fishing are sports I am familiar with, but definitely not an expert in, and I won't attempt to give you information that is better sought from someone who really knows these activities.

Nonhunters visiting the area may be interested in some aspects of hunting as it relates to other outdoor activities. Nearly all of the hiking trails in *Beyond Acadia* are open to hunting. All state parks (but not other state-owned land) are closed to hunting. As far as I know, there haven't been any major incidents in which a hiker was injured by a hunter on these properties. Different user groups have coexisted peacefully, and I consider it a fairly safe activity to hike these trails during the hunting season. With that said, you and your pets should wear blaze orange during the deer firearms season (generally all of November but often a few days of either October or December), just to be sure you can be seen by hunters. You may also want to avoid hiking early in the morning or shortly before dark, as these are prime times for hunters. Few hunters are out at midday unless it is overcast or rainy. There is no hunting anywhere in the state on Sunday, so if you are still nervous to be out in the woods with hunters, Sunday is your day. Finally, be aware that people may be out hunting for many kinds of birds and mammals, though deer hunting gets most of the attention. Hunters also take moose, coyotes, ruffed grouse (also called partridge), wild turkeys, crows (but not ravens), small mammals, and various kinds of ducks. Overall there is some animal that can be hunted all year-round (except on Sunday).

Some trailheads have notices about hunting, but you should assume hunting is allowed at all of the trails, with the exception of state parks.

In general, the Maine Department of Inland Fisheries and Wildlife regulates **hunting** and determines the seasons each year. A license is required to hunt. They offer lots of information about the laws, regulations, procedures, and dates when you can hunt. You can find more info at maine.gov/ifw.

Freshwater fishing is also regulated by the Maine Department of Inland Fisheries and Wildlife, and their website (maine.gov/ifw) has information for fishing. A fishing license is required to catch fish in fresh water.

Saltwater fishing is not a common activity here, but there are exceptions. Striped bass, mackerel, and a few other species may be hooked if you know where to go at the right time. There are also deep-sea fishing charter boats that leave from Eastport. With a few exceptions, saltwater fishers will need to register with the Maine Department of Marine Resources. You can find more info at maine.gov/dmr.

Villages

Considering the size of the region beyond Acadia, there is a surprising diversity of characters, aesthetics, and amenities among the villages. Eastport and Lubec, for example, are separated by just two miles of water across the mouth of Cobscook Bay, or almost forty miles and an hour by road around the perimeter of the bay. Despite the geographic proximity, the differences in scale of the two towns should be considered when you decide where to go. Go to Eastport for art galleries, restaurants, and a little hubbub around town in the early evening. Go to Lubec for hiking, sightseeing, and a simple dinner with craft beer at one of the several restaurants. Compare Eastport further with Jonesport, which has a pizza place, a grocery store, two banks, and a couple of gas stations, but few other retail businesses. Go to Jonesport for the beautiful views and exposure to an authentic fishing village. A little bit of forethought about what you're interested in and, particularly, what amenities you need can make the difference between eating dinner from a gas station or sitting down to a meal overlooking the water. Like the rest of the chapters of this book, the descriptions in this chapter will start at the southwest end of the region and work their way up the coast toward Eastport.

These are the towns with the largest concentrations of people and/or businesses. There are plenty of other hamlets and small towns to explore and discover on your own.

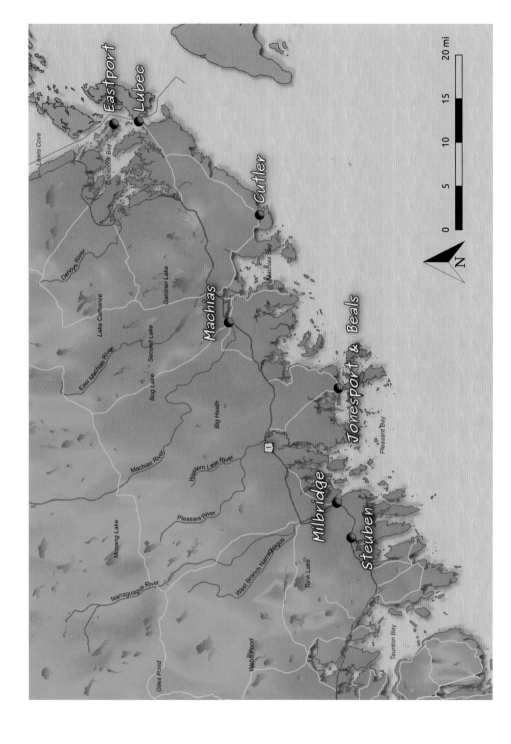

Steuben

Steuben is a cluster of homes with no real commercial center. In fact, Maineayr Campground is the only business in the village open to the public, so it is hard to spend a dollar here. The area is rich, however, in free stuff to do. Three hikes in this book (see listings beginning on page 183 for the Hollingsworth Trail, Birch Point Trail, and Pigeon Hill) are within the town's boundaries. There are also several places to access the shore.

Milbridge

Route 1 through Milbridge is bookended by beautiful water views at both ends of the village, including the always-pleasurable-to-cross bridge over the tidal part of the Narraguagus River, with its view of the town's fleet of fishing boats and the opportunity to watch the tide rush in or out under the bridge. Other than a trip down Wyman Road to McClellan Park, there isn't much to draw you off the main road through town.

In recent years a surge of civic pride has overtaken Milbridge that is transforming the downtown. A small number of interesting shops and galleries have popped up. A local group known as the Women's Health Resource Library started the wildly successful "Incredible Edible Milbridge" that provides a "help yourself" garden scattered across town in small raised beds tended to by volunteers. The same group enlisted the help of the Maine Coast Heritage Trust to help them purchase what will become a new in-town park. An ambitious plan to revive a local theater is gaining steam through grassroots fund-raising, and one of the first steps was to erect an outdoor performance stage that hosts contra-dances and concerts throughout the warm season.

Interestingly, Milbridge is known as the most diverse village in the region. Being close to the blueberry barrens, a large contingent of migrant workers from Mexico came to the region in the early 2000s to pick berries. Several families ended up settling permanently here, starting businesses and making themselves an inseparable part of the fabric of town. Since then, immigrants from other countries have found the beauty of Milbridge. The most visible and popular result of this diversity is Vasquez Mexican Takeout, hands down the best Mexican food in eastern Maine.

The Milbridge harbor is at the head of Narraguagus Bay.

Jonesport and Beals

Jonesport and Beals are a pair of towns that are often lumped together because they are so far from everywhere else and so entwined with each other. Jonesport sits at the far tip of one of the longest peninsulas in the region. Beals is even a step more remote—on a pair of offshore islands called Beals Island and Great Wass Island. Beals is connected to the center of Jonesport's village by a narrow bridge that is well known in the area for the view it provides of the two fishing villages. A trip to Jonesport and Beals is all about the scenery, particularly since there is little else for visitors to enjoy. There are no hotels or inns and very little shopping, and the only restaurants are Jonesport Pizza and Bayside Takeout. There are a handful of Airbnbs, and you may be able to find a seasonal rental, but more than anywhere else beyond Acadia, you're on your own if you want to really experience Jonesport and Beals. Nevertheless, the scenery is worth the trip if you have the time, and particularly if you can hike at the Great Wass Island Preserve or catch the Jonesport Beals/Moosabec Summerfest.

For the most part, staying on the main roads in Jonesport and Beals will reveal the best views, but one destination that is slightly off the beaten path is the town marina. If you're coming from the Machias side of Route 187, turn left at the Moosabec Variety gas station/convenience store and continue to the parking lot for the marina. Park out of the way of commercial fishers, who may be launching boats or bringing in their catch, and enjoy a short walk out on the public dock. This is a wonderful place to watch the summer afternoon fog roll in, though once it is in, Jonesport and Beals are a wall of white.

Birdhouses look like real houses in Jonesport as viewed from across Moosabec Reach on Beals Island.

Machias

Sometimes locally referred to as "The Shiretown" (meaning "county seat"), Machias is one of the full-service towns in the region. Lodging, food, bars, live entertainment, banking, car repair, a small airport, an open-air market, hardware and housewares, a small thrift shop, a beautiful historic library, and locally made art and gifts are all found here. Along with these commercial necessaries, Machias boasts a couple of worthwhile parks and preserves that highlight the Machias River and its smaller tributary, the Middle River. The Machias River defines the center of downtown, hearkening back to the bustling days of log drives and sailing ships when the river was the center of it all. Today the river is being rediscovered as an attraction and recreational destination.

The Bad Little Falls (roughly translated from the Passamaquoddy word *machias*) are a series of waterfalls that run through Bad Little Falls Park and underneath the Jeremiah O'Brien Bridge (Route 1). Everything downriver of the falls is tidal and brackish, meaning that it is part of the ocean but heavily influenced by the fresh water pouring in from the river above. The view from lower parts of downtown changes dramatically as the tide rises and falls as much as fifteen feet every six hours. Many people wonder why there isn't more boat traffic in the large bay across from Helen's Restaurant, and a big part of the answer is visible when the bay essentially disappears to a narrow trickle at low tide.

History runs deep in Machias, where local residents celebrate the first naval battle of the American Revolution with the annual Margaretta Days Festival in early

Machias is an ideal home base for an exploration of the region, with its stores and central location.

June, complete with historical reenactors and a small encampment. If you happen to visit at a different time of year, you can learn the full tale of how the battle came to be at the Burnham Tavern (built in 1770), which is now a museum. The tavern is where a small group of local revolutionary sympathizers plotted to take on a sizeable British warship with a far smaller vessel. Remarkably, they succeeded! Read more about it on page 54.

The Dike (or, sometimes, the Dyke) across the mouth of the Middle River is one of the centers of activity in town. On a daily basis during the summer, vendors set up on folding tables or the tailgate of their truck to sell whatever they've got. Some are professional vendors who are there nearly every day, usually trading in vintage or used goods they pick up from somewhere else and sell here. Some just come to sell something specific or to have a yard sale in a central location. The end of the Dike closest to the village is also the home of the Machias Farmers' Market. The Down East Sunrise Trail crosses the Dike on its ninety-mile path from Ellsworth to Calais. Locals use the Dike as a meeting place, and you'll often find clusters of two or three trucks pulled up with their windows close and people talking over the rumble of idling engines. Finally, the Dike is just a nice place to pull over and watch the view over the water. The public dock is just outside Helen's Restaurant next to the Dike, and it's another great place to experience the Machias River and Machias Bay.

Cutler

Like Jonesport and Beals, Cutler is a fishing town from start to finish. Despite the fact that the town contains some of the most dramatic and beautiful coastline and a picture-postcard marina with its fishing fleet, there are virtually no services for visitors. The A to Z Variety store and gas station is out on the fringe of town toward Machiasport, and the only other place one could buy something in Cutler is at Little River Lobster, a well-hidden-in-plain-sight place to buy live lobsters right off the boat. They are located right at the public boat launch, but ask anyone in town if you aren't sure where they are.

Public events that may draw visitors to Cutler include the annual July 4 celebration, held during the day rather than in the evening. The highlight is the "lobster crate race" that tests local youths' balance, speed, agility, and tolerance for ice-cold ocean water. The other event to watch for is the open house, when the Friends of Little River Lighthouse provide boat transportation out to Little River Island at the mouth of Cutler Harbor for visitors to enjoy the scenic lighthouse.

Other than the previously mentioned attractions, Cutler is all about hiking and scenery for visitors. About 65 percent of the land area of Cutler is protected from development to retain the incredible views and opportunities for remote recreation. The most popular of these protected lands is the Cutler Coast Unit of the state's Bureau of Public Lands. This property was more commonly known for years as "The Bold Coast" trail, but this name has fallen out of favor, because these days "Bold

The protected harbor in Cutler is straight out of a postcard.

Coast" refers to the area from Milbridge all the way to the Canadian border (see Bold Coast Scenic Byway, page 94).

Cutler is also home to the "Cutler towers." If you've been anywhere within about twenty miles, you probably noticed the towers on the horizon, particularly at night when red lights mark this hazard to aviation. The towers are on a US Navy base that dates from the Cold War era. They are essentially a remarkably strong radio station that played a critical role in keeping the US fleet in communication across the globe. Today the towers are apparently kept in working condition as a backup to modern technology, but they don't seem to be actively used these days. The towers themselves are more than eight hundred feet tall and are connected by an intricate network of cables.

Lubec

Once primarily a fishing village, Lubec is haltingly moving toward more of a tourism economy based on its identity as a fishing village. Don't misunderstand—the tourism aspects of Lubec are not souvenir shops and chain restaurants. Far from it. A very authentic selection of small restaurants, a microbrewery with organic and natural food, and just a couple of shops make up the heart of downtown, along with the views of the ocean and nearby US and Canadian islands. Except on summer weekends, the village looks all but abandoned, but don't be fooled. There are lots of people doing very interesting things here. They just don't gather on the main drag to do them.

Lubec claims that it is the first piece of the continental United States to receive the sun's rays each morning. This is partially true. For a couple of weeks around each spring and fall equinox, the sun rises first at Quoddy Head State Park. At other times, it may rise first on Eastport (see the next section), Cadillac Mountain in Acadia National Park, or Mars Hill, which is a mountain 150 miles or so north of Lubec.

The town, along with the unorganized territory of Trescott Township, is a peninsula that forms the southern shore of Cobscook Bay and separates it from the Atlantic

Pop Island sits right off the shores of Lubec but is often draped in fog.

Ocean. Between the open ocean and the convoluted shoreline of Cobscook Bay, Lubec boasts more than ninety-five miles of coast. Much of this coast is conserved by a group of land trusts and government agencies that have been working for decades to protect the rich wildlife habitat and scenic beauty of the region (see page 261).

Eastport

The city of Eastport is on Moose Island, which is the last of a string of islands stretching out from the mainland to form the eastern edge of Cobscook Bay on one side and the western edge of Passamaquoddy Bay on the other. The islands are all connected by a series of causeways, making it seamless to travel the seven miles or so from Route 1 to the commercial district of Eastport.

Eastport has a history, like many towns in the area, as a booming sardine fishing town. When the sardine fishery collapsed in the mid-1900s, the once bustling downtown became a depressed stretch of boarded-up windows and "Closed" signs. Little by little, though, the town began a comeback thanks at first to the lobster fishery, which didn't get really good in this region until later in the twentieth century. This brought some much-needed life to the town. Next, a small community of artists opened several galleries and shops in the downtown, attracting other artists and tourists. Restaurants and evening life followed, and today Eastport has it all. It still retains its authentic working waterfront with a fleet of lobster and scallop boats, which provides a perfect backdrop for the thriving arts community, including the visual and performing arts.

The port of Eastport, on the opposite side of the island from the village waterfront, is the deepest natural port in the Lower 48 states and can accommodate a ship up to nine hundred feet long. The port's depth and position as the closest to Europe has brought a lot of business to Eastport, including shipments of thousands of cattle to Turkey and countless loads of wood chips bound for other countries for making paper.

All of Eastport gets in the "pirate spirit" for the annual Eastport Pirate Festival, including Moose Island Bakery.

Festivals and Seasonal Events

L ike most places that are as tied to the natural world as this region, the year unfolds with the changing seasons. Just when you get used to the summer heat, for example, temperatures will drop, and that first hint of fall makes you wonder how you wasted away the "hot" (for Maine) weather. The passing of the seasons is not just a matter of the thermometer going up or down, or even the trees changing colors from brown to green to all shades of red and yellow and back to brown once again. For many locals, the changing seasons also mean changing jobs to reap the bounty of what nature provides in each season. One person could conceivably earn money in the course of the year by mowing lawns, selling produce from the garden at a farmer's stand, digging clams, raking blueberries, gathering wreath tips (more on this activity later), plowing driveways, making maple syrup, cleaning up from winter's mess, and harvesting river herring and baby eels, among many other natural resource jobs.

In a region where locals spend most of their time holed up on their own property and engrossed in their own business, great value is placed on occasions to gather together. Over the years the number of local festivals has ballooned, so that barely a week goes by in the summer without a special event somewhere in the region. They are also scattered throughout the rest of the year, so a visit during any season may allow you to take in a local festival or event.

The sections that follow outline not only festivals and human-centered events but also notable natural events that you will see and perhaps wonder about if you're less familiar with the way of life Down East.

Spring

Apple trees blossom in the late spring and are promptly visited by pollinators.

The spring freshet (high flow in rivers and streams due to snowmelt) is a key event in the natural year and it can have effects throughout the growing season, from the timing of fish migration to the quality of the blueberry harvest in August. Following a mud season that spans the transition from winter to spring that can be anywhere from a few to six weeks long, spring really comes when the leaves begin to appear on the trees. Grass turns green and begins to grow around the beginning of May.

Smelt Fry & World Fish Migrations Day Celebration

The first notable festival on the calendar each year is the annual Smelt Fry & World Fish Migrations Day Celebration, held each April around Earth Day, but check current listings at the Downeast Salmon Federation's website to be sure. The festival has grown organically over the years and now virtually takes over the sleepy village of Columbia Falls, with events at the Wild Salmon Resource Center, the Wreaths Across America museum, a portable fish smoker, and other locations within about a quarter mile of each other on Main Street. The focal point of the festival is a meal, served by volunteers, featuring fried smelt that were caught in local rivers over the previous winter as well as venison, moose stew, and prodigious quantities of blueberry cobbler. This is an opportunity for the community to come together and celebrate the positive effects that sea-run fish have on the life in this area and to shine a spotlight on the work of the Downeast Salmon Federation, which for decades has been leading the way to bring back wild Atlantic salmon and other diadromous fish. Find more info at mainesalmonrivers.org.

Down East Spring Birding Festival

Later in the spring, on Memorial Day weekend, the Down East Spring Birding Festival celebrates the diversity of birds that make their way through the region on their way north each spring, or that settle here to breed before migrating south again in the fall. The event spans the whole weekend and features a host of outings from roadside samplers to longer hikes into the habitat to boat trips to see the iconic Atlantic puffins

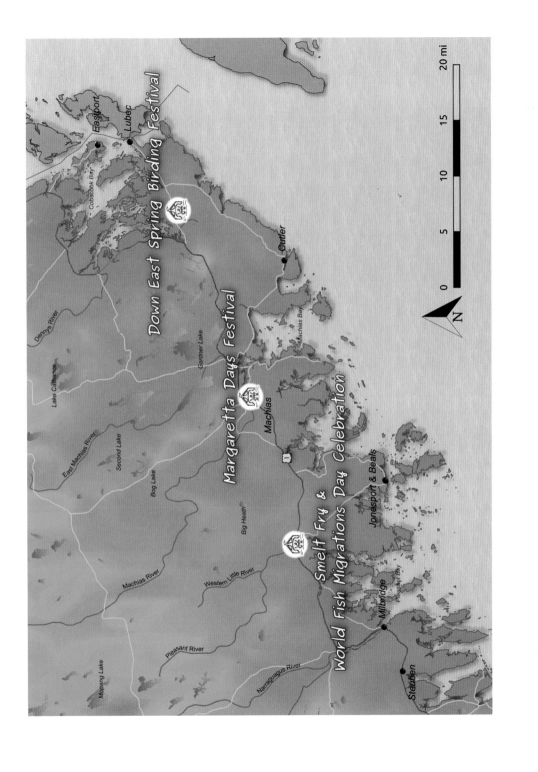

Down East Spring Birding Festival

Margaretta Days Festival

Smelt Fry &
World Fish Migrations Day Celebration

Easport

Lubec

Cobscook Bay

Denny's River

Lake Cathance

Gardner Lake

Cutler

Machias Bay

East Machias River

Second Lake

Machias

Bog Lake

Big Heath

Jonesport & Beals

Machias River

Western Little River

Pleasant Bay

Milbridge

Pleasant River

Narraguagus River

Steuben

Mopang Lake

N

0   5   10   15   20 mi

Black guillemots are one of the many seabirds you may see on a trip to the puffin nesting islands.

that breed on offshore islands. There is generally a fee for each event to cover the costs of organizing the festival. Find more information at thecclc.org/birdfest-intro.

Margaretta Days Festival

The most significant day in recorded history for Machias is celebrated every June at the annual Margaretta Days Festival. Revolutionary War reenactors, musicians, vendors, and state and local dignitaries, as well as Passamaquoddy Elders, gather on the grounds of the University of Maine at Machias to remember the first naval battle of the American Revolution. Most of the local colonists had become Revolutionary sympathizers after hearing of the battle at Lexington and Concord, Massachusetts, which sparked the Revolutionary War. Ordinary farmers and townsfolk who made up the minutemen had successfully defended Concord and the countryside by driving the far more numerous redcoats back to Boston. Less than two months later, a critical supply ship arrived in Machias from Boston. Owned by a loyalist to the crown, and supported by the presence of the *Margaretta*, a British warship, the townspeople were denied their supplies unless they agreed to fill the ship with their lumber haul. Such cargo was intended to build extensive barracks to house more British soldiers. The story of how the patriots deliberated what to do, the true tale of the men making a symbolic leap across a creek to indicate their willingness to die for the cause of liberty, followed by them actually capturing the British ship and its crew with their tiny boat *Unity*, is a source of immense local pride—and perhaps a bit of legend as well. The local chapter of the DAR (Daughters of the American Revolution) is named after sixteen-year-old Hannah Weston, who, as it is told, carried heavy sacks of ammunition several miles through the woods at night from Whitneyville to Machias Bay to assist the patriots. Some parts of this story are undoubtedly true, but pretty much everyone avoids too much scrutiny over specific details. The point is that Machias townsmen rose up and rebelled against the British navy at a time when the course of the Revolutionary War was far from a sure thing and they had much to lose. This battle did in fact have a significant impact on the British mentality, for it impressed upon them that this region was too risky to attack for the purpose of commandeering resources. The names of these brave men can still be found in their many descendants in the town. Before and during the festival, Machias is festooned with colonial era flags and other decorations to call those days to mind. Up at the university, a period encampment is established, demonstrating the use of old tools and equipment, clothing and cooking, and games and crafts that would have been common 250 years ago. Try your hand at hatchet throwing, or stick your head in the stocks! Eat some venison stew, watch the blacksmith, and don't forget to dress up if you like! When you are at the festival and you think of it, walk across the Jeremiah O'Brien Bridge (named after the captain of *Unity*, the vessel that captured the *Margaretta*) and peer down into the rushing river. The festival often overlaps the alewife migration already described, and you might just see the fish making their way up the Bad Little Falls below. You can find more information at margarettadays.com.

A group of young history buffs play the part of the first naval battle in the American Revolutionary War at the Margaretta Days reenactment.

Summer

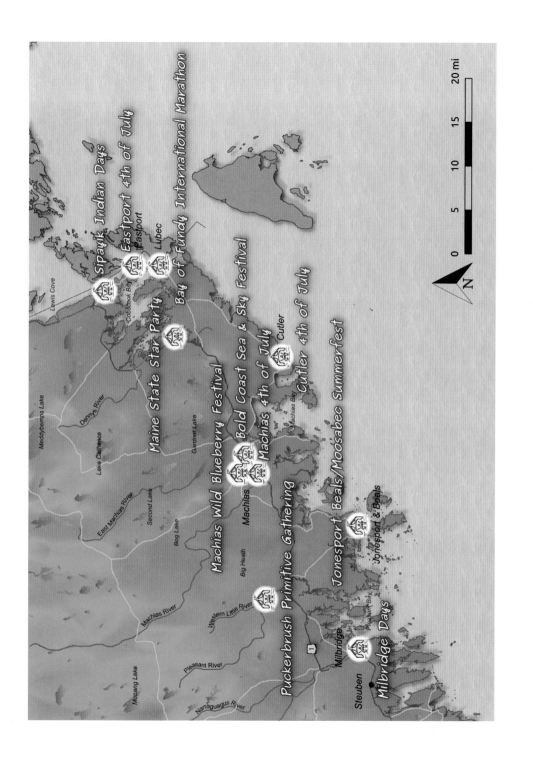

As spring transitions to summer (or leaps, as is often the case), the natural world really gets going on its annual business. At this latitude the long, dark winter robbed plants and animals of opportunities to feed and grow as they struggled to survive. The reverse happens when the long summer days send plants into overdrive with up to fifteen and a half hours of sunlight. Most locals see this most clearly when the grass grows so fast you can practically see the blades get longer if you rest in your hammock long enough. Trees fill out, ponds and lakes grow aquatic plants that can render a river unusable by motorboats, and the forest floor becomes a jungle of greenery.

For people, this is a busy and social season. When not tending to their gardens (which also grow at unbelievable speeds, both crops and weeds), locals spend more time out at festivals, at public suppers, or with friends—perhaps at their favorite fishing spot. A very popular summer activity is gathering with friends and family at their "camps," the colloquial term for a little cabin in the woods or on a lake. Apparently even people who live in the Maine woods need a getaway that's *more* woodsy! Traditionally, even hard-working folks of low economic means could manage to have a weekend camp for their family, as land was relatively inexpensive or leased by the big paper companies for practically nothing and virtually everyone could swing a hammer. In this isolated area there is a great deal of pride in being self-sufficient, whether that be "putting away" summer produce for winter, cutting firewood off your own woodlot, repairing most anything needing to be fixed, or building a camp to last generations.

Alewives, a kind of river herring that spends most of its life out at sea, migrate en masse to Maine's rivers and streams early every summer to spawn. In bodies of water that do not have manmade dams or other obstructions, hundreds of thousands of ale-

Cormorants and gulls line up in anticipation of the beginning of the alewife run, when these herring return to fresh water to spawn.

wives may rush in. This influx of easy prey creates a frenzy by all kinds of predators, including eagles, ospreys, gulls, seals, and people. The harvest of alewives is strictly regulated on a town-by-town basis, usually with a single individual buying the right to harvest a certain amount of fish. In turn, most of those fish are processed to be used as lobster bait, but smoked alewife is a local delicacy that can be hard to find. The meat is oily and smoky and definitely not for everyone, but many people get a wild gleam in their eyes when they taste the wild flesh of the alewife.

The incoming alewives flood predators with food, which provides cover for a much smaller number of young Atlantic salmon, called smolts, which are undertaking their migration out to sea at about two years of age. Even if there were many salmon, the numbers of smolts would be dwarfed by the incoming horde of alewives. But, sadly, there are very few smolts, and many of those that do migrate out were grown in hatcheries and then released into the river to mature in the wild, at least in a few select rivers. Atlantic salmon are the most charismatic of the endangered species in the region since bald eagles were delisted in 2007. After decades of work, fisheries biologists feel like they are finally getting a toehold and will be able to start bringing salmon numbers back from the brink. Climate change will not be kind to salmon in US waters, but even so, a positive trend in the numbers will be welcome news for many people.

Bay of Fundy International Marathon

Sometimes an event happens that is an immediate success, and everyone wonders why we haven't been doing this all along. Such is the case for the Bay of Fundy International Marathon and 10K, which was founded in 2013. The marathon is one of the only international running races involving the United States in which runners cross the border and must complete parts of the course in Canada and the United States. The 10K race is strictly in Lubec, on the US side of the border. Although the terrain is overall relatively flat, the frequent small hills make this one of the more challenging marathons on the circuit, and the race grows in popularity every year. Find more information at bayoffundymarathon.com.

Open Farm Day

One of the longer running traditional events is Maine's Open Farm Day, which happens on a Sunday in June. Each farm decides whether and how to participate, so you can either contact your favorite farm to find out what's happening or go to the state's website at maine.gov/dacf/ard/market_promotion/open_farm_day.shtml for a listing of participating farms. Typically there may be opportunities to tour a barn, pet a cow, pick your own produce, and enjoy hayrides.

Independence Day Celebrations

As in most places in New England, July is the high season for festivals and events with a local flair to them. Take, for instance, the **Moosabec Reach Lobster Boat Races,**

You'll have your choice of Independence Day fireworks in Jonesport, Machias, or Eastport.

which are a part of the annual **Jonesport Beals/Mooseabec Summerfest**. These events take place for several days around the Fourth of July but are timed each year so they don't conflict with other major commemorations in the region. A series of lobster boat races occur up and down the coast, but I dare say that none take it as seriously as the Mooseabec racers. Participants are lobstermen through and through, and their boats are a source of pride and honor among their colleagues. Summerfest also features lobster crate races, in which (usually) young people run across a string of lobster crates that are roped together across a stretch of water between two docks. Quick feet and good balance are the keys to not taking a bath in the icy water. There is also a parade and fireworks to mark Independence Day. There doesn't seem to be an official website or social media presence for the Summerfest and lobster boat races, but information is often posted on a blog at maine-lylobster.com.

Similar to the Moosabec Summerfest, the town of **Cutler** holds a real Down East Independence Day celebration, including a much-anticipated Lobster Boat Race, lobster crate races, a road running race, a church lunch, a parade, and children's activities. There are no fireworks, so head in to Jonesport, Machias, or Eastport (in order of the magnitude of the fireworks display) for the evening's festivities. Learn more at facebook.com/Cutler4thofJuly.

Independence Day Fireworks in **Machias** on or around the Fourth are best viewed on the Dike with the display happening over the Middle River. Fog has canceled these fireworks on more than one year in the recent past, so watch the weather. The most extensive fireworks display in the region happens in **Eastport**. Thousands gather during the day for a parade, games, a few rides for the kids, live music, special events at businesses all over town, and finally the fireworks after dusk. The single road into Eastport is busy all day as people trickle into town, but everyone trying to leave after the fireworks causes the only traffic jam you're likely to encounter in the region all year. If you're headed out of town at the end of the night, be sure everyone has what they need and has used the facilities, because it will be a while before you finally hit the open road. Find more information at eastport4th.com.

Bold Coast Sea & Sky Festival

Later in July, Machias celebrates the annual Bold Coast Sea & Sky Festival. Events are planned all over town, including live music, boat races, kite flying, drone demonstrations, bounce houses, laser tag, an airport fly-in, and much more. The festival takes place over the course of two days and there is no charge to enter, though some of the individual activities do require a fee. Find more information at boldcoastseaandskyfestival.com.

Milbridge Days

Taking place over a full weekend in July, Milbridge Days has a variety of fun activities for all ages. Of particular interest is the Codfish Relay, in which contestants carry a huge codfish across a course while being sprayed by a firehose and then pass it to a teammate. Other activities include a cribbage match, a game show, garden tours, a car show, fireworks, and more. You can find more information about the current year's event on Facebook by performing a search for "Milbridge Days."

Puckerbrush Primitive Gathering

The Puckerbrush Primitive Gathering takes place each July at the Pleasant River Fish and Game Conservation Association facility in Columbia Falls. This event is an opportunity for enthusiasts of woodcraft and survival methods to camp out, show off their skills, compare notes with other aficionados, and help newbies get hooked on things like fire-making, emergency camping techniques, hunting with bow and arrow, leathercraft, flint knapping, and more. Learn more at prfgca.org.

Sipayik Indian Days

Sipayik Indian Days at the Pleasant Point Reservation is an annual opportunity to celebrate the history of the First Peoples who still live here. Over the course of three days, there are traditional meals, drumming, dancing, sports and games, fireworks, prayer meetings, and a pageant. Search the Internet for "Sipayik Indian Days" for the current year's information.

Machias Wild Blueberry Festival

The last major event of summer is the annual Machias Wild Blueberry Festival. Held over three days toward the end of August, the celebration commemorates the blueberry harvest. Though often done mechanically or with migrant labor these days, locals remember when nearly every child earned money for their school clothes by raking blueberries in the summer heat for a few weeks. The festival has become primarily a commercial happening, with more than one hundred vendors selling art, crafts, clothing, food, and jewelry. A big attraction every year is the book sale at Porter Memorial Library, with thousands of books being sold for pennies on the dollar to support the library. Each year there is also a well-attended blueberry pie–eating contest (once televised on ESPN) high on the steps of the historic Congregational church (which houses a working Paul Revere bell) and an original blueberry musical written just for that year's celebration. A blueberry quilt raffle, a blueberry pancake breakfast, and a popular early morning 5K run round out this signature event. Visit machiasblueberry.com for more information.

Maine State Star Party

Every August, the Downeast Amateur Astronomers group holds the Maine State Star Party at Cobscook Bay State Park. Washington County is one of the best places on the eastern seaboard to view the night sky (see page 5), and this event is designed to recognize, observe, and protect that status. There are lectures, viewing opportunities, and, of course, camping under the stars at the state park campground on-site. Search the Internet for "Maine State Star Party" to find information about the current year's event.

Autumn

Fall weather usually arrives right about on time in the third week of September. Early September can be very summer-like with temperatures that may reach into the eighties, though most nights are cool. One day, there is a hint of coldness in the air and the slightly sweet smell of moist humus on the forest floor. Ready or not, temperatures will now regularly be in the sixties or even fifties during the day, dipping down to the freezing point or lower at night. By the equinox, the first maple trees will have begun to turn brilliant red, and the blueberry barrens, which were tinged blue just a few weeks earlier before the harvest, also turn a shocking shade of crimson. One by one, the other deciduous trees and plants join in the riot of color. The forest can seem like a kaleidoscope, but people who know their trees can identify them from afar by the color the leaves turn. Red for maple, yellow for birch and aspen, brown for oak and beech. The last to turn color is the hackmatack, also known as larch, which is the only deciduous conifer in the region, meaning that it has needles instead of leaves, but these turn color and drop off each fall. The larch needles turn an orange-yellow, like the color of ground turmeric, and stand out from the drab gray that adorns most of the trees by that time. Eventually nearly all color is gone from the forest, and enthusiasts revel in the various shades of brown, gray, and green that will dominate the forest for the next seven months or so.

The State of Maine maintains a website (mainefoliage.com) with foliage observations around the state to help you find the right time to go leaf-peeping. According to this website, the peak in this region typically falls during the period from October 22 to October 27, though I would say it really happens earlier, from around October 10 to October 20. This varies from year to year, so if fall colors are your thing, check the state's website for that year's foliage observations.

Beginning just after the blueberry harvest in August and continuing through the fall and even into early spring, each field is burned every other year. This keeps the weeds and pests at bay and rejuvenates the blueberries, which produce a much higher crop when managed this way. In recent years, growers have begun to mow the fields instead of burning them, which is a more environmentally sensitive and safer alternative. The fields that are burned will turn black for a few weeks until the rain washes all the ash away. This forms an amazing contrast with the crimson fields right next door that were not burned.

The other color that makes its appearance each fall is safety orange. Hunting season, which is never really over for some species, like coyote and some small game, heats up in early September with bear season, followed by deer season. There are several weeks of archery-only deer hunting, into October, with the month-long November rifle season finishing off the hunting year for most hunters. During this time orange becomes a fashion statement, along with camouflage. Locals wear their colors like a flag of support for the hunting lifestyle, even if they never set foot in

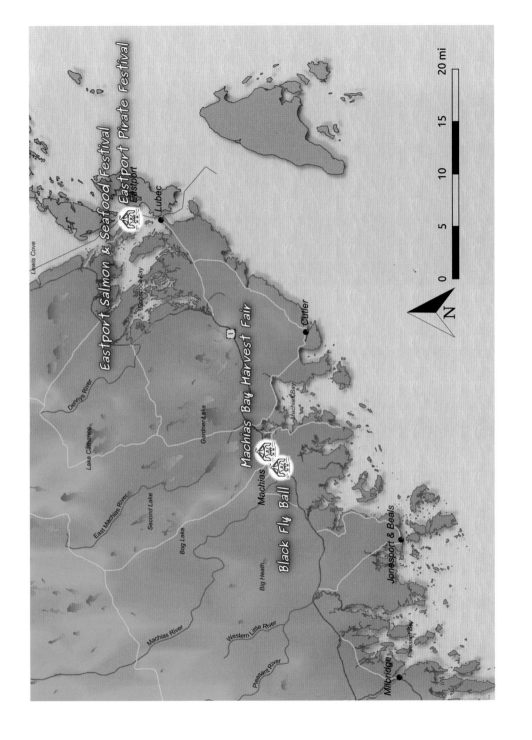

Blueberry barrens turn a nearly unbelievable shade of red each autumn.

the woods. Orange is also recommended for visitors, because virtually all trails in the region permit hunting alongside hiking and other uses. This can frighten those who are less comfortable about people hiding in the woods looking to shoot something, but the truth is that hunters in this region have proven that they are careful and safe, with very few accidental shootings over a history of many years. The recommendation is to wear orange from October through the end of November, and don't let fear keep you from enjoying this magical period in the woods. Also remember that there is no hunting of any kind on Sunday, so you can always enjoy a hike without worrying, at least once a week.

Black Fly Ball

The annual Black Fly Ball should not be missed if you're in Machias at the time. For many years the ball has been held in August in conjunction with the Machias Wild Blueberry Festival, but in 2019 it will be held in October for the first time. There may be some changes in the program or feeling, but there is no doubt that locals and visitors will turn out in droves for the best musical event of the year. Up to five stages are used for a rotating list of bands, beginning with open mics and lesser-known local bands in the late afternoon and moving to touring bands later on. The options include indie rock, country, jazz, klezmer, and gypsy music. A predictable favorite at the Black Fly Ball is the Machias Ukulele Club, a ragtag group that gathers for many special events throughout the year to play feel-good standards and songs you know by heart. The evening usually closes out with a raucous steampunk brass marching band (this is not your high school marching band, by the way). The event is billed as a "Dress Up Party for All," and that means whatever you want it to. People arrive in gowns and suits, in something resembling Halloween costumes, or in their jeans and muck boots right off the lobster boat. It's all up to you, as long as you're kicking up your heels and partying (alcohol- and drug-free) at what is, for many people, the most anticipated public event of the year. Find information on Facebook by watching the Beehive Design Collective's page. The Beehive Collective is a group of artists dispersed across the country, and even the globe, but is based in Machias and the Black Fly Ball is their signature event each year.

Eastport Salmon and Seafood Festival

On Saturday and Sunday of Labor Day weekend, Eastport celebrates the end of summer with the Eastport Salmon and Seafood Festival. This festival is a lead-up to the Pirate Festival the following weekend, so don't be surprised to see a few people in shiny black boots, waistcoats, and maybe an eye patch. The festival includes art shows, public suppers, a silent auction, live music, boat tours, beer and spirit sampling, and much more. Of course, salmon and other seafood are the star of the show, but really it's just a great excuse to stroll around Eastport and take in the last few days of the summer season. Learn more at eastportchamber.net/eastportsalmonfest.

Eastport Pirate Festival

Local legends have it that more than one pirate took refuge in the hidden bays of Down East Maine. To commemorate, the Eastport Pirate Festival is held each year during the

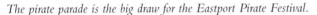

The pirate parade is the big draw for the Eastport Pirate Festival.

weekend following Labor Day. The festivities actually begin on Labor Day weekend when "pirates" from Eastport arrive in Lubec by boat and proceed to rampage around town causing havoc and making more than a few stops at bars in town. It's all in good fun and sets the stage for a pirate festival that is more Pirates of the Caribbean than Blackbeard. On Pirate Festival weekend, men, women, and children roam the streets of Eastport dressed in pirate garb (eye patches, fake parrots, and fake swords are standard). Many women dress as wenches—usually in a tasteful way, if such a thing is possible, given that this is a family event. A packed agenda will keep scallywags busy from early on Friday straight through to Sunday afternoon, with a parade, costume contests, live music, boat tours and whale-watching trips around the bay, and lots more. The whole town gets in the act, but even at its height, parking is relatively easy within a few blocks of Water Street, and you won't wait too long for a lobster roll at Quoddy Bay Lobster Company. Find more information at eastportpiratefestival.com.

Machias Bay Harvest Fair

With more than thirty vendors taking part, along with children's games, a chili contest, and even a "Seagull Calling Contest," which debuted in 2018, the Machias Bay Harvest Fair is a great excuse to get out and celebrate the bounty of nature as the growing season draws to a close. In the past they have also held a pumpkin chucking contest in which catapults and trebuchets were used to launch pumpkins out into the bay, so you never know what they might add in future years. There is also a fly-in event at the Machias Valley Regional Airport on the same weekend as the fair. The date of the festival floats but is usually in the middle of September. Information is available from the Machias Bay Chamber of Commerce at machiaschamber.org.

Contestants try their hand in the seagull calling contest at the Machias Bay Harvest Fair.

Winter

Winter here is defined by the incredibly long nights and achingly short days. The sun is low on the horizon, even in the middle of the day, and is gone before you know it, with darkness coming before 4 p.m. for nearly the entire month of December. The darkness leaves plenty of time for quiet times—reading, playing games, feeding the woodstove, and getting plenty of sleep. Meanwhile, the short days are all that much more precious. There is nothing like a winter day with cold air, fresh white snow on the ground, and a brilliant blue sky above—a bluebird day, as one of my bosses used to call it. For those who are prepared for the elements, the long nights and high heating bills are well worth it for the outdoor recreation opportunities the region offers (see page 131).

The social gatherings during the winter can be amazing. You bundle up and brave the cold wind to get from your car door to the brewery or restaurant, the air burning your cheeks as you walk briskly to the door. You open the door and slip inside as quickly as possible to avoid letting all the heat out. As you strip off the hat, gloves, scarf, and jacket, the feeling of camaraderie with the other customers is unmistakable. You're all in this together, this monumental challenge of surviving the winter, and you've made it out to enjoy a beer, maybe a pizza, and some live music with your peers.

The main events that gather many people together are clustered around Christmas and the New Year.

The winter sun, hanging low on the horizon, is brilliant but doesn't offer much warmth.

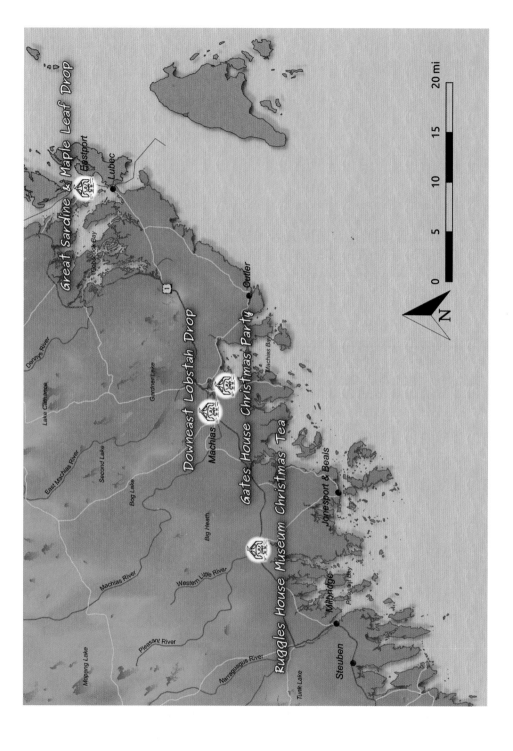

Ruggles House Museum Christmas Tea

At the Ruggles House Museum in Columbia Falls there is an annual tea in December, often with live music that evokes the seafaring life. The Ruggles House is a restored Adamesque Federal-style home that is now a historical museum. The home, built in 1818, features a famous flying staircase. Learn more at ruggleshouse.org.

The Gates House Christmas Party

The Gates House, a restored sea captain's home from the early 1800s right on Machias Bay, hosts an annual Christmas party. Members of the Machiasport Historical Society (and anyone else so inclined) dress in period clothing, sing old-time Christmas carols, and share in traditional finger foods and cider. The place is decorated to the nines with authentic holiday decor. Find more information at machiasporthistoricalsociety.org.

Downeast Lobstah Drop

The Downeast Lobstah Drop is a relatively new celebration in Machias. A crane is brought in to hoist a giant lobster that is dropped at the stroke of midnight. Leading up to this climax is a varying schedule of events and shows around Machias and the nearby region. Find more information at downeastlobstahdrop.com.

The Great Sardine and Maple Leaf Drop

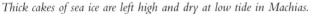

The Great Sardine and Maple Leaf Drop is a two-nation celebration in Eastport. At 11 p.m. Eastern time (12 a.m. Atlantic time), a giant maple leaf is dropped from the

Thick cakes of sea ice are left high and dry at low tide in Machias.

third story of the Tides Institute while a band plays "O Canada." At midnight Eastern time a giant sardine is lowered from the same place to the tune of "Auld Lang Syne." The whole day includes live music and special events all over the city. Lodging space is limited, so make reservations early if you plan to spend the night. If you don't spend the night, have a designated driver if you are drinking; the single road in and out of Eastport makes it easy for law enforcement to find impaired drivers. Learn more at tidesinstitute.org/new-years-eve.

View!

Destinations

Driftwood and cobblestones.

The places I'm calling "Destinations" are, in some cases, just my idea of a great place for a picnic, even though not all of the locations have a picnic table. These are the places that may warrant a longer visit than just an opportunity to stretch your legs or use the bathroom. Of course, it's fine if that's all you do, but if you're on the lookout for a great spot to spend part of your day, this list will be helpful. See page 84 for my "Quick Stops" list, with beautiful places to visit but that may not warrant going far out of your way to see.

Tidal Falls Preserve

Tidal Falls Road, Hancock; picnic tables, restrooms, visitor center

Twice each day the tide rushes through the narrows at this location, filling Taunton Bay with water and creating rushing whitewater at the Tidal Falls Preserve, a property owned by Frenchman Bay Conservancy. Twice each day the tide reverses itself

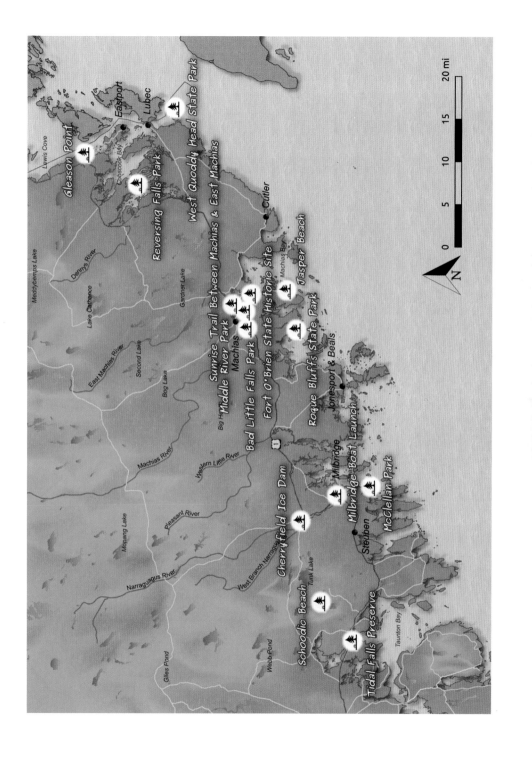

and rushes out, nearly emptying Taunton Bay, creating rushing whitewater in the opposite direction. Enjoy the sounds of the rushing water, seals, eagles, and water birds frolicking and feeding in the bay. Catch Frenchman Bay Conservancy's Monday night music concert series at Tidal Falls during the summer.

Schoodic Beach at Donnell Pond

no street address, T9 SD (see page 175 for driving directions); picnic tables, beach, swimming

This is the only picnic area in this section that requires a short hike from your car, but it is well worth including it in your itinerary if possible. The hike to the beach is about half a mile on relatively easy and wide trails. Many people use sturdy carts or all-terrain baby strollers to carry their gear to the beach. Once there, you can find a picnic table or spread out on the sand to enjoy the views of Donnell Pond and Schoodic Mountain. This is one of the most exquisite freshwater beaches in the state, which is one reason that you may find it quite crowded on summer weekends, at least by Down East standards. Combine a picnic here with a hike up either Schoodic Mountain or Black Mountain, and then cool off afterward with a swim at the beach. Camping is also permitted here.

A stop at Schoodic Beach is well worth the half-mile walk from the parking lot.

Cherryfield Ice Dam

*Cable Pool Road, Cherryfield; picnic tables, seasonal outhouse,
hand-carry boat launch*

A quaint town park on the outskirts of the village of Cherryfield with some grassy areas, a few picnic tables, and access to the Narraguagus River (pronounced nar-a-GWAY-gus). This is a historic salmon fishing pool that was known across the state before Atlantic salmon became an endangered species. It is also accessible from the Sunrise Trail, which crosses the river on an old railroad bridge near the park.

Milbridge Boat Launch

*Bay View Road, Milbridge; picnic table, horseshoe pits (bring your own
horseshoes), seasonal outhouse*

This is very much an active working waterfront location, so leisure activities must defer to the needs of fishers. Enjoy the view and the occasional activity on fishing boats moored nearby, but please do so without getting in the way.

The Milbridge public boat launch has a picnic area with a view that can't be beat.

A picnic table at McClellan Park is literally on the shore.

McClellan Park

Wyman Road, Milbridge; picnic tables, short trails, camping

McClellan Park is a relatively wild town park in Milbridge. While enjoying the rocky ledges at the shore, watch fishing boats coming and going as they pass from the town harbor out to the open ocean. Campsites are also available for a fee (see page 268).

Bad Little Falls Park

Elm Street, Machias; picnic tables

This is a somewhat hidden park in the center of the village of Machias with stunning and varied views of the waterfalls that earned the town the name of Machias (roughly translated as "Bad Little Falls" in the Passamaquoddy language). A grassy lawn area offers a place for young ones to run and play, but use caution when they approach the river. Guardrails here will not prevent them from falling off of cliffs. A footbridge crosses a branch of the river, taking you to an island with several viewpoints, a small gazebo, and pedestrian access to the main part of the village. There is also a short riverside trail that heads downriver from the grassy section of the park.

The footbridge at Bad Little Falls Park gets you up close and personal with the Machias River.

Middle River Park

Kilton Lane, Machias; picnic tables, walking trails, sledding, hand-carry boat launch

The picnic area here is part of a Downeast Coastal Conservancy preserve with two miles or so of hiking trails, access to the Sunrise Trail, and the only canoe and kayak

The picnic area at Middle River Park is an easy walk from most of the town's restaurants.

access point on the Middle River, one of two rivers that run through Machias. The picnic area is set on top of a hill with beautiful views of Middle River and the Machias River estuary. In winter the hill is a very popular place for families to go sledding. You can grab a lunch at one of several nearby restaurants and be at Middle River Park in just a couple of minutes to enjoy the view or give the kids a chance to burn off some energy.

Fort O'Brien State Historic Site

Port Road, Machiasport; no amenities

The park centers around the remains of Fort O'Brien, also once called Fort Machias, which played a role in the American Revolution and the War of 1812. Perched atop a bluff overlooking all of outer Machias Bay, you can imagine a British war sloop coming toward town. Large mounds that are remnants of battlements and a cannon complete the picture. This stop is well worth a visit for the view alone, but the history is also very important to this region.

Jasper Beach

Port Road, Machiasport; no amenities

Jasper Beach in Howard Cove is one of the most popular attractions in the Machias area. The beach, made entirely of rounded rocks about the size of walnuts to apples,

Sunrise at Jasper Beach.

is quite amazing to walk on and explore. The once-popular idea that this is a genuine jasper beach is inaccurate (although a very small percentage of the stones do contain jasper). Rather, it is volcanic rhyolite that gives the smooth rocks their reddish color and gemlike look, especially when wet. Anyone who had a rock tumbler when they were a kid knows what I mean. A highlight of a visit here is listening to the rocks as they "sing" when waves crash on the beach and the water is pulled through the gaps among the billions and billions of stones. It is claimed that only one other beach of this geology exists in the world, although I cannot verify this. Regardless, it is truly a magical place to visit.

Roque Bluffs State Park

Schoppee Point Road; Roque Bluffs; fee charged, picnic areas, seasonal outhouses, swimming, ocean beach, freshwater pond

Despite being one of the only places in this chapter to charge admission, Roque Bluffs State Park is the most popular ocean sand beach in the region (see Schoodic Beach for a lake beach). On one side of the road is the expansive beach, accessed through a variety of paths through the beach rose bushes that smell heavenly in season. Although the water is frigid year-round, hearty souls at least dip their toes in the ocean before spending their time walking the beach looking for shells and interesting rocks, watching the interesting assemblages of seabirds that raft just offshore, and enjoying the view of offshore islands. On the other side of the road

The wheelchair-accessible platform at Roque Bluffs State Park allows all users to enjoy the beauty of the beach.

are picnic tables, barbecue grills, outhouses, and a freshwater pond that kids enjoy swimming in since it is much warmer than the ocean. See page 128 for swimming at Roque Bluffs State Park.

Sunrise Trail between Machias and East Machias

Route 1, Machias

The stretch of Down East Sunrise Trail between Route 1 in Machias and where it rejoins Route 1 in East Machias is one of the most stunningly beautiful areas in the region. There are two picnic tables along the route, including one that is easily accessible right off Route 1 and the other that is a mile and half toward East Machias. You can also simply walk down the trail and sit on the waterside rocks nearly anywhere along the first half mile or so of trail.

Quoddy Head State Park

South Lubec Road, Lubec; picnic tables, seasonal outhouse, hiking trails

The red-and-white candy-striped lighthouse at the easternmost point in the continental United States is the subject of thousands of visitors' photos every year, and with good reason. The rocky shore, steep cliffs, interesting birds, occasional whale sightings, and excellent views of Canada's Campobello Island and Grand Manan Island are definitely worth the stop if you are near Lubec. A small museum and gift shop at the base of the lighthouse are open seasonally. More than six miles of hiking trails are accessible from here. See page 109 for more on the lighthouse and page 230 for the hiking trails.

Reversing Falls Park

Reversing Falls Road, Pembroke; picnic tables, hiking trails

This is one of the most popular, but hardest to find, attractions Down East. The field, parking area, and main viewpoints are owned by the town of Pembroke. Similar to the Tidal Falls Preserve, the incoming and outgoing tides produce wild whitewater that reverses direction with each change of the tide. Eagles and seals are commonly seen here. To the left of the upper viewing area, blue blazes mark the beginning of a half-mile hiking trail (on land owned by Downeast Coastal Conservancy) that offers several other vantage points from which to view the action.

Gleason Point is a great place to watch fishing boats on the bay and let the kids blow off some steam.

Gleason Point

Gleason Cove Road, Perry; boat launch, picnic tables, charcoal grill

Not far from Eastport, this is a beautiful spot for a break or a picnic. There are nice views out to Canada's Deer Island across the channel, and local fishing boats are always in view. An old fish weir (a pen for catching fish) is still visible, though it hasn't been used for several years.

Quick Stops

My "Quick Stops" list consists of some of my favorite places to stop and smell the roses as I'm out and about in the region. These are places that may be worth a stop if you're in the area but probably don't warrant a long drive out of your way. In some cases a major road is too close for a peaceful rest, and in an area that has so many secluded places, there is no point in spreading out the picnic blanket and napping in the shade listening to cars and trucks whizzing by. Nevertheless, these quick stops are perfect as places to stretch your legs, have a cup of coffee, or check the map to plan the rest of your day's adventure.

Many of these locations have few, if any, formal amenities like restrooms or picnic tables. As with most things Down East, it is up to you to make do without the luxuries of organized town park departments. The reward is enjoying a sublime rest stop, often with no other people in sight.

Long Cove Rest Area

2180 US Route 1, Sullivan; picnic tables, restrooms open seasonally

Right on Route 1, this is a convenient and scenic location for a picnic or a break on the drive east. At high tide, Long Cove fills with just a few feet of water and is frequented by an assortment of birds, often including eagles. At low tide, you might see people digging clams on the exposed mudflats.

Long Cove Rest Area has a series of educational signs to help kids learn fun facts while they wait for lunch.

Sipp Bay

Shackford Head

Eastport Breakwater/shore path

Eastport

Eubec

Lost Fishermen's Memorial

Mowry Beach

Morong Cove

Patrick Lake

Gardner Lake Dam

Reynold's Marsh Overlook

EMARC

Machias

Cutler

Columbia Falls Boat Launch

Mason Bay Conservation Area

Jonesport & Beals

Milbridge

Steuben

Pinkham Bay Bridge

Prospect Harbor

Fox Pond

Long Cove Rest Area

Lewis Cove

Meddybemps Lake

Dennys River

Lake Cathance

East Machias River

Second Lake

Bog Lake

Big Heath

Machias River

Machias Bay

Pleasant Bay

Pleasant River

Narraguagus River

West Branch Narraguagus

Tunk Lake

Webb Pond

Mopang Lake

Taunton Bay

N

0   5   10   15   20 mi

Prospect Harbor

200 ME Route 186, Gouldsboro; no amenities

This is simply a dirt pull-off in the middle of Prospect Harbor with a gorgeous view of the working harbor. With room for only one vehicle and no real space to play, this is pretty much a place for a quick stop but worth knowing about if you are headed east from the Schoodic section of Acadia National Park.

Fox Pond

ME Route 182, T10 SD; no amenities

The very scenic Blackwoods Road (Route 182) touches several lakes and ponds with boat launches where you might want to stop and enjoy the view. Fox Pond is unique in that the road runs right along the shore of the pond for half a mile, with several wide dirt areas where you can pull over to enjoy the view without losing much time along your way.

Pinkham Bay Bridge

Pinkham Bay Bridge Road, Steuben; no amenities

This is a place that few people know about, other than locals. At both ends of the Pinkham Bay Bridge, which makes it sound much bigger than it is, there are dirt areas where you can pull over and watch the tide rushing under the bridge, birds and wildlife out in the bay, and clam diggers turning over the mudflats in search of clams. This is a great place for a quick stop. Be sure not to park in front of the boat-loading ramp to avoid irritating the fishers who earn their living on the bay.

Columbia Falls Boat Launch

Maine Street, Columbia Falls; picnic table, hand-carry boat launch

This small park in the village of Columbia Falls on the shore of the Pleasant River estuary is an excellent opportunity to view eagles and interesting water birds. Learn about efforts to restore salmon and other sea-run fish at the adjacent Wild Salmon Resource Center run by the Downeast Salmon Federation. (See also the picnic area at the related East Machias Aquatic Resource Center, also run by Downeast Salmon Federation.)

The Wild Salmon Resource Center is the headquarters for the Downeast Salmon Federation.

The Pleasant River rushes through a rocky channel at the head of tide.

The expansive field at Mason Bay Conservation Area is maintained for bird habitat.

Mason Bay Conservation Area

Route 187, Jonesport; picnic table, walking trail

A delightful place for a relatively quick stop. The picnic table is a little exposed to the main road (which isn't all that busy), but the pastoral view is worth the stop if you're whizzing by on the Scenic Drive on Route 187. If you have a little more time, informal trails take you through the field and to the shoreline of Mason Bay.

EMARC

Willow Street, East Machias; picnic table, restroom (during business hours), access to Sunrise Trail

Situated right on the banks of the East Machias River, the picnic table at the East Machias Aquatic Resource Center (EMARC) is a lovely place to pause during a summer day. During the spring alewife runs, this location is in the center of the action as seals, eagles, ospreys, cormorants, and gulls gorge on this herring species that migrates up the river to breed each April (see page 59). Take advantage of the visitor center at EMARC to learn about aquatic ecology and the efforts of the Downeast Salmon Federation to restore and protect Atlantic salmon and other sea-run fish (including alewives).

Gardner Lake Dam

Chases Mill Road, East Machias; picnic tables, outhouse, small sand beach, boat launch

A favorite spot for locals to cool off in the summer (see page 130), this can also be a great spot to stretch your legs, enjoy the view of Gardner Lake, and check out the fish ladder in the dam.

Patrick Lake

ME Route 86, Marion Township; hand-carry boat launch

There are few amenities here, and it's probably not worth a long drive out of your way to see, but if you are traveling between Dennysville and East Machias on Route 92, it's worth a look and can be a good resting spot. The lake is almost completely wild, with no houses bordering it, so the view even from the parking area is serene.

Patrick Lake is a small but very beautiful lake.

Reynold's Marsh Overlook

Route 1, Whiting; picnic table, hand-carry boat launch

This location is part of Downeast Coastal Conservancy's Orange River Conservation Area. A single picnic table is available to enjoy the view of a freshwater marsh that is usually buzzing with life during the summer, including a nearby beaver lodge, plenty of ducks, dragonflies, and, unfortunately, mosquitoes and blackflies (depending on the season). See page 155 for paddling opportunities here.

Morong Cove

Straight Bay Road, Lubec; bench, accessible parking and path to viewpoint

This section of the Cobscook Bay Wildlife Management Area (owned and managed by the Maine Department of Inland Fisheries and Wildlife) is an old farm field with bucolic views of the old hay field and the bay beyond. An interpretive panel describing life along the margins of the sea marks this as a site on the Downeast Fisheries Trail. As an aside, this is a site that I'm proud to say I created. It is a small part of the Wildlife Management Area from where I enjoyed the view occasionally. Thanks to grants, and help from the Downeast Fisheries Trail, we built a parking lot and installed a bench and interpretive sign.

The Morong Cove stop overlooks an old farm field and the inner parts of Morong Cove.

Mowry Beach

Pleasant Street, Lubec; no amenities

This section of beach and adjacent marsh boardwalk are owned by Downeast Coastal Conservancy. This is a favorite place for locals to enjoy the beach and for visitors to marvel at the dramatic differences between high and low tide. At low tide the water is nearly a half-mile away or close to the iconic "spark plug" lighthouse in the middle of the Lubec Channel. Views of Canada's Campobello Island make it a year-round destination, but the thousands of migrating shorebirds that feed here in early autumn make this a must-see location for birders.

Lost Fishermen's Memorial

North Water Street, Lubec; bench

Set right in the village of Lubec, the memorial is a sobering and heartfelt reminder of the risks associated with making one's living from the ocean here in Maine. The Lubec breakwater and harbor are close by, as is Mulholland Light, just across the channel on Canada's Campobello Island. Grab a lunch or snack at any of several restaurants in Lubec and sit near the memorial to watch the tide rushing by. When fish are running, you can watch dozens of seals and several eagles just offshore.

The Lost Fishermen's Memorial is Lubec's testament to the dangers of working on the North Atlantic.

Sipp Bay

Birby Road, Perry; boat launch, picnic table

The site of a former campground, the Sipp Bay Preserve is now a Maine Coast Heritage Trust preserve (see page 253 for the hiking trail). There are great views of inner parts of Cobscook Bay here, including an excellent look at boiling and rushing tides near the end of the peninsula (at the end of the road past the picnic area).

The Eastport shore path is right next to downtown and offers beautiful views of several islands in Canada.

Eastport Breakwater/shore path

Water Street, Eastport; picnic tables, benches

In downtown Eastport you can't miss the large breakwater that forms a protected harbor for much of the town's fishing fleet. The breakwater is open to the public, and you can fish for mackerel when they run. At the landward edge of the breakwater, the Eastport shore path picks up. This is just a short paved path between the backside of the town's businesses and the waterfront. As part of the town's revitalization from purely a fishing village to a tourism- and visitor-based economy, the path has been spruced up with a small amphitheater and several sculptures. This is the place to be for the annual Independence Day fireworks.

Shackford Head State Park

Deep Cove Road, Eastport; picnic tables, small pavilion, toilet, access to Cony Beach

Near the trailhead for the Shackford Head trails (see page 258), there is a small picnic area with excellent views out into Broad Cove, a beautiful but industrial landscape with the Eastport cargo pier and floating salmon aquaculture pens, in addition to the forest, beach, and abundant waterfowl.

Boat Launches

Several of the quick stops detailed in this section are also boat launches. The truth is that nearly any public boat launch in the area would make an excellent place to stop and enjoy the view or eat a picnic lunch. If you want to find your own secret spot, consult the *Maine Atlas and Gazetteer*, which shows boat launch icons up and down the ocean shore and on the majority of the lakes and rivers that dot the region. You can also consult the *Coastal Access Guide*, published by the state of Maine. Just be sure to stay out of the way of commercial fishers (if there are any), and make room for people loading or unloading boats.

Scenic Drives

One activity almost anyone can enjoy is a nice scenic drive, whether that means taking the long way to get somewhere else or the whole point of the outing is to see some scenery. The extensive forests, amazing coastlines, colorful blueberry barrens, and quaint villages make it hard to decide where to go. In a place where pretty much every road is a scenic route, how do you choose? Below are a few of my favorite stretches of road with some hints about what you'll see along the way.

In general, these directions are given as if you're headed north on Route 1 toward Eastport, so they tend to originate in the south or western extent of the drive and proceed north or east.

Bold Coast Scenic Byway

Milbridge to Eastport

The Bold Coast Scenic Byway is a 125-mile-long driving route that runs through the heart of the Bold Coast region. It incorporates a couple of scenic sections that I detail here. You can drive the whole byway, or just know that while you are out exploring on your own, this scenic route is a great way to get from here to there. Information at discoverboldcoast.com/bold-coast-scenic-byway.

Blackwoods Scenic Byway/Route 182

Hancock, Franklin, T10 SD, and Cherryfield

The Blackwoods Road, also known as Route 182, is an alternative to Route 1 while traveling from the Ellsworth area to farther Down East. The byway runs through the middle of a large block of public land (the Donnell Pond Unit of Public Reserved Land), with access to several hikes, at least five lakes, and a very diverse forest. The road is quite twisty and hilly for this region, so use caution at night or in bad weather. This is a must-see if you happen to visit during fall foliage season.

The stretch of Route 1 that you bypass is also very beautiful, so you may decide to take this road one way and Route 1 the other direction.

From the intersection of Route 1 and Route 182 in Hancock, take Route 182 for 23.8 miles to Cherryfield. In the first few miles, you'll get a couple of glimpses of Taunton Bay on your right before entering the village of Franklin. Other than a gas station/convenience store, there are no retail businesses in Franklin. Within a few miles of leaving Franklin, the Blackwoods Road enters the Donnell Pond Public Reserved Land. Blue road signs indicate trailheads and lake access points, including Fox Pond (see page 86), the Caribou Loop Trail (see page 178), Tunk Mountain (see page 172), Tunk Lake (see page 127), and Spring River Lake.

A steep hill along the way is known as Catherine's Hill. This is the site of one of the most famous Maine-based ghost stories. The story varies from teller to teller, but it usually revolves around a bride-to-be, Catherine, who was killed on the way to her wedding and is forever seeking a ride to make it to the nuptials. If you see someone in a long, flowing dress along the road, especially on a foggy night, you'd better stop and give her a ride to the wedding or risk her wrath. This tale, and other spooky stories, is told well in the book *Dark Woods, Chill Waters: Ghost Tales from Down East Maine* by Dr. Marcus LiBrizzi of the University of Maine at Machias.

The Blackwoods Road ends at the intersection with Route 1 in Cherryfield.

Route 187

Columbia Falls, Addison, Jonesport, and Jonesboro

Route 187 is a U-shaped road that leaves Route 1 in the town of Columbia Falls and arrives back at Route 1 in Jonesboro (or vice versa). The trip is roughly thirty minutes if you don't take a side trip to Beals Island from Jonesport (which you should if you have time). Allow another twenty minutes for a quick look at the fishing village of Beals. By comparison, the direct route from Columbia Falls to Jonesboro takes about six minutes on Route 1.

The route begins at Wild Blueberry Land (a giant domed blueberry selling all things blueberry!) in Columbia Falls and proceeds south and east on Route 187 through parts of Addison and Jonesport. For an even longer trip, you can combine the Basin Road scenic drive by turning right onto Wescogus Road 1.8 miles from Route 1 (see page 97 for the rest of that route). Route 187 continues toward Jonesport, and you'll start to see glimpses of the ocean where Indian River empties to the sea under the road. From here it isn't far to downtown Jonesport. See page 43 for a description of Jonesport and its amenities. At 10.4 miles from Route 1, you can turn right to take the bridge across to Beals Island and the town of Beals.

Other than the Great Wass Island Preserve (see page 197 for the hiking trail), the Downeast Institute, and a single takeout restaurant, there isn't much for a visitor to do in Beals, but just driving the main road offers a glimpse of the truest authentic fishing village. From the bridge continue straight on Bay View Drive and bear left onto Alleys Bay Road about 1.6 miles from the intersection of Route 187 (bear right here to get to the Great Wass Preserve or the Downeast Institute). This road eventually ends at some marine businesses that have no public services, so turn around when it feels right and return to Jonesport. Be sure to call ahead if you'd like to plan a visit to the Downeast Institute (207-497-5769), a marine research facility on Great Wass Island, in Beals.

Back on Route 187 in Jonesport, continue east and eventually north through the rest of the village of Jonesport. As you leave the village, views begin to open up over Chandler Bay. A few places have wide spots where you can pull over to enjoy the

One of the many beautiful views from Route 187 in Jonesport.

Bar Island sits just a few yards offshore and is accessible at low tide.

view. Roque Island beckons from across the water. The entire island and an associated archipelago are owned by a single family. On the southeast side of the island is a dreamy sand beach that the owners have opened for boaters, who can also anchor in the somewhat protected cove. Continuing north on Route 187, the road skirts the edges of some commercial blueberry barrens overlooking the ocean before heading inland for the rest of the drive back to Route 1.

East Side Road to Basin Road

Addison

Basin Road is an add-on to the Route 187 loop already described to explore a little deeper off Route 1. From the intersection of Route 1 and Route 187 at Wild Blueberry Land, head south on Route 187 for 1.8 miles and bear right onto Wescogus Road at a sharp bend in the road. The scenery begins immediately with views of the Pleasant River and the village of Addison in the distance beyond a cemetery placed at the edge of a blueberry barren (not an uncommon co-location). Wescogus Road ends after 1.4 miles. Turn left onto East Side Road, which you'll follow for 5.9 miles. The first few miles of the East Side Road offer close access to the Pleasant River (the tidal portion that is part of Pleasant Bay) and views of salt marsh and mudflats. At a sharp bend to the left, which marks the beginning of the Basin Road, you can also bear right to go down onto Cape Split, the farthest point of mainland in the town of Addison. The Ingersoll Point hike is on Cape Split. Toward the end of the cape is a

This view from Wescogus Road in Addison is quintessential Down East beauty.

small town landing with some associated hiking trails (not detailed in this book) and a larger commercial boat launch, each of which offers views in different directions. Back on the Basin Road, continue generally northeastward for 5.8 miles to Route 187. Along the way there are beautiful stretches of rural homesteads, shrubby headlands overlooking coves and bays, and some stellar views.

Centerville Road to Station Road

Columbia Falls and Jonesboro

This byway parallels Route 1 from Columbia Falls into the village of Jonesboro but offers a great look at some relatively large blueberry barrens. For a trip through really extensive barrens, you can research a route that includes Pea Ridge Road and Schoodic Road in Columbia. There are a number of ways to access those roads, and I'll leave it to you to explore if you're interested.

From the intersection of Route 1 and Tibbetstown Road in Columbia Falls, turn onto Tibbetstown Road and make a right turn after less than five hundred feet. Drive for 3.7 miles, beginning in forest but eventually breaking out into the blueberry barrens. At the end of the road, turn right onto Station Road, which takes you 6.0 miles back to Route 1 in Jonesboro. Along the way the road goes through some forested stretches and some blueberry barrens and also offers a glimpse of a forest that has been converted to produce primarily balsam fir that is used to make holiday wreaths each late fall. To be precise, these trees produce the wreaths that adorn the headstones of veterans at Arlington National Cemetery and at veterans' graves across the country, a project of the Wreaths Across America Foundation.

Port Road/Route 92

Machias and Machiasport

The road from downtown Machias to Machiasport, known locally as the Port Road or Route 92, is about 11.2 miles to the very end. Along the way you'll pass a Revolutionary War historical site, several wide views of parts of Machias Bay, and access to Jasper Beach.

From the intersection of Route 1 and Route 92 in the center of Machias, turn onto Route 92. Almost immediately, you'll pass Bad Little Falls Park on the left, at a sharp bend to the right. In 3.0 miles, a left turn would take you to the Rim Bridge with its stunning views and into East Machias. Continuing on the Port Road, the road quickly meets the waters of Machias Bay on your left.

At 3.8 miles, you'll reach the Gates House, a beautifully restored sea captain's house, owned by the Machiasport Historical Society (see page 71 for the annual Christmas party here). You can launch a boat behind the Gates House for access to inner Machias Bay (see page 143). From here the road quickly climbs a steep hill to

A cannon at Fort O'Brien State Historic Site stands guard over Machias Bay and the entrance to the Machias River.

the First Congregational Church, with a cemetery overlooking Machias Bay with graves dating back to the Revolutionary War era.

At 4.6 miles, the entrance to Fort O'Brien State Historic Site is on your left. The road then sweeps around Sanborn Cove and down the western edge of Machias Bay. After 8.7 miles, Pettegrow Point Road leaves from the left side. This short, dead-end road goes into the village of Bucks Harbor, a fishing hamlet within Machiasport. There are nice views of the working waterfront and a real taste of Down East. Literally, you can purchase lobsters right from BBS lobster pound, a company that purchases directly from the boat captains. Turn around at one of the public water access points and return to the Port Road.

The entrance to Jasper Beach is 9.5 miles from the beginning of the drive. This is a must-see stop if you've made it this far down the road (see pages 80 and 129). Finally, the road ends at 11.2 miles in a place with stunning views of outer Machias Bay and several of its islands. Private dirt roads continue from here, but the public is not invited. Return to Machias the way you came.

Route 191 through Cutler

East Machias, Whiting, Cutler, Trescott Township, Lubec

If you're doing any hiking at all while you're in this region, you'll probably find yourself on Route 191 through Cutler. This book includes five trails accessible from this route (Long Point, page 208; Eastern Knubble, page 213; Cutler Coast Unit, page 214; Norse Pond Trail, page 220; and Moose Cove, page 224). There are several other trails on this stretch that you might happen across as well. The entire route is about twenty-seven miles and takes roughly thirty-five minutes without stops.

From the intersection of Route 1 and Route 191 South in East Machias, take Route 191 South for 27 miles to the intersection of Route 191 and Route 189 in Lubec. Along the way you'll have varied views of Machias Bay, Little Machias Bay, and Cutler Harbor and a couple of glimpses of small coves and tidal rivers beyond that.

Seven miles from Route 1, you'll see a sign on your right for A to Z Variety, which is your last opportunity to buy anything other than lobsters. Just beyond A to Z, you'll have an opportunity for the closest approach allowed to the Cutler towers, the US Naval facility used to search the horizon for enemy submarines during the Cold War. The eight-hundred-foot towers are visible, especially at night, for miles in every direction and it is interesting to get a better look at this complex facility.

As already alluded to, the village of Cutler has no real public businesses to speak of. Little River Lobster Company is right on a wharf in the middle of town, and they sell lobster to the public, but their main business is buying lobsters from fishers and shipping them off to be processed or eaten elsewhere, so don't expect a fancy store or a smiling salesperson. Some of the best views of Cutler Harbor are from the parking lot of the US Post Office, perched on a hill above the harbor. The fleet of fishing boats rides the enormous tides up and down as much as twenty-five feet every six hours. If you didn't realize that and are there near low tide, you might wonder why

Foggy days provide some of the most picturesque moments in Cutler.

the boats are so far below the deck of the wharves. More than once a newcomer has tied up his or her boat too tightly to a pier in the Bold Coast region and come back to discover the sea has dropped out from below the hull, leaving the boat dangling precariously from a hopefully very sturdy rope!

The remainder of this drive is through a variety of forested stretches, homesteads, and fishers' homes. Turn right onto Boot Cove Road 24.2 miles from the beginning of this route to take an additional scenic route toward Quoddy Head State Park and the town of Lubec.

Eastport/Sipayik on Route 190

Perry, Sipayik, and Eastport

This scenic drive is the route you must take to get to Eastport, unless you're arriving by boat. From the intersection of Route 1 and Route 190 in Perry, take Route 190 for 7.1 miles to the downtown waterfront. The road begins adjacent to a residential neighborhood, but it isn't long before water views open up on both sides of the road. To the right is Half-Moon Cove, a part of Cobscook Bay. To the left, across a grassy wetland, is Passamaquoddy Bay. Shortly thereafter you'll see signs that you are entering Sipayik. The entire town of Sipayik consists of the Pleasant Point Reservation of the Passamaquoddy tribe. It is a tiny town that you'll pass through in just a minute or two. There is a Wahponahki Museum here, and the trailhead for the Sipayik Trail (see page 255).

The town of Sipayik is a small island connected by bridges to the mainland and other islands.

After passing through Sipayik, the road crosses a causeway that connects the mainland to Carlow Island. There isn't much on Carlow Island except a handful of homes on both sides of the road. Following this, the road crosses another causeway onto Moose Island, which holds the main part of the city of Eastport.

There are a couple more nice water views on the right (Cobscook Bay) side before entering the built-up part of the city. When the road bends sharply to the left, you can turn right for the Shackford Head hiking trails (see page 258) or the Shackford Head picnic area (see page 92), or you can follow the road left toward the downtown. The road ends at a stop sign on Water Street, where you'll find the waterfront, shops, restaurants, whale watching, and more.

Driving "Trails"

Each of these three driving trails can be seen as an individual activity that would occupy a day or more, or you can review the maps of each tour and see whether any of the stops is particularly interesting or near another activity you'll be engaged in.

Downeast Fisheries Trail

As you can see by a quick skim of this book, the region beyond Acadia is steeped in maritime history, and fisheries in particular. The Downeast Fisheries Trail identifies forty-five different locations from Searsport on Penobscot Bay to the west (well outside the region covered in this book) to Eastport and Lubec on Cobscook Bay. Each site along the trail has an interpretive sign that tells the story of that location's ecology, history, or current use as it relates to fisheries. Information is available in a printed brochure available at various places around the region or at downeastfisheriestrail.org.

A stop along the Downeast Fisheries Trail at Long Cove Rest Area.

Ice Age Trail

The Ice Age Trail is a list of forty-six places, from Ellsworth and Aurora in the west (outside the region beyond Acadia) to Lubec and Eastport in the east, where you can see evidence of the effects that the Ice Age had on the geology and ecology of the area. Sites include peat bogs, places where glaciers scraped across bedrock, and a flooded forest that is preserved in mud and salt water, among others. The Ice Age Trail has an app for iPads only, or you can find information on printed brochures available at various places around the region or at iceagetrail.umaine.edu.

Maine Sculpture Trail

The Maine Sculpture Trail is the product of the Schoodic International Sculpture Symposium, a multiyear project to inspire public sculptures scattered around the region. There are thirty-four sculptures in places from Castine and Bangor in the west (outside the region beyond Acadia) to Eastport and Lubec in the east. The website has a very informative profile of each sculpture and sculptor at schoodicsculpture.org.

Eastport hosts Nature's Grace, one of the Schoodic Sculpture Symposium's many public artworks scattered across the region.

Lighthouses

The region covered by this book is home to eight lighthouses that have been used by mariners for decades as an aid to navigation in the perilous environment of the North Atlantic.

The details of many lighthouses marry form and function.

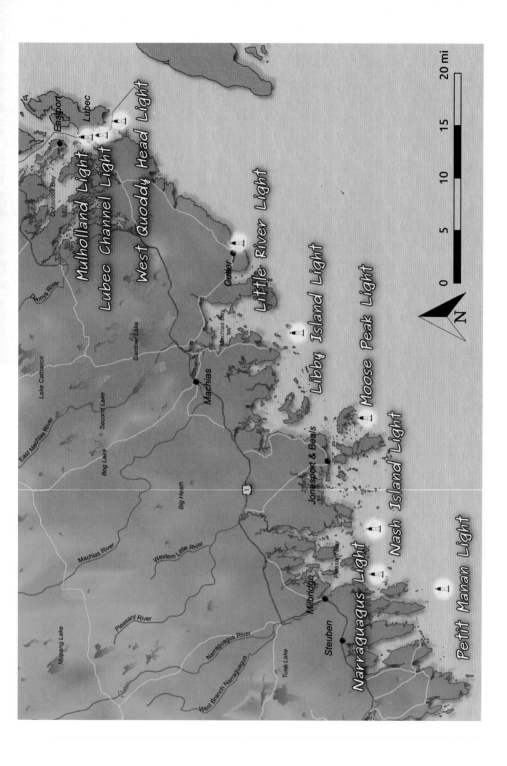

Petit Manan Light stands on an offshore island inhabited by fascinating seabirds.

The **Petit Manan Light** is generally off-limits to the public, as it sits on an island that is critical to the recovery of endangered Atlantic puffins and other seabirds. The island is owned and managed by the Maine Coastal Islands National Wildlife Refuge. Tour boats and experienced sea kayakers can approach the island for a view of the birds and lighthouse, but landing is forbidden without authorization. The lighthouse, at 119 feet tall, was built in 1855 and is still in service. The best way to see the island from the mainland is to hike to the shore on the Hollingsworth Trail on another section of the Maine Coastal Islands National Wildlife Refuge (see page 183). From here the lighthouse is about 2.75 miles across open ocean.

Narraguagus Light is a privately owned lighthouse on Pond Island, off the coast of Milbridge. Neither the island nor the lighthouse are open to the public, but the lighthouse can be viewed by boat. The lighthouse was built in 1853 and has been out of service since 1934. The tower is thirty-one feet tall. Narraguagus Light is not viewable from the mainland and can only be seen from boats or nearby islands.

Nash Island Light is owned and maintained by the Friends of Nash Island Light. It was constructed in 1874 and taken out of service in 1982. The tower is just thirty-six feet tall, but it is noticeable and distinctive for its square, rather than round, shape, and because Nash Island is bare of trees, which helps the lighthouse to stand out. Nash Island Light can't be seen from any public vantage points on the mainland and can only be seen from boats or nearby islands.

The distinctive Nash Island Light is square, not round, like most other lighthouses.

Moose Peak Light is located on Mistake Island, in the town of Beals. It is privately owned and not open to the public. It can be seen by boat, or a distant view is available on a clear day from Great Wass Island. The lighthouse is fifty-seven feet tall and was constructed in 1851. It is still in service.

Lobster fishers ply the waters around Moose Peak Light.

Libby Island Light, similar to Petit Manan Light, is on an island that is now owned by the Maine Coastal Islands National Wildlife Refuge and is managed to support the seabird breeding colonies found on Little Libby Island (where the lighthouse is) and the adjacent Big Libby Island, which is owned by the Maine Department of Inland Fisheries and Wildlife and is similarly managed for seabird restoration. Libby Island Light, at forty-two feet tall, was built way back in 1823 and is still in use today. The lighthouse is visible on the horizon from Jasper Beach in Machiasport (see page 80) and is best seen by boat.

Little River Light, on Little River Island at the mouth of Cutler Harbor, was built in 1876 and is still in service today. The island and forty-one-foot-tall lighthouse are owned by the Friends of Little River Lighthouse, who hold Open House Days most summers, when the public is invited to take a free boat ride out to the island to visit the lighthouse. The lighthouse is only visible from boats, on Little River Island, or from the Fairy Head portion of the Cutler Coast Trail (see page 214).

West Quoddy Head Light is one of the most photographed and recognizable lighthouses in the northeastern United States. With its red-and-white candy-striped pattern, it is hard to miss. Its appeal is further augmented because it sits on the easternmost point of land in the continental United States. The current forty-nine-foot-tall lighthouse was built in 1857, but the station was established back in 1808. The lighthouse is still in service today. The lighthouse is owned and maintained by the Maine Department of Agriculture, Conservation, and Forestry on its Quoddy Head State Park (see page 230 for a description of the trails). The West Quoddy Head Light Keepers Association runs a visitor center and museum in the former lighthouse keeper's house adjacent to the tower. It is open Memorial Day through mid-October.

The West Quoddy Head Light receives the first hint of sunlight.

The Lubec Channel Light is often referred to as "the Spark Plug."

The tower itself is only accessible one day each year on the Maine Open Lighthouse Day in September. This is the only lighthouse in the region that is open to the public on this day. Information about Maine Open Lighthouse Day is at lighthousefoundation.org/maine-open-lighthouse-day.

Lubec Channel Light (also known locally as "the Spark Plug") sits in the water of the Lubec Channel, not far from the international border with Canada. The forty-foot tower was built in 1890 and is still in service today. The lighthouse is not open to the public, but can easily be viewed from many places around the Lubec Channel, including Mowry Beach (see page 90), the approach road to Quoddy Head State Park, and Campobello Island.

Mulholland Light gets an honorable mention in this category since it isn't technically in the region covered in *Beyond Acadia*. Sitting on Campobello Island, right across the Lubec Channel from the Lubec public wharf, the Lost Fishermen's Memorial (see page 91), and the heart of downtown Lubec, Mulholland Light is a Lubec landmark every bit as much as the Lubec Channel Light. You'll need a passport or passport card to cross the bridge into Canada to visit the light, but photos from the Lubec side are easier than dealing with customs.

Mulholland Light, on Canada's Campobello Island, as seen from downtown Lubec.

Boat Tours

For a region that is so entwined with its maritime history and culture, there are surprisingly few professional boat tour operators. What follows is a selection of several scattered across the region beyond Acadia.

Robertson Sea Tours & Adventures

Bayview Street, Milbridge

A broad array of maritime activities are available from Robertson Sea Tours (robertsonseatours.com). Available tours include lobster fishing demonstrations, lighthouse tours, whale watches, puffin and seabird cruises, or private charters specializing in whatever your interest may be.

Bold Coast Charter Company

Cutler Harbor, Cutler

Bold Coast Charter Company (boldcoast.com) specializes in excursions to Machias Seal Island, which is ten miles across open ocean from Cutler. Bold Coast is the only US company that is licensed to actually land and disembark passengers on the island. All other companies are permitted only to circle the island. Generally one tour per day actually lands, and tickets are in high demand, so plan ahead if this interests you.

Inn on the Wharf Whale Watching

69 Johnson Street, Lubec

Whale watching tours leave right from the wharf on this scenic stretch of Johnson Street. The *Tarquin* holds up to twenty-six people. Get more information at innonthewharf.com.

Downeast Charter Boat Tours

31 Johnson Street, Lubec

This company offers tours of Passamaquoddy, Cobscook, and Fundy Bays aboard a modified lobster boat that holds six passengers. The owner-and-operator couple specialize in trips to the Old Sow, which is the largest whirlpool in the Western hemisphere; tours are timed to ensure that the whirlpool is at its peak of activity when the boat passes through. The company also offers whale-watching and private charter trips. Information can be found at downeastcharterboattours.com.

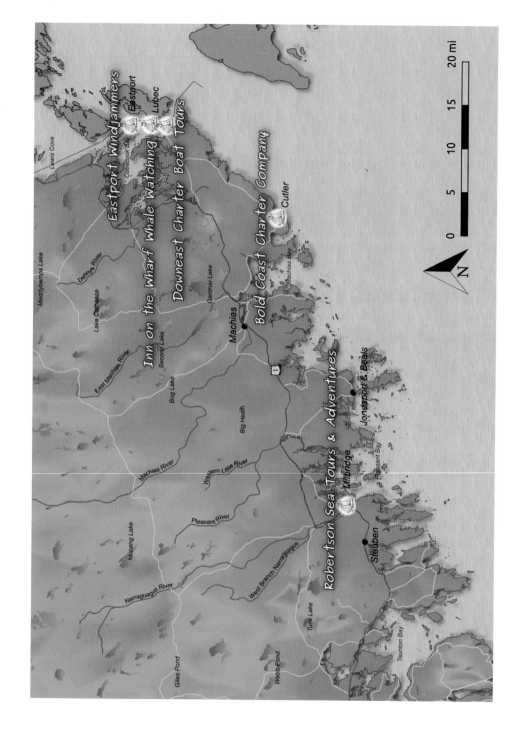

Eastport Windjammers

Eastport Breakwater, Eastport

This company traditionally used a schooner for their tours, but the *Ada C. Lore* was heavily damaged when the Eastport Breakwater collapsed several years ago. They now run a custom-built lobster-style boat with lobstering and whale-watching tours, deep-sea fishing expeditions, sunset cruises, and private charters. Find information at eastportwindjammers.com.

Ferries

There are a few ferries that serve the far eastern edge of the region beyond Acadia. The Eastport–Lubec Ferry is a seasonal service that transports passengers the roughly two miles between these two population centers. Other ferries, capable of transporting cars and trucks, connect the city of Eastport with Deer Island, New Brunswick, and then Campobello Island, New Brunswick, which is connected with the town of Lubec by a bridge. Another ferry connects Deer Island, New Brunswick, with the Canadian mainland. Check ahead for any of these ferries, as they typically run seasonally but can unexpectedly cancel service. Find more information at downeast windjammer.com and eastcoastferriesltd.com/index.html.

Do!

Down East Sunrise Trail

The Down East Sunrise Trail is a rails-to-trails project on the former Calais Branch of the Maine Central Railroad Company. The trail stretches about ninety miles from the edge of Ellsworth all the way to Calais, making it a notable feature of the region beyond Acadia. Its gravel surface permits use by walkers, bikers, skiers, snowshoers, equestrians, ATVs, and snowmobiles. The multiuse nature of the trail requires everyone to use caution and courtesy to avoid conflicts. Generally speaking, motorists are considerate as they approach non-motorized users. The only real problem is on especially dry days when a cloud of dust can't be avoided no matter how slow the driver goes.

The gravel surface is good for mountain bikes and hybrids with tires that are wider than street tires. The gravel is groomed periodically, and, paradoxically, it is much harder to pedal right after grooming. As ATVs use the trail, they kick smaller pebbles out of their tire tracks, and eventually you end up with a pair of clear, hard ruts that are easy to bike on. When the trail is groomed, all of the pebbles are redistributed, making it feel like you're pedaling through an inch of sand.

Since it is a rail trail, the path is nearly straight except for wide, gentle bends and only gradual hills, making it not the most interesting place to walk for long distances, but there are a few stretches worth checking out. By far the most popular and beautiful stretch of the trail starts at the Route 1 crossing in Machias, just across from Dunkin' Donuts. Parking is available either on the nearby dike or informally on a wide gravel parking lot directly adjacent to the trail. This parking lot is privately owned but open for public use.

From here the Sunrise Trail carves a path along the Machias River, in many places between a marsh on one side and the river on the other. Birding is excellent here, but

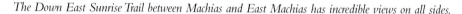

The Down East Sunrise Trail between Machias and East Machias has incredible views on all sides.

you don't need to be an expert birder to enjoy watching the eagles, ospreys, herons, and other species that feed or nest here. The river will stay immediately on your right side for 2.25 miles, until you cross Rim Road (next to the large Rim Bridge that can't be missed). The trail enters the woods here, but only for a short stretch before opening back onto the East Machias River in the center of the village of East Machias. The beautiful scenery continues for another 1.5 miles before the trail leaves the river and heads straight into the forest for a long stretch.

Another of my favorite places to explore on the Sunrise Trail is Northern Inlet. Parking is at the intersection of the Sunrise Trail and Route 191, 7.0 miles north of the intersection of Route 191 and Route 1. From the parking area, cross Route 191 and follow the Sunrise Trail for about 0.4 mile. The forest opens up to a large marsh with a small stream channel, called Northern Inlet, flowing through the center. The marsh is abuzz all summer long with wildflowers, insects, birds, turtles, and the occasional deer or moose. You can continue for another 1.9 miles to an even larger marsh and river crossing at the upper reaches of Gardner Lake, but this is probably only worth it on a bicycle or other means faster than walking.

Bicycling

Bicycling in the region beyond Acadia really came on the map (literally) in 2016, when the Bicycle Coalition of Maine chose to run their annual week-long bike ride, called BikeMaine, on the Bold Coast. Before then you might have occasionally seen bikes along the road, but it was fairly rare. It is a long distance between towns with supplies and lodging, the roads are rough, and there was absolutely no source for bike repair or parts in the entire area. A few intrepid cyclists making their way from Florida to Maine, or from Washington or California to Maine, would pedal through these last miles of their ride, ending at the easternmost point of land in the continental United States, at Quoddy Head State Park.

When the BikeMaine team first came to community organizers to ask about holding the event here, the response was somewhat incredulous. We all thought that our region was terrible for biking. The BikeMaine team did a series of test rides around portions of the route they had planned and had news that was pretty shocking to many of us: The Bold Coast is an incredible place to ride. Sure, our roads are rough, but no more so than many other rural areas. Sure, our roads don't tend to have shoulders to get cyclists out of the flow of traffic, but we have so little traffic that a rider can relax and enjoy the ride on most stretches of road. And sure, it's a long way between towns, but, actually, it's often just about the right distance for an afternoon or a day's ride. Plus, we have scenery that simply can't be beat all along the route, and although we do have hills, they tend to be short and not all that challenging.

BikeMaine is committed to helping the communities that they ride through each year, so they offered our local community organizers assistance to set up our own biking routes and to train local businesses to offer services that cyclists need, from water to Wi-Fi to commonly needed tools for repairs. The result is the Bold Coast Scenic Bikeway, the very first Scenic Bikeway in the state of Maine.

The interest in biking didn't end there. At the same time that our group was planning the Scenic Bikeway, the Adventure Cycling Association and the American Association of State Highway and Transportation Officials unveiled their bicycle route from Florida to Maine, stringing together some of the most picturesque stretches of road along the way. The route is called US Bicycle Route 1. It overlaps with legs of the Scenic Bikeway but also provides some alternate ideas of where to ride, especially if you're just passing through on your bike.

Let's not forget the East Coast Greenway, which is creating yet another Florida-to-Maine network of bike paths. They adopted the Down East Sunrise Trail (see page 116) as the chosen route through the Bold Coast region. This is the only unpaved stretch of the Greenway, at least thus far, to be incorporated into the route. The ninety-mile length of the Sunrise Trail right along the targeted route of the Greenway made it an obvious choice to include.

The result of all of these factors that came together at about the same time is your opportunity to bike the Bold Coast while it is still an unusual activity. Whether you want to bring your bike for a multimodal adventure that combines biking with hiking, or you want to ride some of the beautiful coastal roads on one day of your vacation, or you want to bike straight through the area over the course of several days, this is the time to do it. Be aware of the risks and particular challenges of biking this area, but don't miss the opportunity if you're up for it. Chief among the challenges is the lack of bicycle services. There is no way around this. At this time there is no dedicated bike shop in the entire region. Service is available in Ellsworth, Bar Harbor, Bangor, or St. Andrews, New Brunswick, so be sure you have emergency tools and extra supplies in case you find yourself stranded with a broken bike. Limited emergency services may be found in Eastport from the Sprocket Society, offering services at Shead High School on Tuesday from 2:30 to 3:30 p.m. during the school year, or from SL Wadsworth, which sells patch kits and basic tools. The only place inside this region to rent a bicycle, that I know of, is from the Inn on the Wharf in Lubec (innonthewharf.com).

What about mountain biking, you ask? This is an activity that, in my opinion, is just waiting to be discovered in this region. The vast network of gravel logging roads and ATV or snowmobile trails is an opportunity that will likely garner some notice when road biking gains some traction in the region. Most of the roads and trails that would be great for biking are privately owned and only open to certain uses, often not including bikes. For now the best place to ride a mountain bike on the Bold Coast is along the Down East Sunrise Trail and the multiuse roads—meaning that they permit vehicles, ATVs, snowmobiles, horses, bikes, and pretty much any other form of transportation you can think of—at the various units of the Public Reserved Land (the Cutler Coast Unit, Rocky Lake Unit, and Donnell Pond Unit) and Moosehorn National Wildlife Refuge. Be sure to check the rules for the particular location you choose before you set out.

The turn-by-turn route descriptions and maps are available on the Internet, so I won't repeat them here. What follows is a description of some of the flavor of each of the route options and recommendations about some of the more spectacular legs of the routes that you may want to prioritize.

Bold Coast Scenic Bikeway

The Bold Coast Scenic Bikeway is a 211-mile-long road-based biking route that begins on Route 1 in Gouldsboro, travels down through the Schoodic Peninsula section of Acadia National Park (not covered in this book), then east and north through the entire region beyond Acadia, and continuing north to Calais and into Canada. The organizers of this route paid particular attention to incorporating some of the most stunning scenery in the region and minimizing the amount of time spent on Route 1, which has the heaviest traffic in the region. Pick almost any stretch of this route and ride for a few miles, or spend days on the whole route. This route includes long stretches of road with views of pristine ocean shoreline, deep forest, lakes, rivers, and blueberry barrens. It would even be great to just use this as a guide for a highly scenic drive through the area. (See page 94 for more on scenic drives.) An interactive map of the route is available at ridewithgps.com/routes/26458033.

US Bicycle Route 1

US Bicycle Route 1 covers 399 miles in Maine, from Kittery in the south to Calais in the north. Compared with the Bold Coast Scenic Bikeway, which has half the miles just within and adjacent to the region beyond Acadia, this is clearly a more direct and quicker route to get through the region, if that's what you're after. The route was chosen to parallel Route 1 and the East Coast Greenway, but it incorporates many of the shorter bypass loops that get a biker out of the relatively heavy traffic on Route 1. It happens that many of these side routes are among the most scenic, with routes through expansive blueberry barrens and along the coast. This route is well marked with dedicated signs at every intersection. An interactive map of the route is available at adventurecycling.org/routes-and-maps/us-bicycle-route-system/usbrs-interactive-map/.

East Coast Greenway

The Maine portion of the East Coast Greenway extends 367 miles from Kittery in the south to Calais in the north, just north of the region beyond Acadia. The official Greenway route through the region is on the Down East Sunrise Trail, which is a gravel multiuse trail open to some motor vehicles. The Greenway also includes a "complimentary route" that parallels the Sunrise Trail but stays on hard pavement. Many people doing long-distance trips on the Greenway do not have the wider tires needed to navigate the Sunrise Trail. See page 116 for more information about the Down East Sunrise Trail and recommendations for individual portions that are particularly scenic. An interactive map of the East Coast Greenway is at map.greenway.org/.

Eastport Bike Routes

The Tides Institute, a nonprofit based in Eastport, has assembled a map of suggested road-biking routes in the city and surrounding area. The routes are all on public roads with no dedicated bike lanes but were chosen for their scenery and relative safety for bikers to use. You can also combine a bike trip in Eastport with a circuit of ferry trips from island to island on the Canadian side of Passamaquoddy Bay. The map and information are at tidesinstitute.org/bike-map. Also, the Sipayik Trail is a two-mile-long paved off-road trail that allows bicycles (see page 255).

All-Terrain Vehicles

There is an extensive trail network for riding ATVs and snowmobiles called the Maine ITS (Interconnected Trail System). Some trails in the ITS are not open to ATVs and are used for snowmobiles only, so check regulations before you ride. There are several ATV clubs active in the region, and they offer information and do a lot of trail maintenance work. The Down East Sunrise Trail is open to ATVs except when posted for muddy conditions or snow (see page 116). Information about snowmobile use is on page 136.

Horseback Riding

There is not a lot of opportunity to ride horses in the region beyond Acadia, but there are a few options.

Whispering Pine Stable

289 Bay Road, Jonesboro, (207) 259-1174

Cottonwood Campground and RV Park

1140 Route 1, Columbia Falls, (207) 598-8497

Stepping Stone East

35 Flaherty Road, Milbridge, (207) 735-3374

If you are bringing your own horse, you can ride on the Down East Sunrise Trail (see page 116) or one of the "multiuse roads" on the various units of Public Reserved Land, like Donnell Pond, Cutler Coast, or Rocky Lake. Cottonwood Campground allows campers to bring their own horses to their campsite.

Running

There are a number of organized runs in the region. Some have been around for many years and some are new. What follows is a partial list, arranged chronologically. Dates may shift from year to year, so search the Internet to get the latest information.

Elaine Hill "Love a Nurse" 5K run

Milbridge, in May

Bay of Fundy International Marathon, Half Marathon, Ultramarathon, 10K, Fun Run

Lubec and Campobello Island, Canada, in June

Wesley 5K and 1-Mile Fun Run/Walk

East Machias, in June

Milbridge Days 5K and Fun Run

Typically in late July

Wild Blueberry 5-Mile Run and 1-Mile Fun Run

Machias, in August

A Dash of Color 5K Color Run

Machias, in September

Suddy 5K and Fun Run

Eastport, in September

Bad Little Trail Run, Machias River Preserve, Whitneyville

7-mile run or 2.5-mile run/walk on hiking trails, in October

Runners compete in the annual Bad Little Trail Run at the Machias River Preserve.

Of course, you can always head out for a jog or run without the fanfare of an organized event. The Down East Sunrise Trail is a great option for off-road running on relatively smooth gravel. A number of hiking trails are also suitable for those who like to run on trails.

Swimming

One of the things many people love about Down East is the moderate summer heat. Sure, temperatures can climb into the nineties on a handful of summer days, and we get our share of eighties, but the typical summer day begins in the low sixties and climbs into the seventies by midday. Afternoon fog can often significantly cool the air. Nevertheless, there are days when you just want to go jump in a river, a lake, or the ocean. Aside from the well-known public places like Roque Bluffs State Park, there aren't a lot of obvious options for a quick dip or a day on the water.

Expect ocean temperatures to remain frigid right through the summer. Most people don't actually swim in the ocean here as much as they might dip their toes or wade to their shins for a little while. It is usually the small children and senior citizens who seem to be able to muster the gumption to dive in. Lakes and rivers do warm up quite a bit as summer wears on and offer a great way to relax and refresh, if you know where to go.

Note that none of the swimming sites listed here have lifeguards or any other support system, so use caution and don't overstep your abilities. The buddy system is a time-tested lifesaver.

Schoodic Beach

Franklin (see page 175 for directions)

Schoodic Beach, on Donnell Pond, should be on everyone's list to go visit during the summer, particularly if you are hiking any of the nearby trails (see pages 76 and 170). From the parking lot, there is about a half-mile walk through the woods to the shores of Donnell Pond. The trail is wide and relatively flat, so many people use wheeled beach totes, all-terrain baby strollers, or something similar to carry their gear. When you break out of the woods and on to the beach, the designated campsites are to your left, but day visitors can use any part of the beach they'd like. The beach is more than one thousand feet long and broad enough to provide plenty of space for your picnic, disc toss, or snooze in the shade at the tree line.

The beach is sublime and the water is clear and relatively warm (at least compared with the ocean). The views of mountains in nearly every direction add to the ambience of the beach. I once heard a former commissioner of the state's Department of Conservation refer to Schoodic Beach as the finest freshwater beach in the state.

Depending on where you set up shop, you might have views of Black Mountain (to your left when your back is to the water), Schoodic Mountain (to your right when your back is to the water), and most definitely distant views of Caribou Mountain and Tunk Mountain beyond it.

It is worth noting that you can also access Schoodic Beach by boating from the public landing in Franklin, off Route 182 (the Blackwoods Road). It is a three-mile

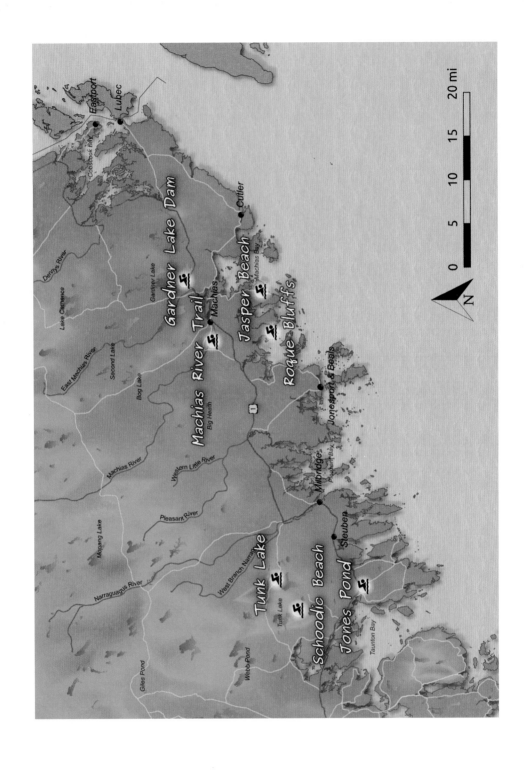

The water, views, and sand on Schoodic Beach at Donnell Pond are simply sublime.

trip by boat to the main beach, but this also gives access to a number of smaller beaches scattered around the lake, many of which permit camping. Find more information at maine.gov/donnellpond.

Tunk Lake

Route 182, T10 SD

There is only one place on Tunk Lake where the public can easily get to the water. The boat launch on Route 182 in T10 SD (one of the state's unincorporated civil divisions) is a scenic and very popular place to pull off the road. The swimming at the boat launch is not really ideal, but if you have a boat, you can reach some of the most beautiful and unknown places to get wet. The lake is essentially a big oval, stretched out toward the south from the boat launch at the northern tip. Almost the entire western shore is privately owned by a single owner who years ago entered into a permanent agreement with the state (called a conservation easement) that guarantees public access to their land. Two sand beaches and a section of rocky outcrops are waiting for those who can get there. The beaches are about 1.5 to 1.75 miles from the boat launch. Continue south from the beaches to reach the rocky outcrops. Watch the beaches carefully for restrictions posted on signs at the tree line. One of the two is reserved for only nonmotorized boats to land, and fires, alcohol, and nudity are not allowed anywhere on the property.

Munson's Pitch on the Machias River is a great place to cool off during a summertime hike.

Machias River Heritage Trail

Park at Heritage Trail parking area, Route 1A, Machias
(see page 201 for directions)

The most popular place to swim on the Machias River Trail is about as far as you can get from the trailhead, so this isn't an option for a quick dip. Rather, it is a welcome break during one of the best hikes in the region (see page 201). The Machias River Trail follows the shoreline of the river for more than three miles, and you can get wet or explore the river just about anywhere along the way, but most people would agree that Munson's Pitch is the place to go. The river plunges a few feet over rock ledges here, creating the negative ions and white noise that make this place hard to leave. Belted kingfishers, ospreys, and eagles are all commonly seen here. Exposed ledges above the summertime river level offer plenty of places to stretch out and warm up in the sun before or after your dip. The water isn't deep, even when the river is reasonably high. This is more of a wading spot than a swimming hole, but well worth taking the time to enjoy. The river bottom is rocky, so a pair of sandals or old sneakers to protect your feet are a good idea.

Roque Bluffs State Park

145 Schoppee Point Road, Roque Bluffs

There are two swimming options at Roque Bluffs State Park. The first is the expansive sand beach that is the focal point of the park. As is the case everywhere in the

Even on a foggy day, Roque Bluffs State Park attracts beachgoers.

region, the ocean water is frigid right through the summer months, so few people really swim here. Most just dare their friends or kids to see how deep they can go before it feels like icicles are forming on their skin, and then warm up on the beach. There are always more adventurous types who set out for a long swim along the half-mile-long beach, often wearing a wetsuit.

There is a handicap-accessible parking spot with a view of the open ocean and a number of islands, which is a great option for someone with limited mobility who still wants to enjoy the beach.

The second swimming option is across the road near the two parking areas. Simpson's Pond is a freshwater lake that is just a few feet from the ocean. The water gets quite warm in the summer, and though few adults take advantage of it, kids seem to love splashing around in the shallows.

There is a fee to enter this state park. Find information at maine.gov/roquebluffs.

Jasper Beach

Port Road, Machiasport

Despite the cold water, many people take a dip at Jasper Beach. The smooth cobble-stone beach means no sand in your shorts and shoes, and it is really a unique experience to walk barefoot into the water on the shifting rocks that constantly massage your soles. See page 80 for more on Jasper Beach.

The Gardner Lake Dam is a popular place to cool off in the summer.

Gardner Lake Dam

Chases Mill Road, East Machias

This park, owned by the town of East Machias, is a favorite local spot to cool off in the summer. It has a tiny sand beach that offers a perfect place for small children to splash around within easy reach of adults. The beach is just feet from the road, so be prepared to keep a close eye on little ones. Late in summer beware of goose poop on the grassy area where you may attempt to lay your towel. There is also a boat launch, picnic tables, and an outhouse.

Winter Fun

The sledding hill at Middle River Park in Machias always attracts a crowd on a nice winter day.

Cross-country skiing on the Down East Sunrise Trail is a great way to see the region.

People love to snowshoe at Middle River Park.

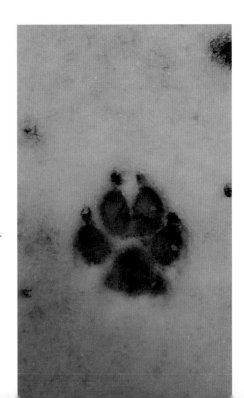

Snow provides an ideal medium to be able to see and identify animal tracks, like this coyote.

The Bold Coast is amazingly peaceful and sleepy in the winter. The year-round residents are still around, so all of the main businesses are up and running year-round, unlike a place like Bar Harbor, where all of the souvenir shops and expensive restaurants close up shop for the winter. Although there aren't many organized winter activities for visitors in this region, self-sufficient winter lovers can find plenty to do if they're willing to do a little homework.

The first consideration is whether there is even snow on the ground. See page 6 for a description of winter weather you can expect.

Those with an interest can snowshoe, cross-country ski, ice skate, sled, or snowmobile all over the region. You'll have to bring all of your own gear. There is no place to rent equipment or repair broken items. Please, please, please do not go out into the wilderness during the winter without the proper clothing, emergency gear, and expertise. Always let someone else know where you are going and when you'll be back.

One of my very favorite aspects of winter is that all of a sudden, when the snow covers the ground, the secret lives of animals can become very clear. Everything from a moose down to a mouse leaves tracks behind them that can be followed to put yourself in the "shoes" of a wild animal. Keep your eyes on the snow ahead and see what you can find!

Virtually every hiking trail can be explored by **snowshoe**. I'm not aware of any trails that prohibit it, except that snowshoers should avoid trampling on groomed cross-country trails. The challenge is finding out which parking lots are kept plowed all winter long. I suggest you call around to the main conservation organizations (Downeast Coastal Conservancy, Downeast Salmon Federation, Maine Coast Heritage Trust) to ask which trails are accessible. For several years, when I worked at Downeast Coastal Conservancy, we published an annual *Winter Access Guide* that

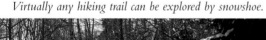

Virtually any hiking trail can be explored by snowshoe.

showed which trailheads are open for the winter, but I don't know whether that will continue. Shackford Head, Cobscook Bay, and Quoddy Head State Parks traditionally keep a parking area plowed for access to the parks all winter, but Maine Public Reserved Lands (Donnell Pond, Rocky Lake, and Cutler Coast) do not.

Snowshoeing is the perfect way to get around the woods in the winter. You can always stick to the marked trails, but some properties allow off-trail use, and it is much harder to get lost if you can just turn around and follow your tracks back to safety.

Places to **cross-country ski** are rarer than places to snowshoe. When most people think of cross-country skiing, it is on trails that have been groomed for either traditional (two side-by-side tracks the width of a ski) or skating (a wide swath that is all smoothed out for skate skiing). The only place in the region that typically offers this activity is Cobscook Bay State Park, which maintains groomed trails all season as long as there is snow.

The **Down East Sunrise Trail** is also open for skiing, but it is not specifically groomed for that use. The trail is groomed for snowmobiles, and even when the groomer doesn't make it out, snowmobiles break the trail and flatten out a path that skiers can use. The conditions often aren't perfect, but sometimes you catch it just right and find smooth snow for miles. Listen for snowmobiles on the Sunrise Trail and step aside to give them room. People on foot have the right of way, but that doesn't pay the hospital bills if you get run over.

Some people enjoy breaking new trail with their skis, and this can be done on many of the hiking trails in this book, though any with long or steep hills are probably out for most people. Any trail that is reasonably level can be skied, but it helps if the turns are relatively gradual and the trail corridor is wide enough to maneuver your skis.

Depending on the weather in a particular year, **ice skating** can be a major activity in the region, or there may be no skating at all. The abundant lakes, ponds, and marshes are all potential places to skate. Beware, however, of any place where you don't see other people, since the locals may know that a particular body of water or a part of it has warm springs that will cause unsafe ice conditions. Always confirm the thickness of the ice before venturing onto it. I remember one winter with bitter cold but virtually no snow. The ice was perfect for weeks on end, and people were out skating all over the place. In other years the temperature never drops low enough for long enough to create good conditions, or heavy snowfall makes it impossible to skate on lakes and ponds. The town of Machias has experimented with an artificial skating rink that can be shoveled, and the pond at the University of Maine at Machias is often cleared by students or community members.

Sledding, sometimes called "sliding" locally, is of course done in every town somewhere. The problem is finding a local hill that is open to the public. The town of East Machias (where I lived for the entire fourteen years I was in the region) owns

◀ *The Machias River Preserve has a trail that is fantastic for snowshoeing.*

A young sledder hits a jump on the East Machias sliding hill.

the premier sliding hill in the area and keeps it open for public use. It can easily be found as you drive through the village anytime there is snow, because there will usually be a line of cars and the hill may be crawling with bundled-up kids and their parents. The hill affords a spectacular view of the East Machias River. This hill is no joke. It is a long, steep, and bumpy ride, and occasionally people have been injured, but the draw is too strong for many people to resist the adrenaline rush.

We are very fortunate to have this sledding hill available. After being used for generations, the property went up for sale in the mid-2010s. Maine Coast Heritage Trust worked with the town to raise funds and purchase the property, and then it gave the land to the town of East Machias to keep it open for winter use.

In Machias, Middle River Park has a short sledding hill overlooking the Middle River right beside the picnic area and trailhead. Because the run is so short, it is much easier to trudge back up and do it again, so people tend to stay here for hours or combine some sledding with a snowshoe hike around the trails in the park.

Ice fishing is a very popular pastime in this region, as it is in every area that gets ice thick enough to safely walk on. As soon as the ice is safe, people venture out, bore holes in the ice, and drop a line into the water. As the ice gets thicker, people sometimes drive ATVs or trucks onto the ice to get farther from shore. Many people even drag out a little shed on skis that will keep them warm for the day (or sometimes overnight). Like warm-weather fishing, ice fishing is regulated by the Maine Department of Inland Fisheries and Wildlife, and a license is required. Find more information at maine.gov/ifw.

Organized and groomed **snowmobile** trails abound in the region, as part of the ITS, or Integrated Trail System. Maps are available from the Maine Snowmobile Association at mesnow.com.

Paddle!

When I first decided to move to this region in 2004, without ever having visited, I studied maps of the area to get a clue about what I would see. I remember being struck by all the blue on the map—rivers, lakes, streams, bays, coves, and open ocean dominated the *DeLorme Atlas & Gazetteer* (you do have one of those, don't you?). The *DeLorme* has excellent information about both hand-carry and vehicle-accessible boat launches. Almost every lake has a public launch of some kind, and they dot the coast and rivers as well. I remember well that I bought a kayak to start my explorations before I even bought a bed to sleep on!

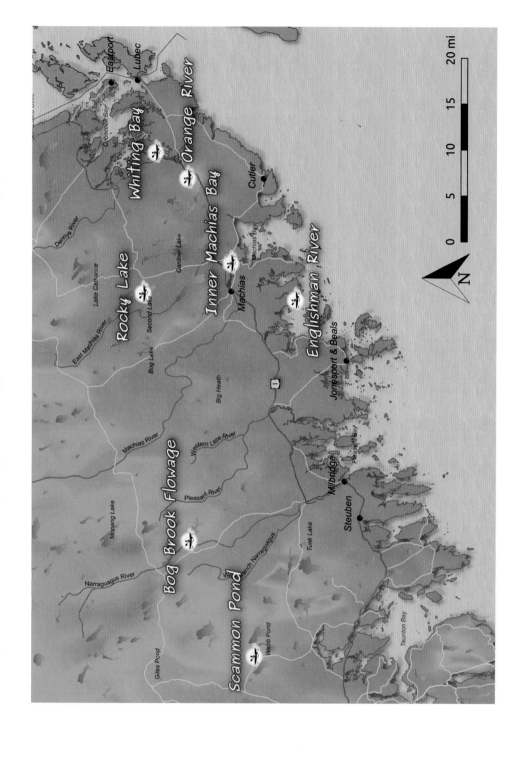

Young paddlers take in the waning autumn sun on an afternoon paddle.

There are truly paddling opportunities everywhere in the region, but many require some inside knowledge for their best use. For example, the water level of most rivers slowly drops from the time of the spring freshet straight through until winter, making them virtually unnavigable by late July unless there is an unusually strong storm. You can ask around to find out how the rivers are doing and whether a paddle is advisable. More than once I've had to get out of my kayak and drag it over some rocky spot exposed by the low water. If that kind of thing bothers you, go early in the year. But be cautious, as certain stretches of river have some serious rapids early on—it is wise to do some research.

Saltwater Paddling

Paddling fresh water has its own risks and rewards, but I want to focus for a moment on the dangers of ocean paddling in this region. There are many reasons why you don't see a plethora of colorful sea kayaks plying the bays, as you do in other coastal regions. Foremost is the frigid water temperature, even into August and September. Just a few minutes submerged in this water can lead to hypothermia and an inability to save yourself. Do not venture into the salt water without a guide if you aren't capable of quickly righting a capsized boat and carrying survival gear to dry and warm you. The massive tides in this region also present a risk to those who don't know the area. As the tide rushes in or out, any narrow passage becomes a raging whitewater. Currents can shift quickly, so you may pass between an island and the mainland fine on your way out but be unable to paddle against the flow to return. Know where you are paddling or get the information you need before blindly giving it a try. Finally, this is a region dominated by working fishing boats, not pleasure craft. Fishers have little patience for kayakers clogging up the boat launches that they need to access to make their living. The frequent sudden fog compounds several other dangers, making navigation by sight impossible and rendering kayaks invisible to lobster boats that may be steaming around using radar that can miss a boat as low to the water as a sea kayak. For all of these reasons, hire a guide service to get out on the ocean, unless you are very confident in your abilities and gear. Even experienced locals who spend their lives on and around the water make mistakes that can cost them their lives or the lives of others. The need for caution can't be overstated.

You definitely need to know what the tide is doing. By this, I mean whether it is coming in or going out. And when is the next change? This information can govern where you can paddle and whether you can even reach the water if there is an extensive mudflat exposed by a low tide.

With all of that need for safety and caution in mind, there are plenty of unbelievably beautiful places to paddle on salt water where the risk can be minimized. Enclosed bays tend to have weaker currents and are easier to navigate, even in pea-soup fog. I recommend a couple of specific places that are on the safer side, but keep in mind the other dangers already mentioned, like frigid water. A good tip, especially if paddling with kids, is to stay within safe swimming distance of the shore and avoid crossing a large stretch of open water. Always wear a life vest, even if you are an experienced adult—it's the law for children, but a smart move for adults.

For more information about where to paddle, the amenities available for kayakers along the coast, and more safety information, consult the Maine Island Trail Association at mita.org.

Roque Bluffs

Roque Bluffs is mostly known by visitors for Roque Bluffs State Park, with its vast sand beach (see page 81). Not far from the beach is a spectacular place to paddle, particularly in the mid-summer. The Englishman River will bring you up a narrow, serpentine tidal river where, if you time it right, the tide will carry you up the river and then turn and bring you back down to your starting point. Along the way you travel through an extensive salt marsh with lots of interesting birds, especially ospreys and, in their season, migratory shorebirds.

Most of the shoreline of the Englishman River is privately owned, so you can't land anywhere, but that isn't really necessary on this short trip. Depending on how much you decide to paddle versus riding the tide, the paddle can be as short as perhaps an hour and a half, or it could stretch to three or four hours if you move slowly and watch birds as you go.

Finding just the right timing is tricky, but, fortunately, there is a lot of leeway, and even if you botch the timing of the tides, the trip will likely be rewarding. The key is to find the tide table for Englishman Bay and look for a day when high tide falls at a time when you can be out paddling. Do not attempt this trip when the tide isn't within a couple of hours of high tide, or you'll find yourself stranded in mud, waiting hours for the tide to float your boat.

Note that the actual time of high tide in the upper reaches of Englishman River will be a half hour or so after the stated time in the tide table. This is because all of the ocean water that fills the river has to flow through a narrow bridge at the mouth of the river. Even after the tide out on the ocean begins to fall, water continues to rush into the river, seeking to equalize the levels on both sides of the bridge constriction.

You'll find just one or two parking spots in a gravel area about a quarter mile down Cow Point Road, just before you cross the very first bridge you come to. Cow Point Road is a dead end road that is an obvious left-hand turn that is just before Route 92 plunges down a very steep hill and arrives at the beach.

If you've timed it right, the water will be rushing through the bridge and up the relatively wide river. Once you launch in the cobbly beach below the parking area, the tide will gently drag you upriver. You can choose to paddle along, or mostly just steer and enjoy the ride. The water in this lower section is very shallow and rocky patches may appear above the water. Just try to stay in open water, and you should be fine. The water here is crystal clear and it is amazing to float just above the ocean bottom.

Before long, the wide expanse narrows to a channel that is little more than ten or fifteen yards wide, and narrower in some places. The higher the tide level, the more you can see above the salt marsh vegetation to get a feel for the whole ecosystem, but even if you're trapped down in the channel, it is a lot of fun to watch the shoreline drift by as you round bend after bend after bend. If you're with a group, you'll see that the channel often makes a hairpin turn and goes in the opposite direction with just a few yards of land between the two stretches.

Once you are in the river channel, you'll see little sign of current human use. There is one homestead, inhabited as recently as the mid-2000s, but no other houses or development can be seen. A careful observer will see many old signs of human occupation of the Englishman River. In many places you may see evidence of old fishing weirs (upright poles stuck in the mud and arranged to form a kind of fish trap), dikes, and ditches. Mostly, though, you'll see birds, potentially a deer, and the tantalizing possibility of encountering an otter or perhaps even a seal in the river.

As high tide approaches, you'll start to feel the tide slow down and eventually come to a standstill. Within a few minutes the tide will slowly begin to fall. You can choose to continue paddling up the river for a while, but eventually the current will get faster and it will feel like you are paddling uphill. At some point your upward passage will be blocked by a beaver dam that marks the upper interface of the freshwater trickle flowing down out of the forest into the brackish water flowing with the tide below.

Above the dam the river becomes unnavigable, so simply turn your boat and return the way you came, drifting with the current or paddling to speed your journey. Do not attempt to ride the current under the road bridge and out into the ocean.

Inner Machias Bay

I have never been able to understand why this area in particular is not crawling with kayakers all summer long. It is protected from the open ocean, has relatively little current, and, except at the extreme southerly reach of the bay, experiences very little motorized boat traffic. Plus, there is spectacular beauty all along the many miles of shore in this body of water. You can start your exploration either at the municipal boat launch in Machias, just outside Helen's Restaurant, or at the commercial landing at what is known as "the narrows," where inner Machias Bay is pinched to just over two hundred yards or so before opening up again to the outer bay. The boat launch is in Machiasport, just behind the Gates House, which is a museum owned by the Machiasport Historical Society, located several miles down Route 192 from Machias. If you launch here, use extreme caution if the tide is running out through the narrows. You probably can't paddle fast enough to beat the current and could be swept out to the outer bay. If the tide is slack or coming in, you should be fine, but remember that later, when you try to land your boat, the tide could be rushing in, preventing you from reaching the landing. Use the Machias town dock option if this sounds intimidating or you are unsure of the tide schedule.

There are several distinct areas you can explore in inner Machias Bay. If you have two cars, you can also start at the boat launch in Machias and follow the outgoing tide all the way to the Gates House, or vice versa on an incoming tide. No point in

Paddling in the Machias River below Bad Little Falls is one of the most underappreciated treats of Machias.

paddling against the tide if you don't have to. Here are the main places to explore, beginning at the upper end in the village of Machias.

No paddle in this area would be complete without approaching Bad Little Falls from below. This is the place where the Machias River tumbles over a series of waterfalls and meets the brackish estuary below. When the river's flow is high, the falls are very dangerous, so approach with caution. The rocky cliffs, wildlife and birds, and negative ions from being so close to the waterfall can all make you forget that you are in the literal center of the village, especially if you position yourself where the gas station looming above the falls is out of view.

Between the falls and the boat launch at Helen's is about a half-mile of history lessons. Unless the tide is extremely high, you'll at least have a glimpse of the old wharf that drove the Machias economy back in the sailing days. Both sides of the river are lined with hundred-year-old (or more) massive logs that are intertwined and were once decked with boards to create a working waterfront where wood and other goods were stacked and loaded onto ships. Old photos of this area portray a vibrant and booming town with tall-masted ships lining the bay.

From the boat launch at Helen's Restaurant headed seaward, both sides offer excellent opportunities to explore. On the left, the Down East Sunrise Trail hugs the shoreline, so you may encounter hikers or people out enjoying their ATVs. The left side is also dominated by interesting salt marshes that, depending on the tide, you may be able to paddle into, crossing the Sunrise Trail under a bridge. On the right side the shoreline veers away from Helen's and opens up into a large open bay at high tide. The shoreline is untrammeled forest for the most part. As the tide falls, however,

History comes alive in Machias as a falling tide reveals the old timbers of the town's long-gone wharf.

the waterway shrinks until at low tide, there is a narrow band of water that is only inches deep in some places. I recommend exploring this area at half tide or greater.

If you follow the river down about 2.25 miles, you'll reach the Rim Bridge, an arching span that appears high enough to allow for large ships to pass underneath. By a quirk of poor planning, the bridge is too low to permit a dredging operation underneath, so the river channel has filled with silt, creating the shallow depth already mentioned. As a result, there is virtually no motorized boat traffic above the Rim Bridge, other than the occasional pleasure motorboat docking for a bite at Helen's around high tide.

Rowing in upper Machias Bay.

The author's wife and dog enjoy an afternoon in upper Machias Bay.

Below the Rim Bridge, the tidal river opens up into a wide bay, about a mile at its widest. To the left (north) is the Rim, which is a peninsula defined by the confluence of the Machias River and the East Machias River. The Rim is dominated by blueberry barrens and is a beautiful sight in any season.

If you continue left around the tip of the Rim peninsula, you'll enter the East Machias River watershed. Simpson Island is off the tip of the peninsula, and behind it you'll find a snaky tidal river that flows through salt marshes for half a mile. Local lore says that the pirate Bellamy hid his ship in this area, since it was out of sight behind Simpson's Island. Heading up the East Machias River, you encounter a bald, rocky headland that is home to a herd of Scottish Highland cattle. Their long, luxurious coats and massive horns, combined with the rugged landscape, make you feel like you've been transported straight to Scotland. It was in this stretch of water that I once met a boy from New Jersey who was staying in the area with his parents. He called to me from the shore, and when I paddled over to him, he asked, "Where can I see some animals?" Nothing is sure, of course, but I told him to walk out to a point near the cattle herd and see what he can see. By chance, I paddled past that point just as he got there. This city kid was completely overwhelmed when within a minute we spotted a bald eagle, a seal, and then a black bear meandering upon the blueberry barren across the river. I hope that boy remembers that day as well as I do.

Money Island sits in the middle of the channel just above the cow pasture. No more than a tiny islet covered with trees, local legend has it that another pirate buried his treasure somewhere on the island. More than a few young people have probably landed their canoes here and searched for hidden treasure, but, as far as anyone knows, it has never been located. Look out for the holes if you go exploring! Continuing up the East Machias River from Money Island, the river makes a sharp bend to the right within view of the village of East Machias. Depending on the tide level, you may not be able to go much farther than the bend, but at higher tides, you

Legend has it that the pirate Bellamy hid his ship in the serpentine river channels in this salt marsh.

can paddle right under the bridge that crosses the river before encountering a set of rapids that you won't be able to paddle up.

Back below the Rim, between the Rim Bridge and Machiasport Narrows, the bay opens up for a very different kind of experience. The water level is shallow in most places, except the channels of the two rivers that flow into it, so you can glide over the surface and clearly see what's below, even when you are a half mile from shore.

If you're headed to the Narrows, they are at the southern extreme of this bay. More experienced paddlers with open-water equipment can head out through the Narrows and explore outer Machias Bay and its islands, but that is outside the scope of this book.

Whiting Bay

Edmunds and Whiting

Whiting Bay is the innermost major bay within Cobscook Bay. As a consequence, less water rushes through the channels than in the outer bays, causing less current. You can launch a kayak at two places—either the public boat launch in Edmunds adjacent to Cobscook Bay State Park (hand carry or drive in) in Edmunds or the

Little Augusta boat launch (hand carry only with a steep slope between the parking area and water) on Route 1 in Whiting.

From the Edmunds boat launch, you can easily reach the coves of Cobscook Bay State Park and the nearby shores, which are plenty interesting enough to keep you busy for a few hours. There are several eagle nests in this area, so if you're there between March and July, you have a really good chance of seeing them. You can also cross the bay to the Trescott Township side or head north into the Dennysville and Pembroke section to check out a number of islands, including many that are owned by the US Fish and Wildlife Service as part of the Moosehorn National Wildlife Refuge. There are dangerous currents in the thoroughfare between Whiting Bay and the opening around Falls Island, so avoid that area or you could get swept into Reversing Falls! Check the map carefully.

From the Little Augusta boat launch the best exploring is just across the narrow bay, along the convoluted shoreline of land owned by the Maine Department of Inland Fisheries and Wildlife as part of the Cobscook Bay Wildlife Management Area. This is the innermost part of Cobscook Bay and much of it is exposed mudflat at lower tides, so watch your tide table carefully to avoid having to pull your kayak through extensive mud at the conclusion of your paddle.

Flat Water Paddling

One of the best ways to get out and be part of nature is to paddle a canoe or kayak on the many lakes and ponds that dot the region. Nearly every body of water has a public boat launch, but that doesn't mean that I would recommend that you paddle just any lake. The first consideration, of course, is safety. You have to choose the right day with the right weather, and make sure you have the skills and equipment for the outing you're planning. After that, it is basically about what you want to see on your trip. Personally, I opt for lakes or ponds with very little human development along the shore. I also prefer lakes that aren't wide-open expanses. Paddling the shores of some-place like Gardner Lake feels like you aren't making any progress. You can see for miles along the shore and even farther on the opposite shore, so, like watching the ground from an airplane, the view changes ever so slowly. What I look for is a medium-size, undeveloped lake with a convoluted shoreline that provides ample opportunity to watch birds and wildlife along the way. That may seem like a tall order, but there are plenty of places to find this combination of features. It bears repeating that the best time to see wildlife of any kind is early in the day or late in the day. Around noon on a sunny day, hardly any birds or animals are up and moving around.

What follows is a description of a few of my favorite paddling spots that you might not otherwise hear about.

Sunrise is an amazing time to be out paddling.

Beddington and Deblois

Bog Brook Flowage is a 625-acre lake in the middle of a 1,600-acre wetland complex that is owned and managed by the Maine Department of Inland Fisheries and Wildlife. The best place to launch a canoe or kayak is from the dam at the northern end of this body of water. Motors are definitely not recommended thanks to the many submerged stumps left behind when the former forest was cut down and then flooded many years ago. Likewise, don't take any canoe or kayak that will be damaged by scraping across trees and rocks. The lake and surrounding forest is home to several osprey nests, usually at least one eagle nest, a great blue heron rookery that has declined in recent years, and countless other birds, otters, beavers, moose, deer, bears, coyotes, and more.

This lake can be a fairly creepy place, to be honest. The shoreline is dotted with stands of dead but still standing trees that have been suspended there for decades. The water is stained very dark with tannins from the surrounding forest, so your paddle disappears from view as soon as it enters the water, and there is no indication of the depth of the lake (though it is actually very shallow). The lake bottom is a murky, unconsolidated mess that you wouldn't want to set foot on. With all of this said, I love paddling here and think it has an innate beauty that is unique in the region.

The shallow, warm, and extremely acidic water fosters aquatic plants that are usually associated with bogs, including sundews and pitcher plants, which are both

The standing dead trees in the water of Bog Brook Flowage give the lake a foreboding and slightly creepy feel.

The floating bog mats at Bog Brook Flowage are interesting to explore.

carnivorous plants that eat insects. There are also floating bog mats, which are tethered to the lake bottom by roots, but that rise and fall with the water level. The flowage can be explored any way you like, but the relatively open character of the lake near the dam quickly narrows as you work your way southeast along either shore. The lake becomes a network of fingers that you can paddle down and back up to see more of the shoreline. At the extreme southeastern tip, the main tributary is usually navigable up to nearby Flynn Pond. There is an alternate boat launch at Flynn Pond that may be used, but it requires passing over private roads that may be restricted by the owner and require a permit. Unless you know how to get such a permit, I suggest you stick to the dam site launch. When you're ready, return to the boat launch the way you came or on the opposite shore.

Scammon Pond

Eastbrook

Not to be confused with Eastport, which is more prominent in other sections of this book, Eastbrook is a town with relatively few people but several nice lakes and ponds closer to the western end of this region. This is a relatively unknown paddling option that is sure to provide a remote wilderness feeling. Virtually the entire lakeshore is part of the Lyle Frost Wildlife Management Area, owned by the Maine Department of Inland Fisheries and Wildlife, except the extreme northwest of the lake near the dam. Once you leave the boat launch at the dam behind, the rest of the lake is wild.

A number of factors lead to so few people knowing anything about this lake. The first is probably that from the one public place to launch a canoe or kayak, the lake doesn't look like much. The northern reaches of the lake are mostly an open bay with a fairly boring-looking shoreline. Not terribly enticing. Also, the lake is shallow, with many stumps of trees that were flooded when the dam was first built many years ago. As summer advances, the lake gets covered with lily pads and bull rush. These last two factors pretty much eliminate anyone with a motorized boat from even considering this lake, and they certainly discourage fishers who tire of getting their hooks tangled in the stumps and vegetation. All the better for the intrepid paddler looking for quiet and solitude.

The secret of Scammon Pond is that it is a long, skinny lake, about six miles long, though you wouldn't know it just by looking from the boat launch. Near the northern access point, it is about a half mile wide, but for most of its length, the lake is only a matter of a few hundred yards or less wide. This keeps you close to shore, so the view constantly changes—more like running a river than circumnavigating a lake where you can see the whole shoreline. Rounding every point or island and exploring every little cove offer a series of adventures. There is also the great possibility of encountering deer, moose, and bears along the shore, all of which I have seen there on various visits. There are also loons, ospreys, and bald eagles that nest on or near the lake, so these are common during the early summer (be sure to give the loons a wide berth if you see them on the water—they are stressed easily and need privacy to successfully rear their young). What you rarely see are other people. In nearly thirty paddles at Scammon Pond, I encountered another paddler exactly once.

You'll find the boat launch 0.3 mile down Sugar Hill Road off Route 200 in Eastbrook. Turn right just past a small bridge into a gravel parking area with a sign that reads "R. Lyle Frost Wildlife Management Area." Depending on your boat and the water level, you may be able to launch right from the cement apron of the lake's dam, or you may have to carry just a few yards to the left around some bushes to find a small access path to the water.

I suggest you choose either the left or the right bank of the lake and follow that down, then cross and return on the opposite side, regardless of how far you intend to paddle. Alternatively, if you have limited time, you could cut straight across the water from the launch and begin to explore the opposite banks when you get to the first narrow place and the really interesting shoreline begins.

Near the southern part of the open section, close to the first narrows, are a series of floating islands that are worth exploring. The islands are essentially mats of water-tolerant shrubs and trees that float but are moored to the bottom by their roots. The acidic water of the lake fosters carnivorous pitcher plants that can be seen along the edges of the floating mats. Beavers and red-winged blackbirds are also common here.

Continuing south, you pass through the first of several narrows and enter the more interesting part of the lake. Near the southern extreme, the lake narrows to the point

Paddling on Scammon Pond at sunrise.

that it is a small channel, which is the main feeder tributary to the lake. If you continue up the tributary, you'll eventually reach a beaver dam that prevents you from paddling farther. Although it is possible to drag your boat across the dam and continue, you won't get far before more dams and/or a rocky stretch end your exploration.

There are several islands and many, many large boulders where you can land for a picnic, a nap, or just a rest. Although some of the islands show evidence of firepits and camping, neither is permitted here.

As mentioned, when you get as far south as you care to go, simply return the way you came, hugging the opposite shoreline.

As a former wildlife biologist for the Maine Department of Inland Fisheries and Wildlife, one of my favorite duties was conducting two annual surveys on Scammon Pond, each June and July. The purpose of my trips was to count the number of ducklings, which I did by carefully paddling the entire length of the pond as close to sunset or sunrise as I could manage. I would begin in the evening, cover half of the lake, and then paddle in the dark back to my truck, where I would catch a few hours of sleep. Well before dawn, which comes at close to 4 a.m. at that time of year, I paddled back to where I left off the previous night, and continued through the early morning until I saw all of the lakeshore.

This repeated experience led to some of the most magical moments of my career, as I paddled quietly in the dim light and watched this lake and its inhabitants—but it didn't start so pleasantly. Just days after moving to Maine and beginning my job as

These massive boulders appear to be in a timeless kiss at the secluded southern end of Scammon Pond.

a biologist, my boss asked whether I was comfortable handling a canoe. "Of course," I replied, thinking about the half dozen or so times I had been in a canoe—none of which had gone very smoothly or was particularly pleasant. He described the duck surveys to me and said to let him know if I needed any help. The next two days, when I carried out the survey, were some of the worst days of my life. The aluminum canoe provided by the State was too long and too heavy for a single person to handle. To access the lake in the preferred location (not the access point at the dam I described), I had to drag the canoe through fifty yards of knee-deep mud while engulfed in a cloud of mosquitoes that seemed determined to suck my blood dry. Wind on the lake reduced the mosquitoes somewhat but also made it virtually impossible for me to steer the boat. This went on and on for the entire evening and next morning. I was determined to do a better job the next time, and for years I polished my approach to the annual survey until it became one of the highlights of my job. This is a good time to remind you to carry your preferred method of bug repellent with you on any Maine adventure!

Rocky Lake

Berry Township

For some reason there are two different Rocky Lakes, separated by just nine miles as the crow flies. The other Rocky Lake, in the town of Whiting, is also a great paddle, but not one that I'll highlight here. The Rocky Lake I want to tell you about is associated with the Rocky Lake Public Reserved Land, which occupies the entire southern half of Berry Township and includes more than half of the lakeshore. There are two boat launches on the lake. The more southerly of the two is at the Rocky Lake campground (see page 269) on Diamond Match Road, off Route 191. Although the southern end of the lake is part of the conserved land and has no development at all, it is not my favorite section to paddle. The wide-open nature of the lake here creates slow paddling and no surprises as you paddle along. You can paddle (or motor) right across the area to get to the more interesting northern half, or you can simply use the other boat launch. The Mud Landing boat launch is at the end of a short dead-end road off Route 191 just north of the Diamond Match Road. There is a shallow boat launch, so small motorized craft can launch here as well as canoes and kayaks.

The Mud Landing boat launch is actually on a tributary stream called Southern Inlet. The way upstream here is blocked by a beaver dam, so you have no choice but to paddle down the backwater (meaning little or no flow) stream. After winding your way through the very beautiful approach stream, you find yourself in the eastern bay of Rocky Lake. From here you can access a number of islands, including one with a campsite! Some of the other islands are privately owned, so be sure to know whether public access is allowed before you land.

You can simply explore the lakeshore and islands and spend the night at the island campsite, or you can continue north to find Rocky Lake Stream, a very remote-feeling tributary to the East Machias River. Continue on Rocky Lake Stream for up to 2.75 miles, when you'll reach the main stem of the East Machias River. A set of rapids just below the confluence means that you'll need to turn back here unless you're planning to paddle down the East Machias River.

Orange River

Whiting

Although this is called Orange River, the stretch I'm describing is a flat water held back by a dam. This is not to be confused with Orange Lake, which is upriver of this area. Orange Lake has its own nice paddling qualities, but it lacks a public boat launch. You may be able to paddle up from Orange River if the water is high enough, but that isn't the best part of the Orange River by far.

There are several ways to explore Orange River, including a unique "paddle-to-hike" option. There are two public canoe or kayak launches, and you can either launch and land at the same place or use another vehicle parked at the second launch to create a one-way trip. One boat launch is at Reynold's Marsh Overlook, which is a preserve owned by the Downeast Coastal Conservancy as part of its Orange River Conservation Area. Reynold's Marsh Overlook is about two and half miles south of Whiting corner (intersection of Route 1 and Route 189). If you launch from or land here, be prepared to get your boat across at least one beaver dam. For the past few years the dam has sat at or just below the water's surface, and I've been able to get a handhold and scoot my boat through rather than having to land, get out, and pull the boat through. Your results may vary. The trouble is worth it, if you're able, because beyond the dam Reynold's Brook flows through a complicated marsh ecosystem that has the stream channel bending back on itself multiple times so that you'll feel like you've gone miles, but you're just a stone's throw from where you started. Finally, Reynold's Brook meets the open water of Orange River.

The other boat launch is near the dam that holds back the Orange River. Take Playhouse Lane, which is three quarters of a mile south of Whiting Corner. For individuals or very small groups, the best access is by turning right on Landing Road and following it to the end. It might look like you are going right up someone's driveway, but the road just passes very close to the home, so continue on through. At the end of the road, there is parking for a handful of vehicles and a shallow gravel ramp for launching a canoe or kayak. You might be tempted to launch a small motorized boat, but the number of submerged stumps and abundant aquatic vegetation don't recommend it. This boat launch is also part of Downeast Coastal Conservancy's Orange River Conservation Area. For larger groups, or if you are towing a trailer, you can continue down Playhouse Lane to the end, where a dirt road takes off on the right. Follow this to the end for a larger parking area with turning space for trailers. You can carry your boat just a few yards to the dam and launch from there. Currents don't tend to be strong enough to pose a risk of being swept over the dam, but if you're brand new to paddling, use caution here.

From this end of the flowage, there is good access to a small offshoot called Little Lake and several other coves and marshes to explore. Downeast Coastal Conservancy has established a number of landing areas around the body of water, where you can stop for a picnic, to stretch your legs, or to consult a map of the river posted at the landing. Much of the shoreline of Orange River has been protected and is open for public access, but there is significant private land, so be sure to use the right places to land.

The Paddle-to-Hike Combo

One option on Orange River is to land your vessel and hike the Estey Mountain Trail, which is only accessible by boat. This hike will only take a half hour, plus any time you take for resting and enjoying the view, so it can easily be just one part of

The view from Estey Mountain is the only way to see Roaring Lake.

a day's exploration of Orange River. The landing is closer to the Reynold's Marsh boat launch, but well within reach of the Landing Road access point. To begin the hike, land on the toe of the peninsula on the north side of the river that looks like Italy's boot (be sure to carry a map). One of the Conservancy picnic sites marks the beginning of the trail, which is three quarters of a mile long one-way. There is one confusing spot on the trail, where the trail meets an old gravel road. Continue on across the road and up a narrower logging path up a hill until the hiking trail takes off into the woods on the left. At the top of a short climb, you are rewarded by a ledge outcropping overlooking Roaring Lake, a tributary of the Orange River surrounded by hills and forest as far as the eye can see. There is no public access to Roaring Lake (unless you bushwhack through the woods on Conservancy land), so this view is the only way to actually see the lake. When you're ready, return to your boat the way you came.

River Paddling

Paddling the freshwater rivers of the region is not an overwhelmingly popular activity. This is probably due to the short period of time when the water level is right for such a trip. Too early and the water, from the melted snowpack, will be too fast and too cold. Too late and the water level is too low to paddle many stretches of the river. Late April to June is generally the time when you might see canoes and kayaks coming down the rivers.

The main choices for river paddling are the Narraguagus River, the Pleasant River, the Machias River, and the East Machias River. For the best experience, consider hiring a guide service, such as Sunrise Canoe and Kayak, which will take care of the all the details and keep you safe, or just rent you equipment and/or provide ground transportation for your trip. If you choose to go on your own, information is available at various sites online.

It is also worth mentioning that the St. Croix River, which is just outside the region beyond Acadia, can be paddled pretty much all summer, thanks to dams that control the water flow and keep it running. Since the St. Croix River forms the border with Canada, there are additional rules and restrictions that you should be aware of. You can find more information at stcroix.org/what-we-do/programs/recreation/planning-your-trip.

Guides and Outfitters

The term "Maine Guide" is an official designation for someone who has passed one of several intensive exams, issued by the state of Maine, and who is permitted to charge money to take people into the wild. Each guide has a specialty. Many are hunting guides, who take "sports," as their clients are called, and help them track down game to hunt. This is a specialty outside the scope of this book. None of the guides I list here offer hunting trips.

It is a great idea to hire a guide for a wilderness exploration in a strange area. Simple knowledge like whether the river is deep enough to paddle on some shallow stretch only comes with experience and a feel for the current year's weather patterns. Guides are all certified in some form of first aid and will help in the case of a rescue. It bears repeating: If you don't have the right equipment and the right skills, don't venture into the wilderness or on to the ocean without a guide.

The services offered vary by the guide but include one or more of the following: equipment rental for your own adventure, shuttle or transportation to and from a starting/ending point of your own adventure, one-day and multiday canoe expeditions on lakes and rivers, one-day sea kayak tours.

Aquaterra Adventures

2695 US Route 1, Sullivan

Aquaterra only recently established their permanent home base in Sullivan, but they have been guiding sea kayak trips in the area for more than twenty years. They rent sea kayaks or sit-on-top kayaks for freshwater use by the day or week. They also offer four-hour guided sea kayak tours of parts of Frenchman Bay. Information can be found at aquaterra-adventures.com.

Hancock Point Kayak Tours & Schoodic Maine Snowshoe Tours

58 Point Road, Hancock

This is the only tour operator that I know of that offers guided snowshoe tours, including rental of the snowshoes. This is a great option for visitors who want to get out into the snow but don't know where to start. They also offer guided sea kayak tours, guided lake paddling tours, and lessons. You can find more information at schoodicmaineguide.com.

Water's Edge Canoe & Kayak Rentals

226 W. Franklin Road, Franklin

This business offers canoes or kayaks to rent. Delivery is available in the area, and reservations are strongly recommended. Information can be found on Facebook by searching "Water's Edge Canoe & Kayak Rentals."

Sunrise Canoe and Kayak

168 Main Street, Machias (next to Dunkin' Donuts)

This is the most full-service guiding and outfitting service in the area, offering canoe trips of varying lengths, sea kayak tours, canoe and kayak rentals, and a full shuttle service for camping, paddling, or bicycling. Get information at sunrisecanoeandkayak.com.

Sunrise Canoe and Kayak rents equipment or provides a full guide service.

Inn on the Wharf

69 Johnson Street, Lubec

This multipronged business not only has an inn and a waterfront restaurant but also offers whale watching and kayak or bicycle rentals. Most people put the kayaks into Johnson Bay right from the inn, but you can also take them to your preferred paddling destination. Find more information at theinnonthewharf.com.

Hike!

Hiking Tips

One foot in front of the other, right? What else do you need to hike? Well, nothing really, but there are some things to consider to keep yourself safe and comfortable while you hike. When I was a biologist with the Maine Department of Inland Fisheries and Wildlife, I spent a lot of time out hiking and exploring. The pack that pretty much lived on my back typically weighed about twenty-five pounds. Not only did I usually carry some kind of gear related to the job at hand, but I always had a full supply of emergency equipment. I got used to carrying the weight and never minded a bit. Nowadays I like to travel a little lighter, so it actually takes more effort before I head into the woods to decide what gear and supplies I should carry given the season, location, time of day, and other factors.

There are a ton of websites dedicated to lists of gear, and I'll leave it to you to do some research, but here are some basic ideas of what you might want to carry:

- **First aid kit:** Years ago I bought a fairly basic backpacker's first aid kit. It weighed only a few ounces; had bandages, moleskin (for blisters), antiseptic, and a few ibuprofen; and just lived in the bottom of my daypack. I have used it probably a dozen times for my own scrapes and for people I meet on the trail. The challenge is to remember to resupply the kit after use. You'll never be sorry that you tossed a first aid kit in your pack and didn't use it, so please do so. Hopefully it goes without saying that if you are on any prescription meds, bring what you need and at least a day or two extra, just in case.

- **Survival gear:** What kind of survival gear you carry depends a lot on where you are going and what you are doing. Most experts would agree that at a minimum, you should have the means to make a fire and a way to signal for help, whether that is a whistle, a mirror, or an emergency beacon. In the winter, or whenever it might get cold in the coming days, I pack extra layers, like socks, light gloves, a hat or neck warmer, and maybe a fleece jacket. These clothes are very light and easy to carry. Lately I've taken to keeping a hunting safety vest in my pack, and I suggest you do so too. It is extremely lightweight, and I really can forget it is there. The blaze-orange color can be useful if you're out during hunting season, to be sure hunters see you, but it will also come in very handy if you get lost or need to be noticed while you're out there. The extra hat that I carry is blaze orange for the same reason. Everyone should also carry a knife.

- **Food and water:** It is a good idea to pack just a little more food and water than you think you'll actually need. In case of an emergency, like an unexpected night in the woods, you'll really appreciate that you threw two granola bars in your pack instead of just the one that you planned on having for a snack in the afternoon. Likewise with water. It is heavy to carry but worth every ounce to have as much as you'll need and more.

- **Navigation:** Somehow you have to know how to get where you're going and, more important, how to get back. You might have a paper map that you print out at home or grab from the trailhead kiosk. Today there is a lot of information online. Nearly every hike detailed in this book is covered by mainetrailfinder.com, so you can just call up the map on your phone. Of course, batteries die, phones fall in streams, and cell coverage can be unpredictable in the wild, so have a backup plan if you rely on technology. You should probably also have a way to navigate across country. A compass that lives in your pack is always a good thing to have, along with the skills to actually use it effectively. A handheld GPS is a good idea, but few people carry these with the advent of smartphones. Phones have built-in compasses and navigation apps can show you where to go, but, again, technology is unpredictable, so plan ahead.

- **Insect repellent:** From roughly May to October, you may be harassed by black flies, mosquitoes, midges (no-see-ums), deerflies, horseflies, and others. Ticks are also a real concern during the same period. See page 25 for more on ticks. Do your research to determine whether you feel more comfortable applying chemicals to your skin or taking your chances with the bugs.

One final tip from someone who has spent a lot of time on the trail: Adjust your gear properly, including your pack and your shoes. I don't see a lot about this in other books, but gear that fits snugly and properly saves energy and makes you more comfortable. Here is what I do to tie my boots for the trail: Usually I'll wear a pair of loose, comfortable sneakers or sandals for the car ride to the trailhead. This helps keep my feet from getting sweaty before I even get started. At the trailhead I tie my

Porcupines are harmless to humans, but dogs running loose on the trail may not fare well if they chase these prickly cuties.

boots as most people would, and then I start hiking. Within about a quarter mile, I stop to retie the laces. This time, I take into account the dominant direction of travel, whether it is up a mountain, down a mountain, or primarily level. For climbing mountains, I flex my ankle upward and tie the lace with my foot held in something like the position it will be in more often as I climb. For downhill, I extend my toes downward and tie the laces in the position that my foot will be in for descending. This is especially useful for over-the-ankle boots, but I usually wear low boots and still find it very helpful. At this point I make the laces fairly snug and then double knot them so they don't slip out or loosen. It may sound like a lot of work, but I've noticed that if I just pile out of my car and start hiking, the movement of the shoe causes my foot muscles to work harder than they need to.

The straps on a backpack all have a use. In some cases it might not make a difference to adjust every one of them, but some straps should certainly be snugged before setting off. If your pack is larger than the gear inside it, it pays to tighten any compression straps you have to keep the load from moving with every step, or even shifting if you bend over. The less movement of the pack and load, the less energy required to carry it. If you have a waist belt, it is the first thing to adjust when you put the pack on. Hunch your shoulders up so that you can tighten the belt, and then let the weight of the pack drop onto your hips. Moving upward, tighten the shoulder straps. These are usually placed so that each hand can grab the free end of the strap and then simply pull down. Adjust both sides together to keep the load balanced.

This should be relatively snug on your shoulders. Many people neglect this step and waste a lot of energy carrying their load down around their behinds. Next, secure and adjust the sternum strap to keep your shoulder straps in place. Larger packs will also have a load-adjuster strap that is near the top, where the shoulder straps meet the pack. Once everything else is adjusted, reach up, grab the free ends, and pull downward on both sides together. This brings the weight of the pack slightly forward and onto your lumbar region, where you can most efficiently carry it. Like tying your boots, these might seem like extra steps, but once you get used to it, carrying a loose, unadjusted pack is really uncomfortable.

Hiking Etiquette

If you're going to go out and use the trails, it is incumbent upon you to do your part to take care of them. This begins with avoiding damage, either to the natural resources on the trail or to other users' experience sharing the woods with you. The latter is relatively easy to accomplish. Don't litter (duh), which includes leaving human and pet waste near the trail. If you have a dog, bring a supply of bags to carry out the waste. For human waste, many people keep a lightweight trowel in their packs to dig cat holes and bury the waste. It is best if you can carry out the toilet paper, but bury it if you have to. The most responsible thing to do usually is to bag your own waste and toilet paper, and then carry it out and dispose of it.

To avoid damaging the resources, follow any posted rules or restrictions, including trail closures. If you are hiking along and come to a muddy spot, the best thing to do is walk right through it if you have waterproof boots. It might feel like you're

You're much more likely to find fox droppings on the trail than to see a real fox.

stirring up muck or making the mud puddle deeper, but this is better than many people all stepping around the edges of the puddle and thereby making the puddle wider and wider. Don't take shortcuts if the trail is switchbacking up or down a mountain. The switchbacks are there not only to make your climb a little easier but also to avoid giving flowing water a direct path down the mountain, which causes erosion of the trail. If a trail is beaten down through the shortcut, water will simply run down it instead of dispersing into the woods at the end of the switchback.

Other recommendations for minimizing our impacts in the woods can be found by researching the seven "Leave No Trace" (LNT) principles. A multiday course is required to be LNT-certified, but a brief list of recommendations is helpful.

- Plan ahead and prepare
- Travel and camp on durable surfaces
- Dispose of waste properly
- Leave what you find
- Minimize campfire impacts
- Respect wildlife
- Be considerate of other visitors

Donnell Pond Area

Donnell Pond Public Reserved Land is unique area within the region beyond Acadia. There is a greater density of lakes, as well as far more and higher mountains, than other sections. The actual block of Public Reserved Land is more than fourteen hundred acres, but this block is augmented by thousands of acres conserved by the Nature Conservancy, Frenchman Bay Conservancy, the Downeast Salmon Federation, and other agencies within the state of Maine. There are at least twenty-five miles of hiking trails accessible from trailheads that dot the region.

Because the block of conservation land is so large, it can take a very long time to get from the more southerly trailheads off Route 1 to the northerly trailheads off Route 182 (also called Blackwoods Road), so be sure to plan your adventure before simply arriving in the area.

For me, this is the section that most reminds me of inland parts of Acadia National Park. A majority of the mountaintops here hover around one thousand feet above sea level. In the case of Schoodic, Black, and Tunk Mountains, the trails are characterized by interspersed forest and exposed ledges that offer excellent views throughout the climb. Caribou Mountain, the other named peak within the trail system, is more densely forested, but with ledge openings at the top that permit varied views.

From most of the mountaintops, there is a clear view to the south that includes the silhouette of Acadia National Park's mountain range. I have often sat atop Black, Schoodic, or Tunk Mountain, enjoying a snack or just feeling the sun on

Hiking in the Donnell Pond area brings you to many "glacial erratic" boulders.

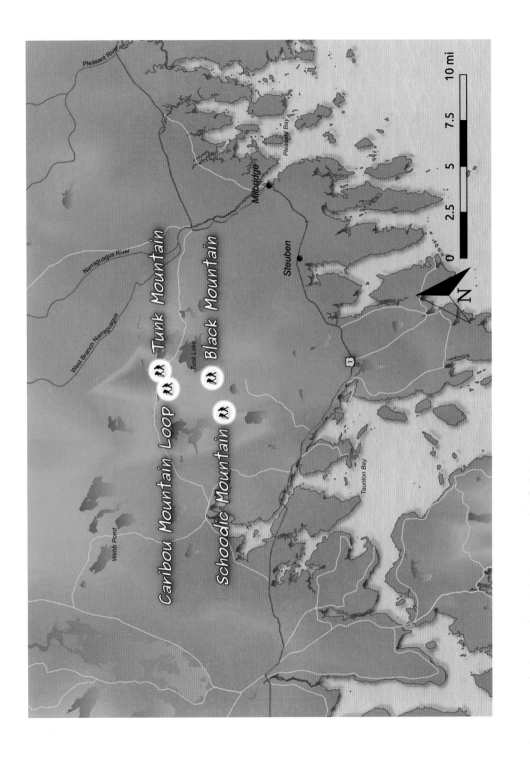

my face with only a couple of people around or even all by myself. I think about the very different scene on Acadia's mountains, with hordes of people, traffic, and trails that are used and abused beyond their capacity. Hiking in the Donnell Pond region on the whole is more peopled than other sections of this book, but with so many different trails to choose from and many miles of trail, you'll probably only run into a handful of other hikers.

Tunk Mountain

Route 182, T10 SD (part of Maine's unorganized territory)

Impressive climb up a challenging and steep, but relatively short mountain. Visit several remote ponds. Incredible views to south and north, sometimes including Katahdin.

Driving directions: From the intersection of Route 1 and Route 182 in Hancock, take Route 182 for 14.3 miles and turn left into the Tunk Mountain parking area marked by a blue sign at the roadside. From the intersection of Route 182 (Blackwoods Road) and Route 1 in Cherryfield, take Route 182 for 9.1 miles and turn right into the parking area.

Length: 4.4 miles round-trip
Difficulty: Challenging. Ascends 750 feet in about 1.2 miles of trail, including a few steep pitches where you need to use your hands. There is one section with several metal rungs drilled into the rock for climbing.

Trail description: The first 0.6 mile of the trail is relatively flat, crossing several small streams on the approach to the base of the mountain. After 0.5 mile, the Hidden Ponds Loop departs to the right. Unless you are in a serious hurry, I suggest you take the extra few minutes to visit the ponds. The loop is about a mile long and provides access to Salmon Pond and Little Long Pond. After rejoining the Tunk Mountain Trail, you'll arrive on the banks of Mud Pond, the third and final of the hidden ponds that the established trails approach. There are two additional ponds in the area that are reached by informal trails that are not part of the established trail system. These ponds are stocked with fish and are open to angling for those who want to fish a pond with no road access.

Shortly after leaving Mud Pond, the trail begins its ascent of the mountain and from here there is very little level ground until you reach the mountaintop. Several views open up to the south as you climb, with amazing views of Downing Bog, Tunk Lake, Spring River Lake, the hidden ponds, the entire Donnell Pond area range of mountains (Schoodic, Black, Caribou, and Catherine), and the ocean beyond them. Near the top the trail becomes increasingly difficult to follow, as multiple routes

The south slope of Tunk Mountain looks across lakes to the open ocean.

A hiker pauses to enjoy the view from the north slope of Tunk Mountain.

One of several "hidden ponds" approached by the Tunk Mountain Trail.

taken over the years blend together. Try to follow the blue blazes on trees or rock cairns. You may find that you aren't on the official trail, but most trails lead to the top.

A sign as the trail levels off on the top indicates that the north side of the mountain is only 0.2 mile ahead. Once again, several different trails can become confusing, including an informal trail that leads about 0.25 mile west to an antenna facility on one part of the summit. The official trail heads directly west and quickly breaks out of the trees to a dramatic view to the north with steeply sloping ledges falling away from the summit.

The first thing that captures your attention as you gaze to the distant horizon is a wind farm several miles away. This doesn't dominate the view by any means, but some people may not be happy to see an industrial facility after an arduous climb through the wilderness. Nevertheless, this is a big view and there is a lot to see other than thirty-something wind turbines. Several lakes, some blueberry barrens, and mountains in the distance make this view worth the climb. On a clear day, Katahdin can be seen almost 100 miles in the distance. It may be hard to pick out, except early in the season, when it will be the only mountain with snow visible.

When you are ready to leave, simply return down the mountain the way you came. **Land ownership:** This trail is part of the fourteen-thousand-acre Donnell Pond Public Reserved Land, owned by the State of Maine and managed by the Department of Agriculture, Conservation, and Forestry.

Online resources: Donnell Pond Public Reserved Land, maine.gov/donnellpond; Maine Trail Finder, mainetrailfinder.com/trails/trail/tunk-mountain

Schoodic Mountain

Donnell Pond Road, T9 SD (part of Maine's unorganized territory)

A short, but steep climb with stellar views in every direction. Combine a hike here with a swim at Schoodic Beach on Donnell Pond.

Driving directions: From the intersection of Route 1 and Route 183, drive north on Route 183 for 4.3 miles. Turn left onto Schoodic Beach Road and go 0.3 mile to an intersection. Bear left and continue for 2.3 miles to a parking lot at the terminus of the road.
Length: 2.4 miles for a loop that includes a stop at Schoodic Beach

Difficulty: Strenuous and challenging
Important notes: Sections of this hike require you to clamber up or down boulders with drops of up to 4 feet in some places. The peak of Schoodic Mountain is treeless and fully exposed with a telecommunications tower. Avoid the summit if lightning is a possibility.

Trail description: Contrary to my habit of starting a loop trail to the right, I prefer using the left-hand trail in this case. The trail leaves the parking lot near the outhouse. The trail is reasonably flat for about 0.5 mile, then begins to ascend the mountain. At 0.9 mile, the trail begins to cross open rock faces and joins the other leg of the loop, which comes from Schoodic Beach. Continue up the mountain for another 0.4 mile to the summit. Schoodic Mountain has impressive views in all directions. The mountains of Acadia National Park are roughly southwest, across Frenchman Bay. To the east is Black Mountain. Donnell Pond, Caribou Mountain, Catherine Mountain, and Tunk Mountain are to north or northeast. Taunton Bay is visible to the west.

From the summit, return 0.4 mile to the trail intersection and bear left to end up at Schoodic Beach on Donnell Pond (see page 76 for a description of the beach). If it's warm enough, take a swim and then walk the easy 0.5 mile back to the trailhead.

Note that another trail heads down Schoodic Mountain on the western side, but this is not covered in this book. The trail was under construction at publication time.
Land ownership: This trail is part of the fourteen-thousand-acre Donnell Pond Public Reserved Land, owned by the State of Maine and managed by the Department of Agriculture, Conservation, and Forestry.
Online resources: Donnell Pond Public Reserved Land, maine.gov/donnellpond; Maine Trail Finder, mainetrailfinder.com/trails/trail/donnell-pond-public-reserved -land-schoodic-mountain-and-beach-trails

Black Mountain

Black Mountain Road, Sullivan
A strenuous but relatively short and steep climb to a summit with views in all directions.

Driving directions: From the intersection of Route 1 and Route 183, drive north on Route 183 for 4.3 miles. Turn left onto Schoodic Beach Road and go 0.3 mile to an intersection. Bear right and continue for about 2.1 miles to a parking area on the right with room for three vehicles. There are often cars parked alongside the road as well.

Length: 2.0 miles, but can be combined with the Caribou Loop Trail or the Black Mountain Cliffs Trail for added mileage.

Difficulty: Challenging and strenuous

Important notes: Sections of this hike require you to clamber up or down boulders with drops of up to 4 feet in some places. The east peak of Black Mountain is treeless and fully exposed. Avoid the summit if lightning is a possibility.

Trail description: This trail is relatively short and sweet with no nonsense. The trail begins to climb almost immediately from the trailhead elevation of about 850 feet and continues until you reach a false summit. From here the trail dips down across the outlet to Wizard Pond, a rare fishless pond amid a patch of old-growth forest, then up to the east peak at 1,049 feet. From here trails head northeast on the Caribou Mountain Loop, or to the west to connect with the Black Mountain Cliff

Bare rocks at the top of Black Mountain offer 360-degree views.

Three different trails converge at the Black Mountain summit.

The author on Black Mountain with Acadia National Park in the background.

Trail, which leads to Schoodic Beach, the Caribou Mountain Loop, or a short trail back to the Big Chief Trail's false summit. You can also return to the trailhead the way you came, but it is roughly the same distance to do the short loop, which takes you through a patch of old-growth spruce trees.

This was one of the first trails I explored when I moved to the region in 2004. It has been a favorite of mine ever since, and I've climbed it at least once every year since then.

Land ownership: This trail is part of the fourteen-thousand-acre Donnell Pond Public Reserved Land, owned by the State of Maine and managed by the Department of Agriculture, Conservation, and Forestry.

Online resources: Donnell Pond Public Reserved Land, maine.gov/donnellpond; Maine Trail Finder, mainetrailfinder.com/trails/trail/donnell-pond-public-reserved-land-caribou-loop

Caribou Mountain Loop

Dynamite Brook Road, T10 SD (part of Maine's unorganized territory)

This hike gives you the opportunity to go for a long day hike or to backpack for one or more nights in one of the most remote areas along the immediate coast. Amazing views, including the mountains of Acadia National Park and the ocean. The hike can be combined with a boat trip and/or a swim in Donnell Pond for a twist.

Driving directions: For the Dynamite Brook trailhead (entering the loop at the northern end)—From the intersection of Route 1 and Route 182 in Hancock, take Route 182 for 14.3 miles and turn right on Dynamite Brook Road. From the intersection of Route 182 (Blackwoods Road) and Route 1 in Cherryfield, take Route 182 for 9.1 miles and turn left onto the Dynamite Brook Road, which has a blue sign indicating the Caribou Connector Trail. Drive 0.9 mile to a gravel pull-off with a sign that says it is parking for the Caribou Connector Trail.

For the Big Chief trailhead (entering loop from the southeast)—See page 176 for the Black Mountain Hike.

For the Schoodic Beach/Black Mountain Cliffs trailhead (entering loop from southwest)—See page 175 for the Schoodic Mountain Hike.

Length: Varies from under 2.0 miles to the top of Caribou Mountain to more than 10.0 miles by using multiple trails in the network. The basic Caribou Loop from the Dynamite Brook Road trailhead described here is 8.9 miles long.

Difficulty: Challenging and strenuous

Important notes: This trail is as remote as it gets in this region, and there is little cell phone coverage in the valleys. Be prepared.

This stand of spruce trees feels like a fairy-tale forest.

Caribou Mountain (right), Black Mountain (left), and Schoodic Mountain (center).

Trail description: To access the loop trail from the north at the Dynamite Brook parking area, walk about 0.25 mile east along the Dynamite Brook Road (farther along the road you came in on) to a sign indicating the Caribou Connector trailhead. From there, the top of Caribou Mountain is 0.9 mile of gradual uphill climbing with a few steep sections. About halfway up that trail, a side trail to Catherine Mountain takes off from the left. That trail goes onto private property that allows public use and offers nice views, though similar to what you'll see on Caribou Mountain. Continuing up to Caribou Mountain, at the first major ledge outcropping with a view of the valley, "Tunk Lake" and "Black Mountain ahead" signs indicate that this is the beginning of the Caribou Loop Trail.

You can go either left or right here to go around the loop. If you go right, you'll walk along the ridge atop Caribou Mountain for about 1.0 mile before beginning the descent toward Black Mountain. The slope is relatively gradual. At the bottom, a trail takes off to the right toward Redman Beach, 1.4 miles away. This would be a great place to camp if you're backpacking, or you can boat across Donnell Pond to Redman Beach and then hike the Caribou Loop from there. There are a number of free first-come, first-served campsites at Redman Beach and at other locations around Donnell Pond. Consult the trail map on the website listed under "Online Resources."

Continuing south on the loop, the ascent up Black Mountain begins almost immediately after the Redman Beach Trail. The trail climbs 600 feet in about a mile with a few steep sections, but it's relatively gradual, particularly compared with the Big Chief Trail or the Black Mountain Cliff Trails on the other side of the mountain. You top out on the western summit, which has no distant views. A trail leaves on the right for the Black Mountain Cliffs and Schoodic Beach beyond, but the loop trail turns left here.

Studies have shown that the forest in this area is one of the very few old-growth forests in coastal Maine. The trees aren't enormous, given the harsh climate and poor soils, but the sparse ground vegetation and thick bed of moss that covers the floor definitely make it feel like a magical forest. Perhaps that's where the name of Wizard Pond comes from. Wizard Pond is a rare fishless pond that is nestled in the valley between the western and eastern summits of Black Mountain. You can catch a glimpse of Wizard Pond if you take a trail with no sign on your right not far from the western summit. Note that there is no good way to actually reach the pond since it is surrounded by thick shrubs. Bear left at the first intersection on that trail, and you'll take an alternate trail up to the eastern summit and rejoin the loop trail.

The main loop trail continues down into the valley between the summits and then climbs a short distance up to the eastern summit. The eastern summit is a treeless and rocky place. In fact, despite its low altitude of just 1,049 feet, this is considered an arctic environment, as is the summit of nearby Schoodic Mountain. The views in all directions can't be beat. To the south, the mountains of Acadia National Park are in silhouette beyond Frenchman Bay. Tunk Lake dominates the eastern view. To the north, you can look back at Caribou Mountain, with Catherine Mountain to

◄ *Cliffs on the north slope of Black Mountain.*

its east and Tunk Mountain behind both of them. Depending on where you're standing, Schoodic Mountain, with its noticeable tower at the top, may be visible to the west. A trail heads south to the Big Chief trailhead, but the Caribou Loop continues toward the northeast. A sign at the summit marks the path.

The descent is similar to the ascent, roughly 600 feet in a mile, with some spectacular cliffs with overhangs and small caves among the trees. The trail skirts the edges of two wetlands that are visible through the trees, but with no obvious route to visit them. It then brushes up against Rainbow Pond, crossing the outlet stream just below the pond. Again, there is no obvious route to the pond, but you can bushwhack over if you really want to see it.

Shortly after crossing the Rainbow Pond outlet stream, the trail begins to ascend Caribou Mountain. This is again a relatively gradual climb through a beautiful boulder-strewn patch of forest. The first open viewpoint you reach is the same one where the Caribou Loop began. Follow the trail down the north side of Caribou Mountain to the Dynamite Brook Road and your vehicle.

Land ownership: This trail is part of the fourteen-thousand-acre Donnell Pond Public Reserved Land, owned by the State of Maine and managed by the Department of Agriculture, Conservation, and Forestry.

Online resources: Donnell Pond Public Reserved Land, maine.gov/donnellpond; Maine Trail Finder, mainetrailfinder.com/trails/trail/donnell-pond-public-reserved-land-caribou-loop

Pleasant Bay

Pleasant Bay is a long arc of mainland coast, interrupted by a series of peninsulas that jut southward, like fingers dangling from the palm of a hand. Along these fingers are miles and miles of coast that is gentle and gradual compared with the Bold Coast farther Down East, with extensive mudflats, salt marshes, and rockweed beds (seaweed that covers rocky intertidal areas).

The payoff for most hikes around Pleasant Bay is some kind of remote-feeling access to the shores of the bay. Except for Pigeon Hill, most of these trails are relatively flat. The forest here tends a little more toward a mixed deciduous and evergreen type than the deep spruce-fir forests farther Down East.

These hikes have the advantage of being near the western end of the region beyond Acadia and so are more accessible to more people. In my own opinion, these are nice hikes that you'll never regret doing, but the real magic of Down East is farther up the coast or in the Donnell Pond area.

Hollingsworth Trail

Pigeon Hill Road, Steuben

A flat hike through a coastal pitch-pine forest to a stretch of rugged and scenic coastline. Excellent choice for a coastal hike if you don't have time to venture farther into the region, or if you are looking for a remote place to just explore the shoreline or rest on the beach. Gorgeous beach is perfect for a picnic or sunning.

Driving directions: From US Route 1 in Steuben, turn onto Pigeon Hill Road at Kennedy Marine Engineering for 6.3 miles. Parking is on the right side of the road, and the trail takes off on the left side.
Length: 1.5-mile loop trail
Difficulty: Easy to moderate. The trail is almost completely flat and plenty wide for single-file hikers. There are a number of places where roots are really prominent across the trail as well as areas of ledge that require a certain degree of agility to easily pass. The trail appears to be well designed with bridges and bog walks to keep you out of wet spots.
Important notes: Thick fog can enclose coastal peninsulas very quickly on summer mornings and afternoons. Ledge- and boulder-strewn shoreline is very slippery when wet. Use caution if you are there on a falling tide, as the shoreline will be wet. The beach is incredibly inviting, but if you are tempted to swim, remember that the ocean is always frigid and it may be difficult to warm up before you get back to your vehicle. Hypothermia can and does happen in the summer in Maine.

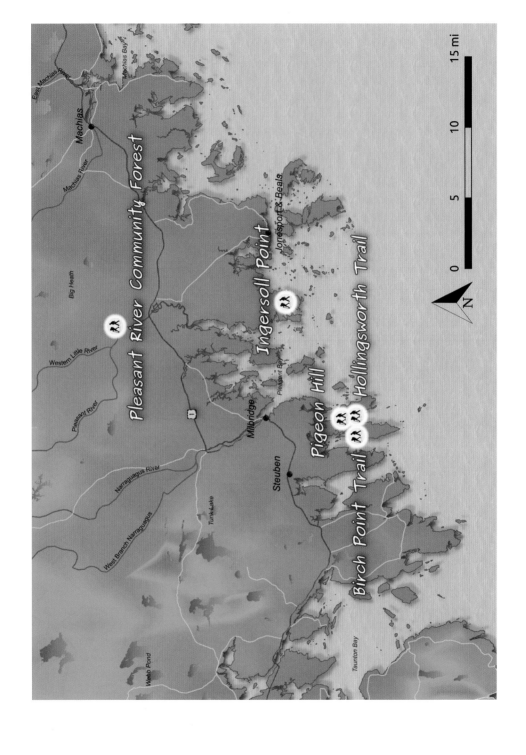

Trail description: This is a very straightforward hike with few options, except how long you choose to dally at the many viewpoints. The trail begins by passing through a field that produces a bumper crop of blueberries in late summer. If you are in the area around the last couple of weeks of August, this could be a great spot to pick a quart of organic blueberries for a pie or smoothies. Once the trail enters the forest, it is only a short walk to where the trail splits to form the loop. A subtle arrow directs hikers to the right for a counter-clockwise trip around the property. There is no reason you can't choose to go left, but if you go with the flow, you have much more solitude along your hike, since you'll likely only see fellow hikers who are passing you, or whom you pass, rather than meeting every hiker headed in the opposite direction.

The forest here is relatively sparse and stunted due to the harsh coastal climate, but there is enough shade to keep it cool on a hot summer's day. One of the botanical highlights is the presence of pitch pines. These are much more common farther south, but the only hikes in this region that feature them are this trail and the Great Wass Trail.

After what seems like a pretty short walk through the woods—just long enough to stretch the legs and get the mind to unwind—the trail breaks out of the woods near Chair Pond, with its sand beach. The sand is mostly at the upper reaches of the beach, so at low tide there may not be any sandy beach at the water's edge. Behind the beach dune is Chair Pond, a small brackish pond that looks perfect for birding and wildlife observation. On a clear day, Petit Manan Island is visible two miles off-shore. Petit Manan Light, at 119 feet tall, is the defining feature of the island, at least at this distance. An active and successful seabird restoration program on Petit Manan is yielding an increase in Atlantic puffins, roseate and arctic terns, guillemots, and others. Boat tours to the island are available (see page 111).

A series of interpretive signs, scattered along the trail but particularly along the shoreline portion, tell the story of the ecology of the area and the work being done by the National Wildlife Refuge to protect or restore it.

There is an amazing array of types of rocky shoreline along a short stretch of the Hollingsworth Trail.

A cobble beach marks the end of the shoreline portion of the trail.

After its first approach to the shore, the trail makes its turn to the left and begins to wind its way back to the trailhead, staying mostly in the forest, but frequently popping out for a view of the ocean and an opportunity to explore a little coastline. Bois Bubert Island (BOY bu-Bear) is the prominent view along this stretch of trail. Before you know it, the trail loop is completed and you're on the homestretch back to the trailhead.

Land ownership: This trail is on land owned by the Maine Coastal Islands National Wildlife Refuge. The refuge owns more than fifty islands and is primarily focused on restoring seabird nesting colonies on the islands.

Online resources: Maine Coastal Islands National Wildlife Refuge, fws.gov/ref uge/maine_coastal_islands/; Maine Trail Finder, mainetrailfinder.com/trails/trail/ petit-manan-wildlife-refuge-hollingsworth-trail

Birch Point Trail

Pigeon Hill Road, Steuben

One of the longer but easier hikes in this book, it offers excellent views of different interior bays within Pleasant Bay.

Driving directions: From US Route 1 in Steuben, turn onto Pigeon Hill Road at Kennedy Marine Engineering for 5.8 miles. Parking is on the right side of the road at a large National Wildlife Refuge kiosk at the edge of a blueberry field.

Length: 4.2 miles round-trip

Difficulty: Easy to moderate. Despite the fact that this is one of the longer hikes in the area, it is one of the easier options. The trail is in excellent condition, with extensive boardwalks and bog bridges where needed.

The footpath is wide and flat. It isn't until the loop near the end of the trail that it becomes a little more narrow and rugged, but it's still quite manageable by anyone who contemplates a 4-mile hike.

Important notes: Thick fog can enclose coastal peninsulas very quickly on summer mornings and afternoons. Ledge and boulder strewn shoreline is very slippery when wet. Use caution if you are there on a falling tide, as the shoreline will be wet.

Trail description: The trail begins in a blueberry barren (field), though there are major differences between this and a commercial blueberry barren. A conventional blueberry barren is treated with herbicides, pesticides, and fertilizer to create a monocrop to maximize the blueberry harvest. By contrast, this barren, which is owned and managed by the US Fish and Wildlife Service, is minimally managed to replicate something closer to the native ecosystem typical of Down East Maine. The blueberry barrens found here are rich and diverse habitats with a variety of plants that grow in full sunlight, unlike the darker forest interior.

The mostly level, or gently sloping, trail is easy and pleasant to walk on. Unlike many trails in the region, nimble hikers are able to take their eyes off the trail and enjoy observing the forest and barrens around them. The total trail is about 2.1 miles

The trail crosses several old blueberry fields on the way to the shore.

A peaceful cove in Pleasant Bay.

A series of informative stops along the route describe the ecosystem.

long and is mostly an out-and-back trail, though there is a loop at the far end on Dyer Bay and a spur trail to Lobster Cove. The loop provides the best views of the trail. Sally's Island is just offshore here, with an eagle's nest that has been used for many years by the resident bald eagles, and the cobble beaches and boulders offer great places to pause to enjoy the view.

Interpretive panels along the trail describe the ecology of the region and point out specific features that may be overlooked.

Land ownership: This trail is on land owned by the Maine Coastal Islands National Wildlife Refuge. The refuge owns more than fifty islands and is primarily focused on restoring seabird nesting colonies on the islands.

Online resources: Maine Coastal Islands National Wildlife Refuge, fws.gov/ref uge/maine_coastal_islands/; Maine Trail Finder, mainetrailfinder.com/trails/trail/ petit-manan-wildlife-refuge-birch-point-trail

Pigeon Hill

Pigeon Hill Road, Steuben

This hike has a short climb to a 317-foot summit with nearly 360-degree views of the ocean, Acadia National Park, and the surrounding forest.

Driving directions: From the intersection of Route 1 and Pigeon Hill Road in Steuben, turn on Pigeon Hill Road and drive about 4.4 miles. The parking area will be on your right, opposite an old cemetery on the left.
Length: The network is 1.4 miles long.

Difficulty: Moderate to challenging. The short but steep climb to the top of Pigeon Hill presents large rocks to scramble up or down, including some that are often slippery. Frequent roots and rocks in the trail require a degree of agility and care.

Trail description: The preferred loop at Pigeon Hill begins on the Historic Trail, which has been in use for generations. Take this trail all the way to the summit, which has multiple views in different directions. A number of interpretive signs along the way and at the summit provide context to the forest around you, its history, and the views from the summit. From the summit, continue to the other side of the mountain and descend via the Summit Loop Trail. For a longer and more challenging hike, you can take an additional loop on the Ledge Woods Trail, which circles through the forest and returns to the Summit Loop Trail. When the Summit Loop Trail rejoins the Historic Trail, turn right and then make a left onto the Silver Mine Trail, which rejoins the Historic Trail at the sign-in box near the trailhead. This route creates a "figure eight" loop.

This trail offers enough challenge and incredible views to be a destination of its own, but at only 1.4 miles for the longest possible loop, it can easily be done in

Pigeon Hill lit up in early fall colors.

combination with a nearby trail, such as the Hollingsworth Trail, or as what I call a "leg stretcher hike" to break up the long drive that passes by the area on Route 1.

This is one of Downeast Coastal Conservancy's most popular trails and is the site of Full Moon Rise Hikes from time to time. At these events dozens of people gather on the summit to watch the sun set and the full moon rise, then walk down in the twilight.

There are nearly 360-degree views from the top.

Land ownership: This 170-acre preserve is owned and managed by Downeast Coastal Conservancy.

Online resources: Downeast Coastal Conservancy, downeastcoastalconservancy .org/dcc-trails/pigeon-hill/; Maine Trail Finder, mainetrailfinder.com/trails/trail/ pigeon-hill

Ingersoll Point

316 Mooseneck Road, Addison

Hike through a coastal spruce-fir forest with carpets of moss to an old homestead right on Wohoa Bay.

Driving directions: From the intersection of Route 1 and Route 187 in Columbia Falls (at the blue dome called Wild Blueberry Land), head south on Route 187 for 1.9 miles. Turn right at the sharp bend in the road and continue 1.4 miles to a stop sign, where you should turn left. Go 5.9 miles and turn right on Moose Neck Road and continue for 1.5 miles. Parking and the trailhead are in the parking lot of the Union Church of South Addison. Please park against the woods in the rear of the church. The trailhead is in the back right corner of the parking lot.

Length: The entire network is 3.4 miles long.

Difficulty: Easy to moderate. There are no particularly challenging sections of this trail, but just enough rocks and roots to make you want to watch your step. The Cove Trail is more challenging, with steep slopes and unstable footing.

Important notes: Be sure to park your car in the rear of the church parking lot, not on the paved church lot, especially on Sunday. A section of the beach along the Wohoa Bay Trail can be unavoidably wet at certain tide stages. If you don't have waterproof shoes, you can take the Moss Trail to bypass this section.

Trail description: The hike begins on the Adler Woods Trail at the rear right of the parking lot and meets the first trail intersection at about 0.5 mile. Ultimately, you can choose among three main trails that bring you to the shore. The Wohoa Bay Trail is the most direct route, but, as mentioned in the **Important notes**, there is a perpetual wet spot along the shore where a freshwater marsh meets the ocean, and it can be impossible to wend your way through without getting wet. The Adler Woods Trail continues all the way to the shore as well, just to the north of Wohoa Bay Trail. After the Cove Trail meets from the left, the Adler Woods Trail joins an old section of woods road that is much wider than the typical trail. At the shore end of this trail, an old cellar hole is engulfed in one of the larger stands of lilac bushes that I've seen. From the shore you can turn right to return by the Wohoa Bay Trail, or you can turn left to return by the Cove Trail, which is my preference. The Cove Trail turns westward almost immediately and hugs the shoreline of Carrying Place Cove for 0.7

The Wahoa Bay Trail stays on the shore for almost half a mile.

Carrying Place Cove nearly empties at low tide.

mile. The cove nearly empties at low tide, so the view is constantly changing. After leaving the shore, the Cove Trail makes its way back and joins the Adler Woods Trail for the last stretch of the walk back to your vehicle.

There are a lot of trails in this book that are described as spruce-fir or boreal forest. All are beautiful and unique in their own ways. This is one of my favorites and is beloved by many people who know this area well. This forest doesn't have a great number of truly large trees, but the average size of the spruce trees is much larger than most stands of this type of forest. There is also very little undergrowth on the forest floor and all of the active growth is high up in the canopy, so the trunks of the trees are prominent and majestic. Ironically, this indicates relatively low-quality habitat for many birds, but it is very pleasing to the human eye.

Land ownership: This 145-acre preserve is owned and managed by the Downeast Coastal Conservancy.

Online resources: Downeast Coastal Conservancy, downeastcoastalconservancy .org/dcc-trails/ingersoll-point/; Maine Trail Finder, mainetrailfinder.com/trails/trail/ ingersoll-point-preserve

Pleasant River Community Forest Trails

Little River Road, Columbia Falls

This is a very nice hike through a diverse forest and along the banks of the Pleasant River and one of its tributaries.

Driving directions: From the intersection of Route 1 and Tibbetstown Road in Columbia Falls, drive north on Tibbetstown Road for 2.8 miles, then turn left onto Cross Road. Drive 0.5 mile and turn left onto Little River Road. A sign at this intersection identifies this area as the Pleasant River Community Forest. Drive down Little River Road for 0.25 mile to a small parking area on the left at Otter Falls.

Length: 2.4 miles for the main loop

Difficulty: Moderate. This trail borders on easy, but the relatively low level of use and sporadic maintenance result in many trees and other obstacles across the trail, requiring agility and an ability to find the trail again after leaving it to walk around a blowdown.

Important notes: Little River Road is a rough dirt road that has been slowly eroding for years. The crown in the center of the two tire ruts is just low enough for most cars to make it to the trailhead. Use caution and move slowly in a low-sitting car. Do not attempt to continue past the trailhead parking area in a car.

Trail description: From the Otter Falls parking lot, be sure not to miss the Otter Falls Trail, which is only 0.1 mile long and begins just behind the parking area, on the same side of the road. This trail approaches a small waterfall on Little River, a tributary to the Pleasant River, and then bends back to the road. Turn right on the

road to return to the parking lot to access the main loop trail. Directly across the road from the parking area, find the "Highland Trail" sign and follow the red diamond blazes nailed to trees. The Highland Trail is about 0.75 mile long and winds through the mixed upland forest. Near the end, the trail breaks out into a clearing and makes a sharp left turn at an old outhouse tipped on its side. It can be difficult to find where the trail continues out of the clearing, but simply follow the path directly ahead through the left-hand side of the clearing and an old road continues into the woods, marked by the red diamond blazes that you'll see when you get close.

The Highland Trail terminates at a woods road called the River Trail, where you can turn right or left. To add about 1.2 mile to the hike, you can turn right and walk to an alternate trailhead on Tibbetstown Road and then back to the same spot. Turn left off the Highland Trail to continue on the main loop, which is now marked with blue diamond blazes. The trail eventually leaves the woods road and makes its way through the forest to the banks of the Pleasant River, which it follows downriver. It can be difficult to follow the path along the river, but always look for the blue diamond blazes. The trail leaves the river at about 1.5 miles into the hike and makes its way across country until it arrives at Little River Road. Turn left onto the road and walk about a half mile back to the parking lot.

Land ownership: The 418-acre Pleasant River Community Forest is owned by the Downeast Salmon Federation with a goal to improve habitat for native fish, animals, and plants, particularly the endangered Atlantic salmon.

Online resources: Downeast Salmon Federation, mainesalmonrivers.org/pleasant -river-community-forest

◄ *For some reason, beavers abandoned efforts to cut this maple tree when they were only part way through.*

The Pleasant River.

Otter Falls can be reached by a short spur trail from the parking area.

Great Wass to Machias Bay

The trails in this section lack a coherent geographical feature to pin them to, but they offer a variety of different types of hikes and experiences, from hikes along rivers to in-town parks to coastal forests with craggy shorelines. Properties here include long-time favorites like the Great Wass Preserve, but the majority are new. The Machias River Preserve, Middle River Park, and Long Point have all been protected since 2013. Nevertheless, these trails are destined to become classics thanks to their accessibility from Machias, their incredibly remote feel despite the proximity to town, and the way they expose the deep beauty of this formerly untrailed region.

Great Wass Island Preserve

Black Duck Cove Road, Beals

Pass through a primeval black spruce and pitch-pine forest to a wild and rugged coastline.

Driving directions: From the intersection of Route 187 and Bridge Street in Jonesport, head south and cross the Beals Island Bridge. Bear left at the end of the bridge and continue straight for 1.7 miles until you cross a small causeway, which marks the entrance to Great Wass Island. Bear right just after the causeway and drive 2.5 miles to the parking area on the left side of the road, just beyond the entrance to the Downeast Institute, on the right.

Length: 4.5 miles of established trails, plus almost 5.0 miles of coast available for exploration

Difficulty: Challenging. Despite the overall flat terrain, the trail is constantly going up or down little dips, often with steps of 2 to 3 feet that are climbed or scrambled down. Exploring along the shore is also challenging, with the need to hop from rock to rock, climb up or down large slabs of rock, or navigate shifting sand and cobblestone beaches.

Important notes: No dogs are allowed on the Great Wass Island Preserve. This is the only trail in this book that does not permit dogs.

Trail description: Great Wass Island Preserve is one of the big three or four hiking destinations that many people already know about when they arrive in the region. Unless you happen to be local to the town of Jonesport or Beals, it is a serious journey just to get to the trailhead, and well worth the time and effort. Great Wass Island is connected by a short causeway to the island of Beals, which is in turn connected to the mainland by a dramatic narrow and steep bridge. The road winds its way down the chain of islands, offering many views of untouched coast as well as taking you through the heart of the fishing villages of Jonesport and Beals.

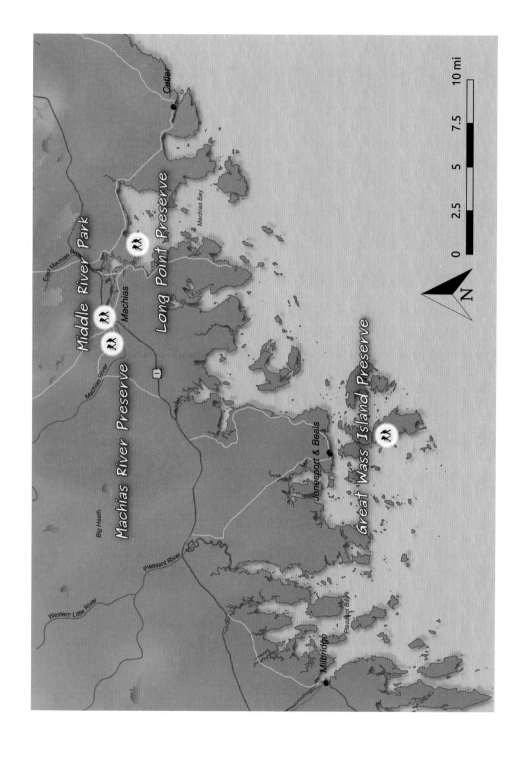

The complex and varied shoreline of the Great Wass Preserve.

Pitch pines and scrubby growth on rocky land with very thin soil.

Rounding Little Cape Point is easiest at low tide.

The trail splits just a hundred feet or so from the trailhead. Head left for the Mud Hole Trail, or stay straight for the Little Cape Point Trail. Looking at a map of the property, it is tempting to plan a loop trail, out one way and back another. There is another option in this case that I recommend. If you have the time to make this a longer hike, stay straight at the split and cross the island on the Little Cape Point Trail (2.2 miles). The hike is just long enough, in my opinion, for you to forget where you are headed. Let yourself get swept in by the scrubby jack pines, the exposed ledge outcrops, and the constant care over your foot placement due to the rooted and rocky trail surface. For me, at least, this became a wonderful hike that could have been almost anywhere and I thoroughly enjoyed it. But then you round a bend in the trail and emerge from the deep forest into a tableau that makes you feel as though you've stumbled onto the set of a David Attenborough documentary. Like most coastal destinations, there is a very different feel to the place depending on whether you arrive near high tide or low tide. My companions and I made it close to low tide, and the scene was positively primeval. The shore is bare granite ledge, broken up by patches of exposed sand or mud. In some places the rocks are broken and jumbled from geological forces over millennia. Farther out in the cove, massive beds of rockweed (a kind of seaweed) blanket the ledge. At low tide the rockweed lays flat and looks like a shaggy carpet. When it is under water, the rockweed floats upward, held to the rocky bottom by a single point of attachment called a "holdfast." The drifting rockweed is similar to the kelp forests of the Pacific, and this ecosystem is every bit as rich and interesting.

One could sit in this spot all day watching the tide come in or go out and gulls resting on top of rocks or bobbing on the water in tide pools. You shouldn't have to sit very long before you spot eagles, seals, and any number of interesting seabirds, all of which live off the churning sea. Nothing in your view is manmade, save the ubiquitous beach litter that washes up and the occasional lobster fishing boat.

As I mentioned, you could head left along the coast, eventually picking up the Mud Hole Trail, which will return you to the trailhead in 2.3 miles. My suggestion, though, is to head right down the shore, wending your way south and farther from the mainland. This stretch of hiking is what makes Great Wass Island one of the most popular and well-known hikes in the region. Be aware, however, that it is slow going on the rocky shoreline. Allow twice as much time as it would take on stable ground. For 2.0 miles, you hop from rock to rock, scramble over massive driftwood trees that lodge in the shoreline, traverse patches of sand beach, and generally make your way toward the tall mass of rock visible down the shore. From there the coast continues in a similar manner to Red Head, where it becomes too difficult to continue. When you are done, return the way you came, or continue up the coast and return on the Mud Hole Trail, which is a little longer than the Cape Point Trail and hugs the shoreline of a cove called Mud Hole for most of its length.

Land ownership: This 1,576-acre preserve is owned and managed by the Nature Conservancy.

Online resources: The Nature Conservancy, nature.org/en-us/get-involved/how -to-help/places-we-protect/great-wass-island

Machias River Preserve

Route 1A, Machias and Whitneyville

This is the best (and perhaps only) hiking trail in the region with more than three miles of trail along a major river. Wading in the Machias River is a great way to cool off in the summer.

Driving directions: For the Machias River Heritage trailhead: From the intersection of Route 1A and Route 192 in Machias, drive south on Route 1A toward Whitneyville for 1.2 miles. The trailhead and parking lot will be on your left.

For the Money Island trailhead: From the intersection of Route 1A and Route 192 in Machias, drive south on Route 1A toward Whitneyville for 3.2 miles. The trailhead and parking lot will be on your left.

Length: Loop trail options vary from about 1.5 miles to 7.2 miles.

Difficulty: Generally moderate. There are a few steep hills, but none are more than a few hundred feet long. There are some rocks and roots to navigate along the trail, but fewer than the average trail in the region.

The railroad bridge over the Machias River is one gateway to the Machias River Preserve.

The Machias River Trail tracks the shore of the Machias River for more than three miles.

The author and companions enjoy the Machias River in the winter.

Important notes: Most trail options will include at least a short stretch of walking on the Down East Sunrise Trail. ATVs and snowmobiles are permitted, so pedestrians should use caution and courtesy by staying right and listening for motors approaching.

Trail description: There are three trailheads to choose from at the Machias River Preserve. From the Machias River Heritage trailhead you can choose to do about a 4.0-mile loop hike, or you can connect with other trails on the preserve for up to 7.0 miles of hiking. You can also choose to simply walk the roughly 0.75 mile to the Machias River and return the way you came. If you're doing the 4.0-mile loop, my strong recommendation is to begin by walking from the trailhead along Route 1 (away from Machias) to the Sunrise Trail, which is the first leg of the hike. There are several reasons for doing the loop in this direction. For about a mile, the Sunrise Trail gradually descends closer to the river level. Moreover, the trail is quite exposed to the sun and is gravelly and dusty, especially if you're passed by any ATVs on the trail. Doing the trail in the reverse direction means finishing with this stretch, going uphill, rather than being able to enjoy it earlier and then spend the rest of your time in the cool, moist forest and along the river.

Keep an eye on the left side of the Sunrise Trail for signs indicating the beginning of the Heritage Trail. If you reach a small gravel pullout with a sign about this Downeast Coastal Conservancy preserve, you just passed the trail you want to take. Enter the trail and bear left at an intersection just a few meters from the Sunrise Trail. Very quickly, you'll cross the first of eight trail bridges that cross tributaries of the Machias River. Don't be surprised if the bridges are a little crooked or even not right where the trail meets them. Nearly every spring, and sometimes during summer storms, the Machias River level rises and floods the tributaries. The wooden bridges float upward and then are dropped somewhere in the vicinity. Ropes and cables hold the bridges in the general location where they should go, but it sometimes takes staff or volunteers some time to readjust the bridges to their proper place. At this point it is important to note that the first bridge you come to, regardless of which direction you are hiking, is an indication of the water conditions ahead. If the bridge is flooded, don't attempt to find a way around and continue, because the other seven bridges are also flooded, and the trail is saturated, so hiking is both dangerous and damaging to the trail. Please turn back and return another time if the trail is flooded.

Soon after crossing the first bridge, the trail meets the Machias River, and for the next 2.0 miles or a little more, the river is rarely more than a few yards from your side. Interpretive signs are scattered periodically along the way, indicating interesting ecological features and the cultural history of the landscape. The focal point of the trail along the river is Munson's Pitch, a short set of rapids with rock outcrops that make a perfect place for a rest or a swim (see page 128). At low water the river barely trickles over the rocks, but in the spring or when the river is higher, it can be breathtaking to watch the water rush by.

The mature forest, featuring tall pines, all along this trail make you forget you are just a mile or so by river from downtown Machias. Occasional canoeists or kayakers will run the river in the spring, but by mid-summer the low water is bony enough to dissuade most paddlers.

At a place called Red Pine Point the trail turns sharply to the left and begins the 0.75-mile return to the trailhead. Immediately across the river from this spot is the Machias Valley Regional Airport. Air traffic safety regulations necessitated the clear-cut you see across the river, as well as the selective timber harvesting you'll pass through for most of the remainder of the hike. The trail winds through a patch of cedar forest that provides winter shelter for herds of deer in severe winters. Please keep dogs on a leash in this area during the winter to avoid unnecessarily stressing the deer. The trail also crosses through the outskirts of what was once called Atusville, a small community of free blacks who lived here in the 1800s and into the early 1900s.

The Money Island trailhead is the launching point for a 3.0-mile loop that includes the Money Island Trail, the Homestead Trail, and the Hemlock Trail. The trail begins in an area of regenerating forest that was harvested back in the early 2000s and follows an old skidder trail for the initial quarter mile or so. Before long the trail veers off the skidder trail and into more mature forest, following the course of a small stream that is known for having a great sea-run brook trout fishery. After about a half mile, the trail meets the Machias River across the channel from Money Island, a tiny wood-covered island in the middle of the River. (Note that this is not the same Money Island described in the **Paddle!** section on the East Machias River.) The trail continues down the river for a short distance to the first intersection. You can go either way, but my suggestion is to take a left turn and begin on the Homestead Trail, which takes you inland, with glimpses of the 65-acre marsh in the middle of this loop trail and on to the old Meadow Farm homestead, featuring a tree plantation with tall red spruce trees in straight lines and an area with a few cellar holes and old apple trees. After 1.25 miles, the Homestead Trail ends at the Sunrise Trail.

From here, you can go right for a 0.6-mile walk on the Sunrise Trail straight through the middle of the marsh and then back to the Machias River. Alternatively, you can take a left on the Sunrise Trail and keep an eye out for the entrance to the Heritage Trail just fifty yards or so on your right. Enter the woods and bear right at the first intersection to join the Hemlock Trail. This 0.7-mile trail hugs the shore of the Machias River, headed upstream. Toward the end the trail makes a sharp bend to the right and then enters a patch of forest that includes some really massive hemlock trees. Tom Wessels, an expert in discerning the history of forests, estimated that these trees could be upward of three hundred years old, but even at that age they are not considered "old growth." The trail rejoins the Sunrise Trail close to a historic railroad bridge over the Machias River, a great spot to watch the river go by and take a break. The trail reenters the woods on the north side of the Sunrise Trail just a little to the right of where the Hemlock Trail ended. This short path parallels the Sunrise Trail back to the Machias River and then turns upriver once again, rejoining the Money Island Trail for the final 0.5 mile to the trailhead.

The third trailhead in this network is in the village of Whitneyville, at the intersection of Middle Street, Route 1A, and the Sunrise Trail. The parking lot includes an ATV or snowmobile ramp for motorized enthusiasts using the Sunrise Trail, but hikers are also welcome here. From the parking area, turn left onto the Sunrise Trail and walk toward the railroad bridge visible up ahead, using caution when crossing Route 1A, as cars tend to drive fast here and the visibility is poor. After crossing the railroad bridge, you can continue on the Sunrise Trail into the marsh, you can turn right onto the Hemlock Trail, or you can turn left and join the Homestead Trail.

This trail system is the home of the Bad Little Trail Run, an event that I started with some volunteers in 2017. Held each fall, the trail run features a 2.5-mile course and a 7.0-mile course. It is part of the Downeast Conservation Trail Race Series, held by six land trusts in the eastern part of the state. You can learn more at downeastconservationraces.org.

Land ownership: The 900-acre Machias River Preserve is owned by Downeast Coastal Conservancy as part of the Two Rivers Conservation Area, which protected this preserve and nearby Middle River Park.

Online resources: Downeast Coastal Conservancy, downeastcoastalconservancy.org/dcc-trails/machias-river-preserve/; Maine Trail Finder, mainetrailfinder.com/trails/trail/machias-river-preserve (note that the trail map on this site is not complete)

Middle River Park

Kilton Lane (just off Route 1), Machias

This in-town park has a surprisingly remote feel on parts of the trail. The picnic area has an excellent view of Middle River.

Driving directions: From Route 1 in Machias, turn onto Kilton Lane directly across from Helen's Restaurant. The road makes a quick left turn and then ends at the wastewater treatment plant. Just before the gates for the treatment plant, take one of the two dirt roads to the right and park in the area indicated.

Length: Varies. There are about 3.0 miles of trail in total, but it can be hiked in many ways to make shorter walks.

Difficulty: Easy to moderate. Many of the trails are grassy paths that are kept fairly well mowed, and this makes for easy walking for those with some mobility issues or even with an all-terrain baby stroller. The trails that enter the woods tend to be a little narrower and may have some roots or rocks to navigate, but none are all that challenging.

Important notes: There are many deer that inhabit the park. Dogs are permitted, but if they are off leash, they are very likely to chase the deer. Use discretion when deciding whether to take a dog and whether to let it roam free or keep it on leash.

Trail description: From the parking area make your way through the split-rail fence and up to the top of the hill, where two trails take off in different directions. There is a complex network of trails with different color blazes that correspond with the colors on the official trail maps, and "You Are Here" maps are posted at most intersections.

Some of the trails at Middle River Park traverse old farm fields that are growing into forest.

A relatively new trail traverses a colonial era berm and ends at the shore of the Middle River.

A maple stand at Middle River Park leaves a blanket of colorful leaves toward the end of autumn.

Land ownership: This 100-acre park is owned and managed by the Downeast Coastal Conservancy as part of its Two Rivers Conservation Area that also includes the nearby Machias River Preserve.

Online resources: Downeast Coastal Conservancy, downeastcoastalconservancy .org/dcc-trails/middle-river-park/; Maine Trail Finder, mainetrailfinder.com/trails/ trail/st-regis-park-on-the-middle-river-hiking-trails

Long Point Preserve

East Side Road, Machiasport

This trail is an easy walk on an old gravel road to a peninsula with stunning views of Machias Bay, cobblestone beaches, and a beautiful forest. A short hiking loop at the end of the road is slightly more challenging but well worth it for the views.

Driving directions: From Route 1 in East Machias, take Route 191 South for 2.3 miles to a sharp right-hand turn on East Side Road. Continue on this road for 1.8 miles to a parking area on your left with a sign reading "Long Point Preserve." For visitors with a designated handicap license plate or placard only, continue on the road to a marked parking spot. This extension of the road is not maintained for passenger cars, so enter at your own risk. (Note that this trail is on East Side Road, which is in Machiasport, on a small sliver of Machiasport that is across the Machias River from the main part of the town.)

Length: 3.0 miles

Difficulty: Easy to moderate. The majority of the trail follows an old gravel road that offers easy walking, though there is one relatively steep hill. At the terminus of the road, a loop trail through the woods is much more rustic and similar to the majority of trails in this book, with roots and rocks that trip the unwary. There is a set of steep stairs that provides optional access to a gravel beach.

Important notes: Although the road continues past the parking lot, visitors to the preserve are asked to park in the designated lot and not on the privately owned beach beyond. The designated path is across private land for the first 0.6 mile. Be courteous and stay on the path until you reach the preserve.

Trail description: From the parking area, walk back out to the road, turn left, and follow the dirt road to a beautiful beach at Randall Point (often called the East Side Beach locally). The beach and land surrounding the freshwater pond adjacent to it are privately owned. You're welcome to enjoy the beach, but be respectful of the owner's property. From the beach the road turns into a seldom-driven gravel road that crosses the beach and then begins to ascend the major hill on the property. At 0.75 mile from the parking lot, you'll reach a kiosk with maps and a sign-in sheet. The road continues to the left of the kiosk (to the right is private property that is not open to the public).

Shoreline lit up by a dazzling sunset.

Long Point Preserve offers access to a number of different gravel beaches.

Salt marsh fringes some of the shoreline at Long Point Preserve.

Views begin to open up on both sides, and pretty soon you'll find yourself at an isthmus, a narrow strip of land that joins the mainland with what would be an island if the isthmus didn't exist. Locally this is usually referred to as a "neck." On the right side of the road, a steep staircase descends to a gravel beach below that could be a destination in its own right. On the left side of the road, a steep muddy path mostly used by commercial clam harvesters (who are allowed to park here) provides access to the mudflats below. The neck itself is just the width of the road and drops steeply on both sides. I'm not aware of another feature just like this in the region. Across the neck the road ends and you have the option of hiking a 0.7-mile loop trail that brings you to the extreme end of Long Point. The views across Machias Bay to Hog, Salt, and Round Islands are absolutely amazing. The trail loops back and rejoins the road close to the neck. From there retrace your steps to return to the parking lot.

Land ownership: Long Point Preserve is owned by Maine Coast Heritage Trust (MCHT). The property was at high risk of being subdivided and closed off from the public, but MCHT was able to keep it available for public use. The property is 163 acres with an impressive 2.3 miles of shoreline.

Online resources: At the time of publication, there were no online resources dedicated to this property.

The Bold Coast

Although the term "Bold Coast" is now used to refer to pretty much the whole region covered by *Beyond Acadia*, the name originally referred to the stretch of coastline that includes Cutler, Trescott Township, and Lubec. With a distance of roughly twenty miles as the crow flies, the area is characterized by its dark spruce-fir forest and its iconic and forbidding craggy coastline with an infinite array of cliffs, boulders, and cobblestone beaches. During storms all year long, but especially in the winter, waves pound against the rocky shore, preventing all vegetation from being established just above the reach of the high tide. This provides us with places to poke out of the interior forest for glorious views of the rushing waves and out across the water toward Grand Manan Island, a Canadian island that is seven miles offshore.

The steepness of the shoreline brings especially cold water that is full of nutrients up from the depths. The churning waves are filtered by abundant seaweed beds that thrive in this environment and create their own habitat niches, where invertebrates proliferate and feed the rest of the food chain, from eider ducks to puffins to whales.

Conservation has a long history in this section, with Quoddy Head State Park in public ownership since 1962. It wasn't until 1989 that what is now called the Cutler Coast Unit of Public Reserved Land was protected. At the time it was known as the Bold Coast Unit, and over the years the term "Bold Coast" became synonymous with that particular piece of property. In the mid-2000s, an effort was made to broaden the Bold Coast to mean this entire region, including actually changing the name of that property.

Views like this are par for the course when hiking on the Bold Coast.

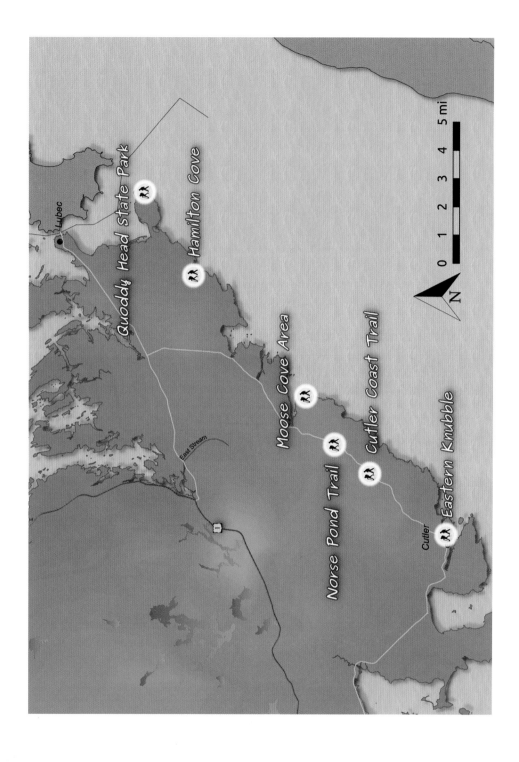

The Cutler Coast Unit definitely gets the most notoriety from the outside world, even though Quoddy Head may see even more visitors and, in my opinion, is a better trail from which to experience the Bold Coast. Nevertheless, the other hikes in the section are well worth the time to visit, especially because they are on the shorter side. They easily can be paired with other hikes but are good options if you only have a limited time to get a sense of the Bold Coast.

Cobscook Trails is a wonderful information source for hikes along the Bold Coast and Cobscook Bay, and it includes most of the hikes I've covered in this book, as well as others I did not profile. A map is available for download or from various sources in the region. Find more information at cobscooktrails.org.

Eastern Knubble

Route 191, Cutler

This is a short walk to a very remote-feeling beach and associated islet. It offers nice views of parts of Canada's Grand Manan Island, the working Cutler harbor, and especially boats traveling in and out of port. It's a taste of the wildness that is the Bold Coast.

Driving directions: Parking is in the village of Cutler, across the street from the US Post Office. It is 13.7 miles from the intersection of Route 191 and Route 189 in Lubec. It is 13.0 miles from the intersection of Route 191 and Route 1 in East Machias.

Length: Total length is 1.4 miles round-trip if you include the spur trail to a historic mining site. It is about 1.0 mile round-trip to the cobble beach.

Difficulty: Challenging. The forest here is among the rockiest and rootiest of the trails in

this book. Sturdy footwear and close attention are suggested. The cobble beach is an integral part of the preserve, and footing on the shifting rocks is unstable and difficult. At lower tides you may be able to cross the beach and scramble up some rocks to an island.

Important notes: The island is accessible at lower tide levels, but watch the time and/or tide carefully, because the water rises quicker than most people expect and you can be stranded on the island or face a dangerous swim back to the mainland.

Trail description: From the parking area cross Route 191 and head down a grassy lane with a sign marking the beginning of the Eastern Knubble Trail. After crossing a field, the trail enters the woods through the site of an old homestead, with a well and old apple trees as evidence of man's hand. Before long the trail enters true forest that, despite being literally inside the village of Cutler, feels surprisingly wild and remote. At this point it is only a short walk to a cobble beach that could occupy a long time of beach combing and searching for heart-shaped rocks.

At lower tide levels you can walk across the beach and access the island known as Eastern Ear (sometimes called Laura Day Island). To access the island, you'll have to climb up some steep rocks. Once there a short path leads to the opposite shore of the island with rocky ledges perfect for a picnic or just watching the waves. From here you can also see the backside of Little River Island, which guards the entrance to Cutler Harbor. A spur trail leaves the main trail a short distance before the beach and goes to a historic mining site with interpretive signs created with the help of local schoolchildren.

This is a short hike, but the rewards are bigger than you would expect with ocean views, a remote feel, and an entrancing boreal spruce-fir forest. This most likely wouldn't be your day's destination, but it fits well as a leg-stretcher if you're passing through Cutler or if you just aren't up for a longer hike.

Land ownership: This 31-acre preserve is owned by Maine Coast Heritage Trust.

Online resources: Maine Coast Heritage Trust, mcht.org/preserves/eastern-knubble; Maine Trail Finder, mainetrailfinder.com/trails/trail/eastern-knubble

Cutler Coast Trail

Route 191, Cutler

A legendary trail along 3.5 miles of truly spectacular rocky, bold coastline, this is the only place to backpack on the coast in this region.

Driving directions: The trailhead is on Route 191, 16.8 miles from the intersection of Route 191 and 1 in East Machias, or 10.0 miles from the intersection of Route 191 and Route 189 in Lubec. There is a gravel parking area on the south side of the road.

Length: Varies. It is a 2.8-mile round-trip to the first set of cliffs; 6.7 miles for the Black Point Loop; 10.4 miles for the Fairy Head Loop. Note that the two loop distances given here are 1.2 miles longer than those in publications by the State of Maine due to a trail reroute on the Inland Trail that added this distance. Signs are posted on-site with information about the reroute.

Difficulty: Challenging and strenuous. The difficulties on this trail are not long or steep hills; in fact, there are no hills that are more than a few dozen steps long, though there are

many of these small dips and climbs. What makes this a strenuous hike are the rugged terrain—with many stone steps and roots up above ground level—and the fact that you have to navigate the bald, rocky shoreline in places.

Important notes: Steep cliffs are hazardous. Use caution when approaching for a view of the coast. The main trail is safe, but many social trails lead to points that may or may not have secure, stable footing.

If you are backpacking, be aware that there are only five sanctioned campsites, which often fill up during the summer. Go during the week or off-season if possible; otherwise, try to get there early to beat the crowd and claim your site.

Fires are not allowed anywhere on the property. Bring along a contained stove to cook meals.

Miles of craggy shoreline stretch into the distance at the Cutler Coast Trail.

Backpacking at the Cutler Coast lets you see the cliffs in different light.

The campsites at Fairy Head are right next to the ocean.

Trail description: There is a reason this trail is labeled iconic, legendary, a must-see, and more. It is one of those that will wow anyone. With that said, read on for my opinion about why this trail is overhyped and some alternatives that may suit some people.

There are essentially three ways to explore the trail system. If you are backpacking, you'll want the Fairy Head Loop, which has the only five sanctioned campsites along the trail. Otherwise, choose whichever length you prefer to hike. From the trailhead, which has a privy to help alleviate waste along the trail, the Coastal Trail makes its way across relatively level ground, though with the constant rocks and roots, which you'll find on the entire trail system.

About 0.4 mile in, you'll reach the intersection of the Inland Trail with the Coastal Trail. If you are bound and determined to make this a loop hike, I suggest you bear right and take the Inland Trail. This will delay the big payoff of your first glimpse of the ocean, but you'll have less of a cross-country slog after leaving the coast if you start at the far end and make your way back toward the trailhead. If you aren't absolutely sure that you want to do a loop, you might want to take the Coastal Trail all the way to the shore. Many people, including me, have decided that after hiking out on the Coastal Trail and then along the shore, they don't want to leave the coast for the return hike and so choose to return the way they came. Ordinarily I prefer a loop trail out and back, but this is a definite exception for me.

◀   *A pair of hikers take a break and enjoy the amazing views.*

Assuming you continue toward the coast, you'll hike through the amazing coastal spruce-fir forest for another mile before actually glimpsing the ocean, at which point the trail heads southwesterly along the shore. For the next 3.5 miles, or as far as you choose to follow it, the trail winds its way along the coast. There are stretches where the ocean isn't visible through the trees, but not for too long, and you are rarely out of earshot of the waves. Views are endlessly changing as you progress down the shore, but always visible on a clear day is the Canadian island of Grand Manan, roughly 7.0 miles across the Grand Manan Channel.

The shoreline is a study in the infinite possibilities of a rocky coast. You'll find every variation of ledge outcroppings at various angles and pitches that tumble from the forest down to the sea below, with veins of quartz and other minerals running in every direction. There are also cobble pocket beaches with smooth stones of all sizes from basketballs (and much bigger) down to pebbles. There is no gentle shoreline, soft sandy beaches, mudflats, or gradually sloping forest that reaches down to the water. This is the heart of the Bold Coast, and that name makes all the sense in the world when you are there.

The Black Point Cutoff is 1.25 miles down the shore from the Coastal Trail, and it will bring you to the Inland Trail and then back to the trailhead for a loop of 6.7 miles. Continuing along the coast, the first two (of five) campsites offer access to different cobble beaches that become private once the day hikers are gone. Farther out, at Fairy Head, there are an additional three campsites, all perched above cliffs of varying steepness that offer great views but no opportunity to actually get in the water (if plunging into frigid salt water is your thing).

All along this path the presence of the ocean dominates your attention, but the forest is truly worthy of at least half of your mind. The trees, which are slightly stunted and growing more densely than a forester would approve, are nevertheless old, but they grow slowly in this very harsh environment. The forest floor itself is impressive here. Thick carpets of moss blanket vast areas of the forest, dampening sound, holding moisture, and making the forest feel like a bewitched land from a fairy tale. Other sections are mature grasslands, with vegetation that crowds the trail from both sides, though the heavily traveled trail is always visible.

There are some confusing places along the trail, particularly where an unmarked social trail heads off in some direction and can appear to be the main trail. Look for the blue blazes, which always seem to be at hand just when you need to confirm that you're still on the trail.

From Fairy Head, which is 4.8 miles from the trailhead along the coast, the Inland Trail takes you 5.4 miles back to the trailhead for a long loop of 10.2 miles.

Personal note: In my first few months living in the region, I hiked here often. Sometimes I just hiked to the shore for a picnic lunch; other times I would continue along the coast as far as I wanted. Only once, in those days, did I hike the Black Point Loop (6.0 miles), but never the Fairy Head Loop (9.0 miles). After hiking the Black Point

Loop, I realized that the inland portion was just as challenging as the coastal portion, but instead of forest on one side and ocean on the other, it has forest on both sides. Wonderful in all the ways that it should be, but less captivating to me than the coast.

For my entire fourteen years in the region, I was part of the group that manages Cobscook Trails, a free local information source for hiking around Cobscook Bay, including the Cutler Coast. In meeting after meeting, the stewards and managers would report trail damage from too many people, a proliferation of unsanctioned campsites, and litter (including human waste) along the trail. We never found a solution to these problems, but we all agreed that the best strategy would be to encourage more use of the other trails in the area to spare the Cutler Coast some damage. Because of this I gave the Cutler Coast a pass, and as time went on I learned about many of those other trails and never went back to the Cutler Coast until doing research for this book.

On a Sunday in September I strapped on my old backpack, seldom used in the past ten years or more, but still a worthy and trusted piece of equipment. I was determined to hike the entire loop so I could better report what you'll find along the route, but I decided to hike along the coast first and return on the Inland Trail. I made it to my campsite at Fairy Head by about 1:30 p.m. and spent the entire afternoon just sitting in the sun on rocky cliffs, watching the ocean, birds, boats, and seals until it started to get dark. I grabbed my cooking stove and sleeping pad and headed back out to the shoreline, where I stayed until the sky had turned black and the Milky Way blazed above my head.

From where I lay my head inside my tent, I could see the glow of both the Machias Seal Island Lighthouse and the Southwest Head Lighthouse at the southern tip of Grand Manan Island. Sometime in the middle of the night I noticed that I could no longer see the lights, and I wondered why they had been turned off. The answer became clear as dawn broke on a fog so thick I could barely see the ocean despite being about twenty yards from it.

I ate breakfast and lingered for a while, hoping the fog would lift somewhat before I headed to the Inland Trail for my return trip, but to no avail. As I lifted my pack to my shoulders and strapped in, I suddenly thought about leaving the sound of the waves, which had been a steady pulse in my being for nearly twenty-four hours. I decided at that moment to return along the coast the way I had come. As I progressed, the fog lifted by degrees until there was a brilliant blue sky above and endless visibility on the horizon. I didn't regret for a moment seeing the same amazing sights I had the day before.

I can't recommend this trail enough for backpackers looking for a coastal route. For anyone else, I suggest you check out some of the other trails in the region and eventually come to explore the Cutler Coast when you've seen what else is out there. My favorite trail that offers a similar experience is at Quoddy Head State Park, which sees as much use as the Cutler Coast or more, but with far more bang for the buck. Right out of the parking lot you're into amazing views of similar shoreline to the Cutler Coast, and it continues for 1.3 miles with very few places where the trail isn't right against the shore. I also love Hamilton Cove, which offers a taste of the Cutler Coast experience in a much shorter length, a more varied forest, and far fewer people. Eastern Knubble is another option to get a taste for the Bold Coast with a very short hike.

Land ownership: The Cutler Coast Unit is owned by the State of Maine through its Department of Agriculture, Conservation, and Forestry, Bureau of Public Lands. The entire Unit is some 12,300 acres. The hiking trail is on an area designated an ecological reserve, which prohibits motorized vehicles and timber management, but the land on the inland side of Route 191 includes miles of multiuse trails (allowing walking, skiing, biking, horses, ATVs, and snowmobiles). Dispersed camping is also allowed on the inland side of Route 191.

Online resources: Property brochure from the State of Maine, maine.gov/dacf/parksearch/PropertyGuides/PDF_GUIDE/cutlercoastguide.pdf; Maine Trail Finder, mainetrailfinder.com/trails/trail/cutler-coast-public-reserved-land

Norse Pond Trail at Bog Brook Cove Preserve

Route 191, Cutler

This is a relatively easy hike through a varied forest to a stunning gravel beach.

Driving directions: The parking area is on Route 191 in the town of Cutler, 18.5 miles from the intersection of Route 1 and Route 191 in East Machias, or 8.2 miles from the intersection of Route 191 and Route 189 in Lubec.
Length: 2.4 miles round-trip

Difficulty: Moderate. The trail is relatively flat for most of the hike, but with the very typical roots and rocks that ensure that you're paying attention to your feet as you hike. The last stretch of the trail down to the beach is steeper and a little more challenging than the rest.

Trail description: The Norse Pond Trail is not about Norse Pond, despite the name. The pond is a scenic stop along the way, but the real destination is the gravel beach at Bog Brook Cove. The hike to the beach and back is about 2.4 miles round-trip and follows a lollipop trail design with a loop for part of the hike. The trail is relatively flat. There is one significant ridge that you climb and then descend, but this is not very challenging. The forest is quite varied, with sections of spruce-fir boreal forest and other sections with deciduous trees. None of the forest is extremely old, but there is little sign of past timber harvesting.

You'll reach a T in the trail after about 0.7 mile that marks the beginning of the loop section of trail. You can go either way, but I prefer to go right to enjoy Norse

The beach and rocky tide pools at the end of the Norse Pond Trail are the real destination.

Norse Pond is mistakenly named for Viking visitors who were thought to have dammed the lake.

Sheep laurel flowers are a tiny, delicate treat to see in early June.

Pond and the longer leg of the loop before reaching the beach, rather than after the beach. The first view of Norse Pond from some high rocky outcrops is absolutely gorgeous. Set amid a lush deciduous forest, the pond looks like a wildlife haven, with dead trees for ospreys and eagles to perch on, visible beaver lodges, and a fringing marsh that looks like it should have some ducks dabbling on the edges of the pond. To the left there is a view beyond the pond to the ocean and the cliffs of Grand Manan Island in the far distance. From that first view the trail continues until a small spur trail takes you the final two hundred feet to a ledge at the edge of the pond. Other than that one ledge, the shoreline of the pond appears to be totally unapproachable due to the marsh and dense vegetation around the edge. This is a great spot for a short break to see whether you can spy some interesting birds.

The trail then approaches the ocean, and for a short tantalizing stretch you can hear the waves breaking on the rocky shore, but you can't see it, and the trail soon turns hard left and the shoreline is left behind for the moment. At a trail intersection, the spur trail to the beach takes off to the right. This section of the trail is the hardest, with some steep sections and a few places of less sure footing. Your arrival at the beach is relatively sudden as you drop out of the trees and on to the gravel. Bog Brook is immediately in front of you. When I visited, the tide was relatively low and the brook, which was running quite swiftly, disappeared into the gravel for the final couple hundred feet to the ocean. The beach is composed of various size smooth

◀ *Extensive bog bridges keep your feet dry through wet forest.*

rocks and pebbles, from basketball and larger down to the size of your smallest fingernail and smaller. The rocks are quite loose, so it feels a lot like walking through deep sand. There are a few buildings visible on the bluff across the cove. Signs and property maps indicate that the beach is all open to the public, but respect private property and don't climb up to the buildings.

After a rest on the beach, and perhaps some wading in the cove, return to the loop trail by climbing the same path you came down on. Turn right at the main trail loop to make your way back to the trailhead. Another trail takes off to the right a little beyond the beach trail. This trail will take you over Bog Brook and eventually to a private road that can be used to connect the Norse Pond Trail with the Moose Cove section of this large property. Most people skip this trail, unless they are looking for a much longer hike.

About a quarter mile from the beach spur trail, you'll reach the end of the loop trail, marking the final stretch of trail and a return to the trailhead.

Land ownership: The Bog Brook Cove Preserve, which includes the Norse Pond Trail and others in this section, was purchased by Maine Coast Heritage Trust beginning in 2005, with the majority of the 1,700 acres acquired in 2008. The preserve is adjacent to the Cutler Coast Unit of Public Reserved Land and forms the largest contiguous block of conserved land along the Maine coast, with the exception of Acadia National Park.

Online resources: Maine Coast Heritage Trust, mcht.org/preserves/bog-brook-cove; Maine Trail Finder, mainetrailfinder.com/trails/trail/bog-brook-cove-preserve

Moose Cove Area at Bog Brook Cove Preserve

Moose River Road, Trescott Township

This is a quarter-mile Universal Access Trail with an amazing view of a rocky beach. One hiking trail has views of the open ocean and the interior of Moose Cove. Another hiking trail has multiple access points to a bold, rocky seashore on the North Atlantic.

Driving directions: From the intersection of Route 191 (Dixie Road) and Moose River Road, turn onto Moose River Road and continue 1.1 miles to the end of the road, where there is a parking area and trailhead.

Length: Varies. There are three trails. The Universal Access Trail to the shore is 0.4 mile round-trip. The Chimney Trail is a 0.8-mile loop. The Ridge Trail is 2.3 miles round-trip.

Difficulty: Easy to moderate. The Universal Access Trail is an easy, smooth, wide gravel path. The Chimney Trail is easy to moderate, with generally stable footing, but a few sections have a lot of rocks in the trail bed. The Ridge Trail is moderate; it has a few steep pitches and is covered with roots and rocks that will trip the unwary.

Just above the high tide line, brilliant orange lichens take hold on the rocks at Moose Cove.

The view from the end of the Universal Access Trail.

The Ridge Trail offers expansive views.

Trail description: From the parking area a wide gravel path leads 0.2 mile to an overlook with views of a cobblestone beach. The more nimble can take a path down to the beach and continue on to another cove beyond it.

The Ridge Trail breaks off on the left from the Universal Access Trail within view of the end of the gravel path. A short flat stretch through a grassy, shrubby area brings you to the first intersection. You can bear left for an easier first section, but if you're able, I suggest that you bear right to climb up on top of the ridge. There are multiple views of Grand Manan Island and the open ocean as the trail traverses the ridge. As you get farther along the trail, the views transition to the interior of Moose Cove. After a short distance the trail rejoins the other loop that stayed off the ridge and continues toward the northwest. After a few more views and short hills, you'll reach the quarter-mile terminus loop that brings you in a wide circle that includes access to a beach composed of rocks the size of a basketball and larger. Walking is difficult on the rocks, but you can explore a little of Moose Cove this way. Back on the trail, continue around the terminus loop and return for some distance on the same path you took out. At the trail intersection you can bear left to return along the same scenic ridge you traversed earlier, or you can bear right for a much easier and more direct return to the gravel path.

The Chimney Trail leaves the parking area from the opposite end that the gravel Universal Access Trail does, meaning back toward the road that brings you into the parking area. For most of its length, the trail is a mowed grassy path through shrubs and patches of forest. There are several places where you can access bold rocky cliffs, either directly from the trail or from short spur trails on your left. Eventually the trail heads inland and toward the top of a small hill. An intersection here offers the option of adding a small loop to the top of the hill with partial views of the ocean. The trail then crosses through the forest back to the Moose River Road. Turn right and it's just a short walk back to the parking area.

Land ownership: The Bog Brook Cove Preserve, which includes the Moose Cove Area and others in this section, was purchased by Maine Coast Heritage Trust beginning in 2005, with the majority of the 1,700 acres acquired in 2008. The preserve is adjacent to the Cutler Coast Unit of Public Reserved Land, and forms the largest contiguous block of conserved land along the Maine coast, with the exception of Acadia National Park.

Online resources: Maine Coast Heritage Trust, mcht.org/preserves/bog-brook -cove; Maine Trail Finder, mainetrailfinder.com/trails/trail/bog-brook-cove-preserve

Hamilton Cove

Boot Cove Road, Lubec

You get a taste of the Bold Coast experience with an easy hike and quick access to an impressive cobblestone beach.

Driving directions: From the intersection of South Lubec Road and Boot Cove Road (in Lubec on the way to Quoddy Head State Park), turn onto Boot Cove Road and drive 2.4 miles to the parking lot on your left.

From the intersection of Route 189 and Route 191 in Lubec, drive 2.8 miles down Route 191 (Dixie Road) and turn left onto Boot Head Road. The parking area is on your right after 3.5 miles on Boot Head Road.

Length: Varies. The Beach Trail, a short path to a cobblestone beach, is less than 0.1 mile.

The Meadow Path is 0.2 mile. The Coastal Trail is about 1.3 miles. Benny's Mountain Trail is 1.2 miles. Multiple destinations can be easily combined in a single visit. (All distances in this section are one way.)

Difficulty: Easy to moderate depending on the trail. The Coastal Trail, the Beach Trail, and the Meadow Path are all fairly easy, though there are extensive bog bridges to navigate, often only 8 inches or so wide. Benny's Mountain Trail is moderately challenging, with sections that are rooted and rocky.

Trail description: From the parking area a very short path brings you to a kiosk and a five-way trail intersection. The Beach Trail and Meadow Path are short, easy, and straightforward, ending at a cobblestone beach and a beautiful meadow, respectively. The Coastal Trail is the real attraction of the property. It travels through a variety of habitat types, from grassland and marsh to mature forest. The trail tends

Even on a foggy day, the bench at the end of the Hamilton Cove Trail offers a beautiful view.

This is one of several stretches of craggy coastline at Hamilton Cove.

A gravel beach at Hamilton Cove.

to be smooth and easy to navigate, but the frequent bog bridges are narrow, making it difficult to keep your balance at normal walking speed. The bog bridges here, in truth, are no more narrow than the thousands of feet of bog bridges found across the region, but I think the grassy trail and typically open habitat make it easier to walk faster than you typically do on a rougher trail, leading to more opportunity to lose your balance. This is just my experience, but you may feel differently.

The Coastal Trail runs mostly inland, but it reaches a viewing platform over steep cliffs at 0.8 mile. You can also take the spur trail to a bench and access to Norton's Rock, which are 1.3 miles from the trailhead. All of the coastal access points offer excellent views out over the North Atlantic to Canada's Grand Manan Island. Return the way you came.

Benny's Mountain Trail takes off from the kiosk and quickly crosses Boot Head Road to bring you to the inland side of the road. The trail takes you through an old field and some younger forest before entering a more mature forest. A small loop near the end of the trail can be done in either direction and takes you to the top of Benny's Mountain (really more a bump than a mountain) with views of Lubec and the surrounding area.

Many people really love this trail and return to hike it over and over again. I would certainly recommend that it be somewhere on your list of things to do, but it wouldn't be a priority for me. Quoddy Head has more viewpoints and a more interesting forest, but it also sees hundreds of users on a summer day. You are quite likely to have Hamilton Cove all to yourself.

Land ownership: The Hamilton Cover Preserve is a 1,225-acre property owned and protected by Maine Coast Heritage Trust.

Online resources: Maine Coast Heritage Trust, mcht.org/preserves/hamilton-cove; Maine Trail Finder, mainetrailfinder.com/trails/trail/hamilton-cove

Quoddy Head State Park

South Lubec Road, Lubec

This is the best bang for your buck! It is one of the best hikes with large quick reward for minimal effort. It should be on your short list of choices if you only have time for one hike. From beginning to end, the hike offers dramatic coastline on one side and primeval boreal forest on the other.

Driving directions: From US Route 1 in Whiting, take Route 189 east toward Lubec for 9.9 miles. Turn right onto South Lubec Road. Drive 2.7 miles. The road ends at the park entrance.

Length: Varies. The full network is 6.4 miles, but you can go any length that suits you, including a short stroll to the shore.

Difficulty: Easy to moderate. The first quarter mile of the Coastal Trail is kept well groomed and relatively flat for easy walking. The rest of the trail is somewhat primitive with muddy spots, exposed roots and rocks, and somewhat tricky steps. Nearly the entire trail is adjacent to steep cliffs with minimal protection. This hike is not safe for unpredictable children or loose dogs, but the area around the lighthouse is safe and provides excellent views.

Important notes: Use care near cliffs. Do not rely on railings or fences. Dogs must be on leash. Stay on trails to protect fragile vegetation.

Trail description: There are a variety of options for enjoying Quoddy Head State Park. The easiest and quickest is to simply park at the end of South Lubec Road in view of the iconic candy-striped lighthouse and walk the manicured grounds around it. The lighthouse itself is only open for visitation on official Maine Open Lighthouse Days. Otherwise a visitor center and gift shop may be open during business hours. The Coast Guard Trail is separate from the rest of the trail network and offers 0.9 mile of easy hiking along the bold headland that forms the easternmost point of the continental United States. Frequent views of the village of Lubec, the Canadian island of Campobello, lobster boats out in Lubec Channel, and the West Quoddy Head Light make this an interesting and rewarding short walk. The rest of the trail network begins at the parking lot that is accessed by bearing right as you enter the park and follow signs for parking. Outhouses and picnic tables are available here.

The Coastal Trail (1.3 miles) is the heart of this property and probably should be mandatory for everyone who visits the region. You simply can't beat the rewards of

The jumbled rocks are great fun to explore, or to nap upon.

The bog boardwalk at Quoddy Head is a fascinating place to see an unusual ecosystem.

The cliffs at Quoddy Head are a great place to sit and watch the ocean.

this hike. Plunging cliffs; amazing waves in the right conditions; old moss-covered forest; interesting seabirds, seals, and even the occasional whale are all found right here. The first 0.25 mile is relatively flat and wide and makes for an easy walk after a picnic or for those who aren't as nimble. This section of trail still offers amazing views of the bold cliffs and boreal forest.

Continuing beyond that section, the trail becomes much more primitive. As you work your way down the coast, new views continually unfold ahead of you, with a few benches or turn-out trails that bring you onto ledges overlooking the sweeping coast. You can continue to the end of the Coastal Trail and pick up the Thompson Trail (1.1 miles), which brings you back toward the trailhead via an inland route that parallels the shore. If the ocean and cliffs are your thing, you're better off just turning around at any point on the Coastal Trail, but the Thompson Trail is easier and faster and offers its own rewards with intimate views of the deep, dark forest and moss-covered boulders.

The Bog Trail is a short 0.2-mile walk that is accessible from either the Coastal Trail or the Thompson Trail, with a raised boardwalk that shows off the amazing beauty of a coastal bog ecosystem with pitcher plants and sundews (both carnivorous plants that eat insects), among other fascinating flora.

Land ownership: Quoddy Head State Park is owned and managed by the State of Maine through its Department of Agriculture, Conservation, and Forestry.

Online resources: Maine Trail Finder, mainetrailfinder.com/trails/trail/quoddy -head-state-park; Quoddy Head State Park website, maine.gov/cgi-bin/online/doc/ parksearch/details.pl?park_id=10; Maine Natural Heritage Hikes, maine.gov/dacf/ mnap/assistance/hikes/quoddy_head_inland_coastal.pdf

The rocky shoreline extends for miles. ▷

Cobscook Bay

Roughly translated as "boiling waters," the name of Cobscook Bay refers to the area around what is known as Reversing Falls, or sometimes Cobscook Falls, the tidal whitewater that changes direction every six hours. But Cobscook Bay is so much more than just the chaotic Reversing Falls. The entire bay is just around ten miles by ten miles, but some say that it has about two hundred miles of shoreline thanks to the convoluted inner bays and coves. This extensive shoreline creates an incredible diversity of ecosystems, from the high-energy boiling waters of Reversing Falls to serene inner coves like Federal Harbor to mudflats in Whiting Bay. All of this water and the cold, rich currents of the North Atlantic make Cobscook Bay the area with the most concentrated population of bald eagles in the Lower 48 states.

Cobscook Bay is bordered by eight different towns, from the city of Eastport to extremely rural places like Edmunds or Trescott Township. The mouths of the bay are formed by the peninsulas that form Eastport and Lubec. Although the two population centers are only two miles or so apart across the bay, it can take an hour or more to drive around the perimeter of the bay.

Hiking around Cobscook Bay offers varied opportunities to explore hidden coves with little or no human development. Trails like Horan Head and Sipp Bay are quite remote and wild. Shackford Head feels wild when you are in the forest, but

The convoluted shoreline of Cobscook Bay creates an incredible variety of coves and bays.

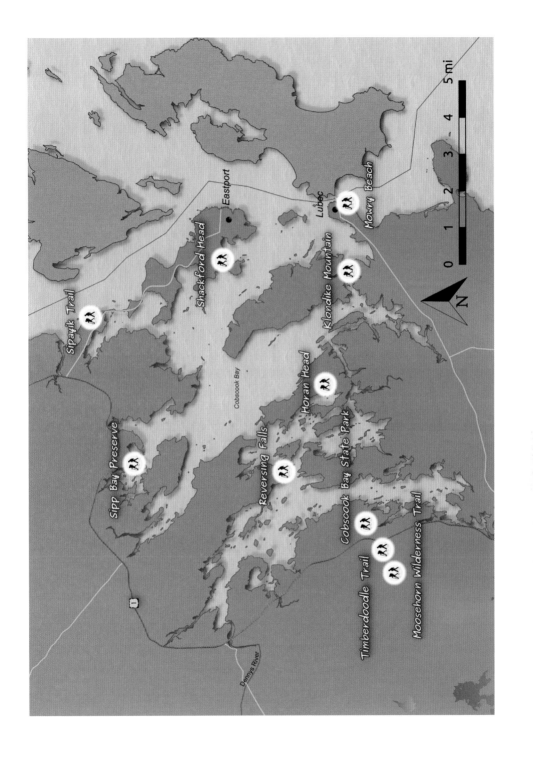

the waters of Cobscook Bay in this area are bustling with salmon aquaculture; lobster, urchin, and scallop fishing boats; and cargo traffic headed to or from the port of Eastport. Cobscook Bay is no less beautiful when there are boats and signs of human use, but there is a contrast with areas that feel pristine and wild.

The forest here is almost completely boreal spruce-fir, except where forces have temporarily changed the composition. Fires, for example, usually result in a birch-maple stand that will last for a few decades before being gradually replaced by spruce-fir. Manmade interventions like timber harvesting are also temporary changes that will eventually revert to boreal forest if given the chance. The Moosehorn Wilderness Trail is a good opportunity to see these transitions taking place.

All of these lands were privately owned at some point, and many are former farms and homesteads. For wildlife and plant diversity, some fields are kept mowed, at least every few years, to keep the grass and the edges of the fields as important wildlife habitat. Klondike Mountain, Horan Head, and Sipp Bay all have managed fields that the trails traverse.

Cobscook Trails is a wonderful information source for hikes along the Bold Coast and Cobscook Bay and includes most of the hikes I've covered in this book, as well as others I did not profile. A map is available for download or from various sources in the region. You can find more information at cobscooktrails.org.

Timberdoodle Trail

South Trail, Edmunds

This is a universally accessible paved path through the woods ending at an observation deck in an area managed for woodcock habitat.

Driving directions: From the intersection of Route 1 and Route 189 in Whiting, drive north on Route 1 for 4.0 miles and turn left onto South Trail, a gravel road that is part of the National Wildlife Refuge. The parking lot is on the left about 0.3 mile from Route 1.

Length: 0.5 mile round-trip

Difficulty: Easy. The trail is completely paved and wide enough for wheelchairs to pass. There are no hills. An observation deck at the terminus has a wheelchair-accessible ramp.

Trail description: The Timberdoodle Trail is a good opportunity to get out into the woods for those with limited mobility. The trail passes through some interesting and varied forest before reaching a wildlife clearing that is managed to encourage woodcock (aka timberdoodles) to find mates, nest, and feed. An observation deck gives a very slightly elevated view of the area. Best times to view woodcock are just before dark and early morning.

A viewing platform at the end of a paved Universal Access Trail is a great place to watch the woodcock in their spring courtship dance at dusk.

Land ownership: This section of Moosehorn National Wildlife Refuge is more than 8,700 acres, owned by the US Fish and Wildlife Service. The primary management objective of the refuge is to provide habitat for woodcock and related wildlife, which require early successional, or young, forests. The Moosehorn Wilderness, also part of the refuge, by contrast, is not managed for young forest but instead will never be managed and will continue on a natural path to an old forest.

Online resources: Moosehorn National Wildlife Refuge, fws.gov/refuge/Moosehorn; Maine Trail Finder, mainetrailfinder.com/trails/trail/moosehorn-national-wildlife-refuge-edmunds

Moosehorn Wilderness Trail

Edmunds

Here is a rare opportunity in the East to hike in a congressionally designated Wilderness Area. It is a relatively smooth and easy-to-follow path through a varied forest, with opportunities to combine a bike route with a hike.

Driving directions: From the intersection of Route 1 and Route 189 in Whiting, drive north on Route 1 for 4.0 miles and turn left onto South Trail, a gravel road that is part of the National Wildlife Refuge. Drive 0.9 mile to the South Trail trailhead. You may also turn right just before the trailhead onto Crane Mill Road. Drive 1.1 miles to the end and turn left onto North Trail. The trailhead is at the end of the road, 1.0 mile ahead. Note that most of the refuge roads in this area are one way only (with the exception of the dead-end at the North Trail trailhead), so you can't backtrack.

Length: Trail is 3.5 miles, but there is an additional 2.1 miles of dirt road that connect the beginning and end of the trail.

Difficulty: Easy, despite the length. The path is basically level (no hills to speak of) and smooth (no rocks or roots to navigate) thanks to being on very old roads. The most challenging part is actually walking the dirt road connection, which can be hot and dusty and has some hills.

Important notes: Although the trail was in good shape when I last hiked it, maintenance in a Wilderness Area is only done using hand tools, so a large tree or cluster of trees that come down may take a while to be cleared.

Trail description: Either before or after you hike the Wilderness Area portion of the trail, you will have to traverse 2.1 miles of dirt road that connect the two ends of the hiking trail. Most people will hike the road as part of a loop trail. Another option is to bike the road, which can be done on a hybrid or mountain bike. Either way, it may be best to deal with the road before hiking the Wilderness Area, just to get it out of the way since it is far less interesting and wilderness-y. You can park at the trailhead on South Trail, bike up Crane Mill Road, make a left on North Trail, lock up your bike at the North Trail trailhead and hike into the Wilderness and back to your car. After your hike, you simply drive to the other trailhead, and pick up your bike. Note, however, that the roads on the refuge are mostly one-way, so trying to do what I described in a different order gets more complicated and may require you to drive the whole loop twice.

From the North Trail trailhead, the hike begins alongside Hobart Stream, which flows out of the Wilderness Area toward the sea. As soon as you leave the parking area, you are inside the congressionally designated Wilderness Area. Trail maintenance is all done with hand tools, and some of the larger trees that have fallen across the trail show evidence of the effort required to clear them. The first stretch is probably the wildest and hardest to follow, as the trail crisscrosses the old roadbed and skirts the stream that drains a wetland. After about 1.0 mile, the main trail makes a hard left onto the Camp Two Trail. The North Trail continues straight into the Wilderness Area and makes a much longer loop before arriving at the South Trail trailhead, but this trail may not be maintained or marked very well. Use the longer loop only if you're confident in your navigation abilities in case you lose the trail. After turning left from the North Trail, the trail becomes much more established and is virtually straight from here on. On both sides of the trail, a constantly changing forest unfolds for the length of the trail. In this section the boreal forest is older, with larger trees and less understory, but the poor soil and harsh climate keep the trees smaller than you'd expect from a similarly aged forest elsewhere. The forest floor in places is blanketed with thick, moist moss. Wispy clumps

Bicycles are not allowed inside the Wilderness Area, but the author combined a short bike ride on gravel roads with a hike through the Wilderness Area.

Much of the forest inside the Wilderness Area was affected by a large wildfire and evidence is still visible.

Nearly all of the Moosehorn Wilderness Trail is on very old roads that are wide, dry, and easy to walk.

Moose are rare in this part of Maine, but hikers occasionally see their tracks or fecal pellets.

of old man's beard (also called usnea) cling to the dead lower branches of primarily balsam fir, red spruce, and the occasional maple or other deciduous tree.

Where the Camp Two Trail meets South Trail, turn left to head toward the trailhead. To the right is the trail that may not be maintained. Before long the forest changes significantly and you begin to see patches of primarily deciduous trees and smaller, thinner trunks. This area burned many years ago and the forest is naturally regenerating.

At 3.4 miles the trail crosses a beaver flowage, or pond, on the old road bed. There were no beavers in the wetland when I visited in 2018, but over time they probably come and go with periods when the pond floor dries into a kind of wet meadow. Eventually young beavers will come across the wetland and will move in, maintaining dams and filling the ponds once again. The beaver flowage is just about 0.1 mile from the South Trail trailhead.

Land ownership: This section of Moosehorn National Wildlife Refuge is more than 8,700 acres, owned by the US Fish and Wildlife Service. The primary management objective of the refuge is to provide habitat for woodcock and related wildlife, which require early successional, or young, forests. The Moosehorn Wilderness Area, also part of the refuge, by contrast, is not managed for young forest but instead will never be managed and will continue on a natural path to an old forest.

Online Resources: Moosehorn National Wildlife Refuge, fws.gov/refuge/Moose horn; Maine Trail Finder, mainetrailfinder.com/trails/trail/moosehorn-national-wild life-refuge-edmunds

Horan Head

Straight Bay Road, Lubec

This is one of the best hikes for sheer solitude and access to remote inner coves of Cobscook Bay. Boreal spruce-fir forest with a carpet of moss adds to the feeling that you've entered a secret world that few have visited.

Driving directions: Coming from Whiting on Route 189, turn left onto Crow's Neck Road 5.6 miles from the intersection of Route 1 and Route 189. Go 0.4 mile and turn right onto Lead Mine Road. Take a very quick left onto Straight Bay Road and continue for 3.1 miles to the Horan Head parking lot on your right.
Length: Various ways to explore. Total trail system is about 6.0 miles.

Difficulty: Moderate. Although the trail is mostly flat, there are steep sections, and the inevitable route-finding over, under, and around trees that fall across the trail increases the difficulty.
Important notes: Trail maintenance is low on the priority list for the Maine Department of Inland Fisheries and Wildlife, so don't expect a clear trail. When going around trees that have

A small island in Federal Harbor is accessible when the tide is completely out.

Trail maintenance is sporadic here, so be prepared to navigate your own way.

The Eastern Trail offers many shades of green.

Federal Harbor can also be explored by boat.

fallen, it is very easy to lose the trail and get lost. Do not attempt this trail unless you are confident in your off-trail navigation abilities and have the tools you need to stay safe, including a compass, water, bug repellent, and anything else you might need if you are out there for longer than you expect.

Trail description: Please read the **Important notes** section above for a warning about this trail.

This is one of my favorite hikes in the region, and probably the one I've visited most over the years, including when I was the manager of the property and did all of the trail maintenance. I don't know of another trail that offers this degree of solitude on the coast.

There are several ways to explore the trail network here, but I like to take the big loop. As usual, I tend to bear right at intersections and do a counter-clockwise loop. The first challenge at Horan Head is finding the trail into the woods. From the parking lot, you climb through or around a metal gate and then enter a small field. Most of the apple trees in the field provide what are called cider apples—too bitter to be eaten by most people, but excellent if mashed and pressed to create cider. However, I have found a couple of trees, particularly in the far reaches of the field away from the trail, that offer excellent sweet eating apples.

A faint footpath through the field can be followed. It turns right and then left to follow the field edge and then goes straight across the field to an opening in the woods where the trail begins. If you lose the path in the field, stick close to the left

A few of the apple trees all around the field yield sweet eating apples. If you're there when the apples are ripe, pick a few and see whether you can find one!

side of the field. When you get to the far end of the field, you should see the opening in the woods and the path that enters it.

After a short stretch of trail that is almost a solid path of exposed tree roots, the trail turns right onto an old woods road that forms the spine of the trail system. The forest here (and throughout this trail system) looks and feels very old, though many of the trees are not as large as you might expect from an old forest. The ground is almost completely covered by a layer of moss that is spongy underfoot. The trail gets so little use that there is moss even on much of the trail.

After about 0.5 mile, the Eastern Trail takes off to the left. I prefer to stay on the main trail for another quarter mile or so until the South Loop Trail departs on your right. The South Loop Trail is about 0.75 mile and offers your first glimpse of the interior of Federal Harbor, a protected cove within Cobscook Bay, but without any real access to the shore. The South Loop Trail terminates back at the main trail, but at the same intersection you can bear right and enter the Shore Trail, a 0.5-mile loop that is one of my favorite parts of the trail network. Before long you begin tracing the convoluted shoreline of Federal Harbor, and there is always something to see. The tide is either coming or going, seals pop up for a breath and look around, and eagles are often found here. In fact, there are several eagles' nests on the property, though only one is usually used each year. At several places you can edge your way out to the shore on a gravel beach or small bit of salt marsh and have a better look around. Toward the end of the loop, there is a small island that is accessible at low tide if you walk across a small mudflat. Just stay aware of the tide so you don't get stranded on the island.

When the Shore Trail rejoins the main trail, bear right again for the walk out to "Land's End," another 0.5 mile to the end of the Horan Head peninsula. A small loop trail was once open that led up a steep bluff and offered one very nice view (including an eagle's nest if you know where to look) and a gorgeous look at the ancient forest here (the terrain is too steep for this to have been logged effectively). On my last visit to Horan Head, the Ledges Trail was all but grown in and no obvious signs marked it. Continuing out to the Land's End Trail, the views begin to open up on South Bay, which is a much larger body of water than the cozy Federal Harbor. There are two main destinations on this section of trail. Look for a left-hand turn out to a point with gently sloping rocks on the shore that offer a perfect place for a rest or picnic. At the very end of the Land's End Trail is another place with rocks on which to enjoy the bay. Keep in mind that at low tide seals may haul up on the rocks to sun, rest, groom, and socialize. If you are here when the seals are out, best practice as a visitor is to avoid displacing the seals and let them enjoy their habitat in peace.

After a break at Land's End, return to the main trail and watch for a right-hand turn a little after the intersection where the Shore Trail joins the main trail. The Eastern Trail is about 0.75 mile long and offers the more interesting way to return to your car instead of following the main trail. Almost the entire length of the Eastern Trail is adjacent to the shore and runs through another section of magical, old forest that has not seen logging for many, many years. A small gravel beach is at the spot where the trail makes a left and leaves the shore for good, so take the opportunity to get out and enjoy one last view of the bay. There are rocks here for sunning also, but beware that as the tide comes up they become an island, and that can happen surprisingly quickly. When the Eastern Trail returns to the main trail, simply bear right and complete the final 0.4 mile back to the parking lot.

Land ownership: Horan Head is a 428-acre unit of the more than 2,300-acre Cobscook Bay Wildlife Management Area, owned and managed by the Maine Department of Inland Fisheries and Wildlife.

Online resources: Maine Trail Finder, mainetrailfinder.com/trails/trail/cobscook -bay-wildlife-management-area-horan-head-unit (but be aware that the map is not completely accurate); Land for Maine's Future Coalition, landformainesfuture.org/ destination/horan-head/

Klondike Mountain

North Lubec Road, Lubec

This short and rewarding hike offers dramatic views from the top of a "mountain" that is just 150 feet above sea level.

Driving directions: From the intersection of Route 189 and North Lubec Road in Lubec, drive 1.0 mile to the Klondike Mountain parking area on the left side of the road.
Length: The entire loop plus a side trail is 0.6 mile.

Difficulty: Challenging. Although most of the trail surfaces are easy, there is a difficult pitch when either climbing or descending Klondike Mountain. A steep slope covered in pine needles is almost impossible to navigate without slipping.

Trail description: From the parking area the trail begins through an arboretum project begun by a local enthusiast who planted varieties of native trees and shrubs in the mid-2010s in a field that has a number of old apple trees. The trail is lined with wood chips for this first section. After leaving the arboretum, the trail turns right and goes down a relatively steep hill and then sets out across an old hay field. A little more than halfway across the field, a fork in the trail can be taken in either direction to begin the loop trail. If you bear to the right, the trail enters the woods and makes its way through some interesting rock features and finally tops out on the bald summit of Klondike Mountain, with views of inner South Bay to the north and west and to the village of Lubec to the east with Campobello Island beyond.

The trail continues down into a small col (a valley between two mountain peaks) and then up to a second summit, with more restricted views of the bay to the west.

View from the top of one of Klondike Mountain's two peaks.

The inner part of the cove below Klondike Mountain is known as Fowlers Mill Pond.

From here the trail descends the mountain. A spur trail, called the Fowler's Mill Pond Trail, takes you through a very nice stretch of forest and ends at a viewpoint with a bench. Return to the loop trail, bear right, and follow the trail back to the parking area.

Land ownership: This 46-acre preserve is owned and managed by Downeast Coastal Conservancy.

Online resources: Downeast Coastal Conservancy, downeastcoastalconservancy .org/dcc-trails/klondike-mountain/; Maine Trail Finder, mainetrailfinder.com/ trails/trail/klondike-mountain

Mowry Beach

Pleasant Street, Lubec

This is an easy visit to a beach with a boardwalk trail through a coastal wetland.

Driving directions: Enter the village of Lubec on Route 189 (coming from Route 1), and bear right onto Washington Street at the IGA (grocery store). Continue until the Roosevelt International Bridge to Canada is right in front of you. Turn right onto Pleasant Street, and the terminus of the road is the parking lot for Mowry Beach.

Length: The boardwalk is 1,700 feet long one-way. The preserve includes 1,800 feet of beach on the Lubec Channel.

Difficulty: Easy. The boardwalk trail is a Universal Access Trail, though the aging boardwalk sometimes has rotten boards or holes that need repair. The beach is not a Universal Access Trail and requires walking through soft and shifting sand.

Important note: Beware of quickly moving incoming tides. If you walk far from shore at low tide, you may be surprised at how fast the mudflat fills with water as the tide rises.

Trail description: There are two separate activities available at Mowry Beach: visiting the beach itself and exploring the wetland boardwalk.

To visit the beach, simply follow the path through the hedge of beach rose to the shore. The tides are dramatic here, with the water line at low tide sometimes as much as a 0.5 mile from the beach. For reference, "the Spark Plug Lighthouse" out in the channel is just beyond the lowest low-tide level. At low tide, you may see people digging clams, and there are abundant shorebirds during the late summer/early fall migration season. At high tide, the channel fills with water and offers a typical beach feeling.

The wetland boardwalk begins at the parking area and wends its way through a diverse freshwater wetland until it reaches the Lubec Consolidated School, some 1,700 feet (about 0.3 mile) away. Along the way the trail brings you to coastal-scrub woodland with good views of a sphagnum bog and a cattail swamp. Consider, as you walk the trail, how rarely you get to see these habitats up close. Without a boardwalk there is no way for a person to walk upright through this ecosystem, so it is usu-

The Mowry Beach boardwalk takes visitors through a freshwater marsh adjacent to the ocean.

ally entirely hidden from us. Enjoy the abundant birds, wildflowers, and insects that inhabit the wetland. At the end, simply return to the parking lot the way you came. Due to changes in sea level and storm intensity that have reshaped the coastal dune, seawater is beginning to infiltrate the wetland more often than in years past. The first bridge on the boardwalk sometimes floats after a particularly high tide rushes into the wetland. Changes in vegetation may be seen in the coming years.

Land ownership: The 48-acre Mowry Beach Preserve was purchased by Downeast Coastal Conservancy (though the organization was called Quoddy Regional Land Trust at the time) in 2004.

Online resources: Downeast Coastal Conservancy, downeastcoastalconservancy .org/dcc-trails/mowry-beach/; Maine Trail Finder, mainetrailfinder.com/trails/trail/ mowry-beach

Cobscook Bay State Park

South Edmunds Road, Edmunds

These are relatively easy options to get out in the woods if you are camped at the state park.

Driving directions: From Whiting Corner (the intersection of Route 1 and Route 189) in Whiting, travel north on Route 1 for 4.2 miles. Turn right onto South Edmunds Road and continue for 0.6 mile to the Cobscook Bay State Park entry gate. A fee is required to enter the park.

Length: The Nature Trail is 1.2 miles one-way. The Shore Trail is a 0.75-mile loop. There is also a 0.2-mile hike to an old fire tower.
Difficulty: Easy to moderate
Important note: A fee is required to enter the park for day use.

Trail description: The Nature Trail begins near the entry gate. Park as directed by the gate attendant. The trail goes through a stretch of mostly mature spruce-fir boreal forest. The trail is generally easy, but there is a short side trail to the scenic overlooks that requires you to scramble up a steep rocky slope. From a pair of rocky ledges, views open up to Whiting Bay and Burnt Cove. The trail ends at the campground loop road. Hikers can return the way they came or on the gravel road, which makes it a 2.0-mile loop.

The Shore Trail is a short path between the campground and the Edmunds public boat launch on Whiting Bay. Ask the gate attendant for directions to the trailhead. The trail begins near campsite number 17 and follows the shoreline to the public boat launch. It then wends its way through the forest to return to the campground near campsite number 20, just a short distance from the starting point.

A short trail climbs 0.2 mile up a steep slope to a discontinued fire tower. The fire tower is not open to the public.

These trails are fun options for people camped at the state park, but they are definitely not at the top of my list for exploring the region.

Land ownership: Cobscook Bay State Park is on land that is owned by the US Fish and Wildlife Service, Moosehorn National Wildlife Refuge, but leased to the State of Maine's Department of Agriculture, Conservation, and Forestry, which manages the park.

Online resources: Cobscook Bay State Park, maine.gov/cgi-bin/online/doc/park search/details.pl?park_id=15; Maine Trail Finder, mainetrailfinder.com/trails/trail/cobscook-bay-state-park

Reversing Falls

Reversing Falls Road, Pembroke

Here is your opportunity to watch one of nature's spectacles as the fast-moving tides create whitewater rapids that churn up fish for seals, eagles, and ospreys.

Driving directions: From the intersection of Route 214 and US Route 1, head south on

Route 214 (right if coming from Dennysville, left if coming from Perry or Eastport) for about

0.2 mile. Turn right and then make a quick left onto Leighton Point Road. Drive 3.3 miles and turn right onto Clarkside Road. After 1.2 miles, at the stop sign, turn left onto Reversing Falls Road. Continue to the end of the road, about 1.5 miles.

Length: Up to 1.2 miles round-trip

Difficulty: Easy to moderate. Though most of the trail is easy, there are a few sections that are more challenging, including sometimes slippery rock faces overlooking the bay.

Important notes: Swimming and wading are never safe in this area. Fast-moving, and sometimes hidden, currents can sweep away even the strongest swimmers. There are steep and sometimes slippery ledges overlooking the bay. Use caution near cliffs, particularly with children or pets.

Trail description: From the parking lot at the end of the road, walk toward the bay down a path to the obvious viewpoint overlooking the bay. Near high tide or low tide, the water will be rushing through the channel between you and Falls Island in one direction or another. When the tide changes, there are a few minutes of stillness, and then the flow reverses, slowly at first and then picking up speed.

To explore the preserve, turn left at the viewpoint and follow the blue blazes painted on trees. After a short distance, you'll arrive at a sign-in registry, which marks the entrance to Downeast Coastal Conservancy's Reversing Falls Preserve. The trail continues for another 0.2 mile to an intersection with a short spur trail leading to an alternative viewpoint of the falls. Continuing on the main trail for another 0.2 mile, the trail ends at yet another view of the bay and part of the Reversing Falls. Return the way you came.

Land ownership: The town of Pembroke owns 32 acres, which includes the field, parking areas, and the primary viewpoint. Downeast Coastal Conservancy owns and manages most of the hiking trail on its 191-acre preserve adjacent to the town-owned land.

The hiking trail at Reversing Falls reveals a boat that apparently didn't fare too well in the rushing water.

Sipp Bay Preserve

Burby Road, Perry

This coastal hike is in Sipp Bay, deep inside Cobscook Bay, with its convoluted rocky shorelines and swift currents.

Driving directions: From the intersection of Route 1 and Burby Road in Perry, turn onto Burby Road and continue for 0.6 mile. Turn right on a gravel road, and the parking area will be on the right. You may also continue on Burby Road to a picnic area, boat launch, and other views of Sipp Bay.

Length: 1.1 miles

Difficulty: Moderate. Although there are no significant hills or steep pitches on these trails, the path is rough and narrow in many places, with exposed roots and rocks.

Important notes: The currents in Sipp Bay move quickly and can change unexpectedly. It is not safe for swimming or wading, and only experienced boaters should attempt to paddle in the bay.

Trail description: For the longer trail, begin at the gravel parking area that is 0.6 mile from Route 1. Walk west along the side road to nearly the end of the road, where it turns back around to form a cul de sac. Watch for the trail sign on the right side of the road and enter the woods. The trail makes its way to the shore and then continues for 0.4 mile, right along the shoreline with constantly changing views and new bays and coves to see. Near the end of the trail it is possible to cross a gravel beach (except near high tide) to explore a small island. From that point the trail cuts inland and follows a very old road through the woods and back to the gravel road. Walk east on the gravel road back to your vehicle.

The shorter trail begins at another parking area that is 0.8 mile from Route 1. From here you can walk right to the shore for a beautiful view or continue walking down the gravel road until a trail takes off through the field on the right side. The trail goes a short distance to the northern shore of the peninsula and begins to work its way around the point of the peninsula. Continue walking along the shore, with varying views of different parts of the bay, until the trail reaches the gravel road once again. Walk along the road back to your vehicle.

Land ownership: The 92-acre Sipp Bay Preserve is owned and managed by Maine Coast Heritage Trust.

Online resources: Maine Coast Heritage Trust, mcht.org/preserves/sipp-bay; Maine Trail Finder, mainetrailfinder.com/trails/trail/sipp-bay-preserve

The coves inside Sipp Bay feel remote and wild.

Sipp Bay nearly empties at low tide.

Most of the Sipp Bay Trail is right along the shoreline of the bay.

Sipayik Trail

Treatment Plant Road, Sipayik (Pleasant Point Reservation)

This is a paved off-road path with excellent access to a variety of undeveloped coastline with red shale beaches and gnarly cliffs.

Driving directions: From the intersection of Route 1 and Route 190 in Perry, drive for 1.4 miles on Route 190. Turn left on Indian Road. After 0.4 mile, turn left onto Side Road. At the end of Side Road, take Treatment Plant Road to the parking lot at the terminus of the road.

Alternatively, you can park adjacent to (but not directly in front of) the New Friendly Restaurant on Route 1 in Perry. The trail's northern end is directly across Route 1 from this gravel parking lot.

Length: 1.8 miles one-way

Difficulty: Easy. The path is paved and the few hills are very gradual. Accessing the beaches and viewpoint can be a bit more challenging, but the main path offers good views for those who can't leave it.

Important notes: The southern half of the trail is on land that is part of the Pleasant Point Passamaquoddy Reservation. Please respect the tribe's generosity in sharing this trail with all users.

Walkers, bicycles, skiers, and snowshoers are allowed on this trail.

The red cliffs on the Sipayik Trail are stunning.

The Sipayik Trail is perfect for exploring by bicycle.

One of several red beaches along the Sipayik Trail.

Trail description: From the parking lot at Treatment Plant Road (which, as you might guess, is next to a wastewater treatment plant that you'll soon leave behind), the trail heads due north along the eastern shore of Sipayik and then into Perry, following the path of an old railroad bed. A few short unpaved spur trails lead to different views or shoreline access points. In particular, the path that leaves the main trail between the 0.3 and 0.4 mile markers offers a sweet spot for a picnic or just a rest. Continuing north on the main trail, you'll reach Kci-peskiyak, which is a salt marsh pond on your left, with a red shale beach (one of several you'll see on this path) on your right. Near the northern end of the paved path, a sign indicates the end of the bike route; however, the trail actually continues after crossing a road for a short distance before ending at Route 1.

Considering the large number of houses you see along Route 190 driving down to Sipayik to begin the trail, it is surprising how remote and undeveloped this trail is. With Passamaquoddy Bay and views of the Canadian islands on the east side and nearly uninterrupted forest on the west, this trail is one that is worth the time if you're visiting Eastport. The Sipayik Trail is nearly unique in this area for being a paved off-road trail. (The Timberdoodle Trail at Moosehorn National Wildlife Refuge is another paved trail.)

Land ownership: The Sipayik Trail is owned and managed by the Passamaquoddy Tribe.

Online resources: Maine Trail Finder, mainetrailfinder.com/trails/trail/sipayik-trail

Shackford Head

Deep Cove Road, Eastport

Experience a working bay from a forest sanctuary. Lobster fishing, scallop dragging, cargo shipments, and salmon aquaculture all take place in the surrounding waters.

Driving directions: From Perry (or anyplace except downtown Eastport), turn onto Route 190 toward Eastport and drive for 6.5 miles. At the sharp left-hand bend, make a right turn onto Deep Cove Road and drive about 0.5 mile. Shackford Head Park is on a short gravel road off Deep Cove Road.

Length: 3.2 miles for the entire network

Difficulty: Easy to moderate. The central, main trail is relatively smooth and quite wide, making for an easy hike out to the viewpoint. For more length and difficulty, the side trails tend more toward the moderate, with some steep pitches and many, many roots or rocks to trip you up.

Important notes: Red fire ants, an invasive species, have taken root along the trail. The short boardwalk section is closed due to their activity, and a new bypass trail was created. Use caution everywhere, particularly with children or pets. Dogs must be on leash. Stay on trails to protect fragile vegetation. This state park charges a fee of $3 for Maine residents or $4 for nonresidents. The fee is paid to an "iron ranger" (a metal pipe with a slot to receive your money) at the trailhead.

Trail description: Shackford Head is a large peninsula that juts out almost 0.75 mile southwestward from Moose Island, which is the name of the landmass that Eastport occupies. The outer trails circle the entire peninsula.

The views from Shackford Head include salmon aquaculture pens (foreground, in the water) and the Eastport cargo terminal (background).

The view from the far end of Shackford Head.

An alluring beach is not accessible from the trail system.

As noted in the **Difficulty** section, the main trail is great for a super-easy out-and-back 1.2-mile hike to a prominent rocky viewpoint with a bench. To add length, difficulty, and more views, you can do a number of side or loop trails. As is my usual practice, I bear right at intersections to make a counter-clockwise loop. At Shackford Head, this brings me on the Schooner Trail, which hugs the coast and offers northerly views of rugged coastline, some salmon aquaculture pens (large round structures out on the bay with netting strung over them), and the northern shores of Cobscook Bay. As the trail rounds the western side of the peninsula, views open up to the west and south, with steep cliffs, rocky beaches, and views of the village of Lubec in the distance. At the junction where Schooner Trail meets Ship Point Trail and the main trail, you can go straight for a short distance to the overlook.

Land ownership: Shackford Head State Park has no on-site staff. All management is by staff from nearby Cobscook Bay State Park.

Online resources: Maine Trail Finder, mainetrailfinder.com/trails/trail/quoddy-head-state-park; Quoddy Head State Park website, maine.gov/cgi-bin/online/doc/parksearch/details.pl?park_id=10; Maine Natural Heritage Hikes, maine.gov/dacf/mnap/assistance/hikes/quoddy_head_inland_coastal.pdf

Conservation Organizations

A huge proportion of the amenities detailed in this book are made possible by the important work done by an array of conservation organizations that have been working in this area for decades. In fact, the places in this book are just a sample of the amazing places that have been conserved. These organizations include both state and federal agencies and nonprofit organizations. Each has played a role in advancing the mission of conserving the most important wildlife habitat, recreational areas, scenic vistas, and places that provide access to lakes, rivers, and the ocean. Without these organizations' work, many of the places covered in *Beyond Acadia* would surely be in private hands and closed to public access.

It is also important to recognize the contributions of private landowners who have donated their land, sold at a bargain price, or placed a conservation easement on their land to preserve it for future generations. None of this work would happen without willing landowners.

I have tried to name the conservation organization responsible for each of the relevant attractions. It is my hope that every time you find yourself someplace with an amazing view, a fantastic hiking trail, or a place to put a boat (or your feet) in the water, you'll take a moment to think about who is responsible for making this place available to the public. The vast majority of these places are free to access, so please consider making a donation to the organization of your choice to support their work. Every dollar makes a difference, and you'll get a wonderful feeling of ownership by being part of something larger than just one person. Also consider joining or volunteering at a conservation organization near your home.

Maine Coast Heritage Trust (mcht.org)

Downeast Coastal Conservancy (downeastcoastalconservancy.org)

Downeast Salmon Federation (mainesalmonrivers.org)

The Downeast Salmon Federation's unique facility in East Machias at night.

Frenchman Bay Conservancy (frenchmanbay.org)

Pleasant River Wildlife Foundation (pleasant-river.org)

The Nature Conservancy in Maine (nature.org/en-us/about-us/where-we
-work/united-states/maine/)

Maine Public Lands and State Parks (maine.gov/dacf/parks/index.shtml)

Moosehorn National Wildlife Refuge (fws.gov/refuge/moosehorn/)

Maine Coastal Islands National Wildlife Refuge (fws.gov/refuge/maine_
coastal_islands/)

Maine Island Trail Association (mita.org)

Camp!

R anging from full-service RV sites to glamping to unorganized car camping on public lands to backpacking options, there is something for anyone who would rather sleep outdoors than in a hotel.

Cobscook Bay State Park offers oceanfront camping.

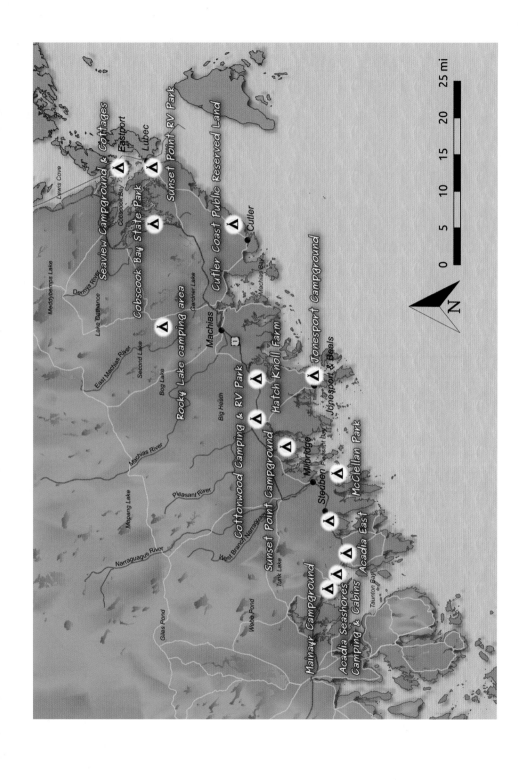

A glamping tent at Hatch Knoll Farm is a great choice if you didn't bring camping gear.

The Jonesport Campground, as seen from the public wharf, with RVs that seem to blend with lobster boats.

Waterfront camping at Maineayr Campground.

Lakeside campsites are free at Rocky Lake Public Reserved Land.

The author's "kitchen" while camping on the Cutler Coast Trail.

Acadia Seashores Camping and Cabins

2695 Route 1, Sullivan

Boasting nearly fifty sites, including tent and RV areas, this is a great place for a home base in the western part of the Down East region, perfect for those who want to spend time at Acadia National Park and also explore farther Down East. An RV is also available for nightly rental. Find information at acadiaseashorecamping.com.

Acadia East

574 Route 1, Gouldsboro

Sites at Acadia East can only be booked online. The campground itself is unattended. Customers with a reservation receive a reserved, named site and there is no need for on-site staff. There are six sites that are relatively close together, but still with a remote feel. There is no water or power, but there are bathrooms with a vault toilet. Find more information at acadiaeastcampground.com.

Donnell Pond Public Reserved Land

Various Locations

There are about twenty-five established campsites on the Donnell Pond Public Reserved Land, accessible from Route 1 and Route 182. Many of these sites are best reached by paddling Tunk Lake, Donnell Pond, or Spring River Lake. Most sites have a picnic table, a fire ring, and a privy nearby, but few other services. Sites are available on a first-come first-served basis. Find information at maine.gov/donnellpond.

Cottonwood Camping and RV Park

1140 Route 1, Columbia Falls

Catering mostly to RVs, Cottonwood Campground is a relatively new facility, so the work of clearing the land and establishing the sites is still evident. There are only a dozen or so campsites, so visitors will never feel overcrowded. A teepee is available for rent, as is a treehouse that sleeps up to four. Find information at cottonwood campingrvpark.com.

Mainayr Campground

321 Village Road, Steuben

There are more than thirty sites at this waterfront campground. Most sites can accommodate an RV of some size, and all are open to tenting. Water and electric are available at or near each site. There is a boat ramp and swimming area on Joy Cove, which nearly empties at low tide. Find information at maineayr.com.

Sunset Point Campground

24 Sunset Point Road, Harrington

On the shores of the saltwater portion of the Pleasant River, this campground offers twenty-one RV sites with water and electric and nine tenting sites with no utilities. There is a scenic shore trail around the property, a dock, and various low-key recreation options such as horseshoes, a basketball court, and a dog walk. Find information at sunsetpointcampground.com.

McClellan Park

Wyman Road, Milbridge

This campground is owned and operated by the town of Milbridge. You can find it about four miles down Wyman Road from its intersection with Route 1 in downtown Milbridge. There are ten sites available on a first-come, first-served basis. None of the sites has water or electric, but there is a bathhouse with running water, flush toilets, and a shower. All of the sites have a picnic table and firepit, and they are an easy walk to the shore, which is a stretch of bold, rocky coast with excellent views of several offshore islands. There is also a free day-use area with picnic tables and firepits (see page 78).

Hatch Knoll Farm

29 Hatch Knoll Road, Jonesboro

If you want to camp but didn't bring any gear, or you just want to sleep outside in a bit more comfort, Hatch Knoll Farm offers a glamping (short for "glamorous camping") site with a canvas tent on a wooden platform with a bed inside. The campsite is set in the woods, just off a wild blueberry field, and within earshot of the farm's herd of goats. Visitors can choose to take part in or observe the daily farm activities, which depend on the season. Traditional campsites are also available for setting up your own tent or small camper. There is no power, water, or RV dumping. Outhouses are nearby. Find information at hatchknollfarm.webs.com.

Jonesport Campground (aka Henry Point Campground)

Kelly Point Road, Jonesport

With about nine RV or tent sites, this small and relatively informal campground is big on views. It is sited on a point of land at the south tip of Jonesport with amazing views across Moosabec Reach toward Beals Island to the south and across Sawyer Cove to the north and west toward the municipal marina. You'll get lots of beauty and fishing village charm, but be forewarned that fishers start their days, and their diesel engines, early. Some sites have access to electric. Drinking water is available to be dispensed into your container from a central location, and there are porta potties but no showers or other bathroom facilities. There is no website or phone number, so treat this as a first-come, first-served campground.

Rocky Lake Camping Area

Diamond Match Road, Berry Township

This is really an unappreciated treasure of the area. The no-fee campground has two large gravel RV sites that are within view of and a very short walk from Rocky Lake. There are also two tenting sites, which require campers to carry their gear up to twenty-five yards or so from their parking spot, but the reward is a lakefront campsite—well worth the effort, in my opinion. There is an additional campsite farther from the lake where you make the last right turn to drive in to the lake. Since this is Public Reserved Land, dispersed camping is allowed anywhere on the property unless otherwise posted. Be aware, however, that if you aren't at an approved campsite like those described, open fires aren't permitted. At the campground there is a very shallow boat launch that probably won't work for most motorboats but could be used for canoes, kayaks, and Grand Laker canoes with motors, and a couple of places with some sand beach when the water level is high enough to reach it. By August in most years, the water level has dropped so that the beaches are high and dry. From the campground the view is open water, surrounded by uninterrupted forest. South Bay, which is the southern half of Rocky Lake, is virtually open water, but the northern half of the lake is much more interesting, with islands that are open to camping and access to the East Machias River. Find information at maine.gov/cgi-bin/online/doc/parksearch/details.pl?park_id=64.

Cutler Coast Public Reserved Land

Route 191, Cutler

There are two primary options for camping here. As Public Reserved Land, dispersed camping is allowed on the big section of the property that is north of Route 191. There are a couple of ways in, but the East Stream Road is the main access road. The second camping option is to backpack in to one of five established backcountry sites. See page 214 for more on the Cutler Coast.

Cobscook Bay State Park

40 South Edmunds Roads, Edmunds

Cobscook Bay State Park is the shining jewel of camping in this region. With more than one hundred to choose from, there are campsites for those who prioritize solitude, views, access to the ocean, or group sites. The park is a wonderful place to use as a base from which to hike or paddle the region, but you can easily park the car and spend a weekend or several days with your feet on the campfire ring watching the impressive tides come and go and digging your own clams from the shore. The nature trails are nice but don't really compare with the other hiking options in the area. Find information at maine.gov/cobscookbay.

Sunset Point RV Park

37 Sunset Road, Lubec

The easternmost campground in the United States has stunning views of Cobscook Bay and easy access to the village of Lubec. There are thirty RV sites and eight tent sites. The campground offers free use of their large pots and burners so you can cook up some lobsters, purchased right in the area. Find information at sunsetpointrvpark.com.

Seaview Campground and Cottages

16 Norwood Road, Eastport

Near the edge of the village of Eastport, right on Passamaquoddy Bay, facing Canada's Deer Island, Seaview Campground is a great home base for exploration of the eastern end of the region. There are more than sixty campsites and several complete cottages for rent. Wi-Fi throughout the campground, an on-site restaurant and store, a playground, and a pier complete this option for "civilized" camping. Find information at eastportmaine.com.

Maine Island Trail Association

Various Locations

The Maine Island Trail Association (MITA) works with a variety of landowners on islands and along the coast to provide camping and day-use sites for sea kayakers, sailors, and motorboaters. MITA works along the entire Maine coast, not just Down East. Their sites are free to use, but you must join MITA for a fee to access maps, descriptions of sites, and an app for phones or tablets. Find information at mita.org.

Downeast Salmon Federation Cabins

Various Locations

The Downeast Salmon Federation (DSF) has acquired a number of properties with cabins, which they have restored and make available for visitors to the region. The cabins are rustic, with no electricity, water, or sewers, and not all of them are easy to find. But the opportunity to stay right on a remote stretch of river in a cabin that has been preserved by a conservation organization makes this a special treat. Find contact information for DSF at mainesalmonrivers.org.

Eat!

Local Food

Local food has made an explosive comeback in the Bold Coast region. This area was once highly self-sufficient when it came to food. Most people had a garden, would eat a lot fish or game, or even keep a pig or cow over the summer to fill the freezer before winter. Over time that practice eroded, with readily available food shipped in so cheaply it wasn't worth the effort to grow or gather your own. In the early 2000s, the once underground health food buying clubs and small farmers' markets grew in popularity. This, in turn, provided the market to encourage many small-scale farmers to begin producing for the local people. Today most towns have a farmers' market of some kind, at least for the summer months, and some run year-round.

In addition to the scheduled markets described here, keep your eyes open for roadside stands all over the region. Small farms and even home gardeners may put out a box of cukes, tomatoes, squash, or whatever is growing faster than the farmer can eat or store it. These are usually paid in cash and on the honor system. You can't beat this option for supporting local agriculture.

Unless noted, the following businesses close for the cold season.

Darthia Farm Stand

51 Darthia Farm Road

Darthia Farm is an organic farm that uses horses to plow the fields and other jobs more commonly done with fossil fuel these days. The farm stand includes their own produce and flowers, locally made artisanal crafts, and a selection of fiber arts. Find information at darthiafarm.com.

Dyers Bay Farm

Dyers Bay Road, Steuben

This mom-and-pop farm stand is located at the farm, and visitors get an intimate look at the barn and some of the facilities around the farm just by driving in. They offer their own grass-fed meat, eggs, maple syrup, and a small selection of veggies. Look for the flag along Route 1 right at the beginning of Dyer's Bay Road.

Milbridge Farmers' Market

29 Main Street, Milbridge

This market is open from May to September on Saturday morning between 9 a.m. and noon. Local produce, meat, dairy, crafts, and live music are all on the agenda. Supplement the offerings of the market by taking advantage of the Incredible Edible

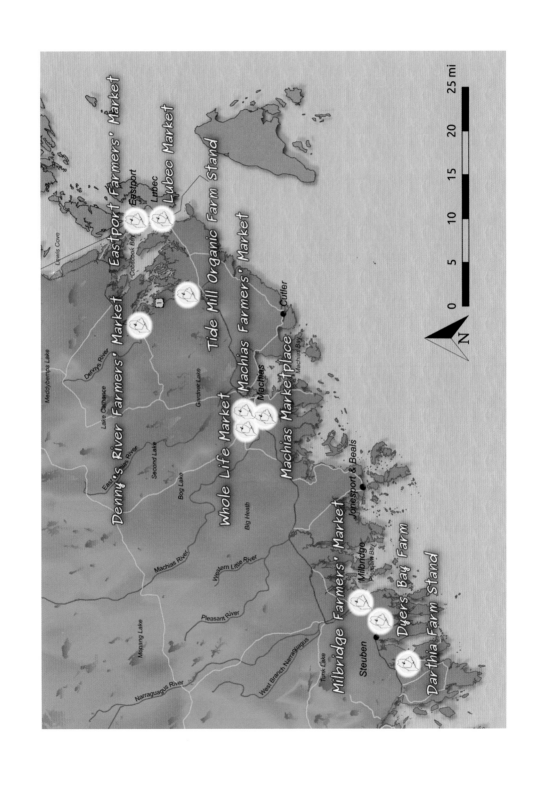

Milbridge free gardens scattered across town. The motto of the organizing group is "If it's ripe, pick it." Everything is free, but be sure to watch for a sign naming it as part of the program to avoid pilfering from someone's private garden. Find information at mainefarmersmarkets.org/market/milbridge-farmers-market.

Whole Life Market

4 Colonial Way, Machias

This is the only full-service health food store in the region. They offer a selection of local produce, meat, books, and arts, as well as the conventional categories you'd expect in a health food store. Vitamins, supplements, a wide variety of teas, alternative soft drinks, healthy pet food, and pre-ordered bulk items are all available. The Salt Water Cafe, which is inside the store, offers up healthy meals for lunch, often featuring local produce, and premade wraps and sandwiches anytime, as well as coffee and espresso drinks. Open all year. Find information at wholelifemarket.com.

Machias Marketplace

76 US Route 1, Machias

The Machias Marketplace is a new breed of farmers' market. At a traditional farmers' market, each farm sets up its own tent and the market runs like a flea market, with customers browsing the many stands and deciding, for example, which broccoli looks the greenest or which farmer looks the most authentic. It can be confusing for customers and a time-waster for busy farmers. At the Machias Marketplace, which is open two to three days per week depending on the season, farmers drop off preordered and à la carte goods the day before the market opens. Similar kinds of produce are placed together in the store, so a customer may have a couple of different broccolis to consider, but they are right next to each other. The Machias Marketplace also sells locally made jams, bread, sweets, preserves, milk, yogurt, kefir, cheese, and sometimes local seafood. It has been a huge success! Open all year. Find information at facebook.com/Machias-MarketPlace-364575833598049.

Machias Farmers' Market

On the dike along Route 1, Machias

The Machias Farmers' Market has a relatively thin selection of goods. Dependable vendors sell potted flowers and various produce that is not necessarily local. Maple syrup and other seasonal goods are sometimes available. The Machias Farmers' Market occupies the section of the dike closest to downtown Machias but is right next to the public area of the dike where anyone can sell anything, so it is often worth slowing down as you drive by to see whether anything catches your eye, be it veggies or some old tools being sold. The market is open Friday and Saturday from 9 a.m. to 1 p.m., from mid-May through October. People can sell goods on the dike any day. Find information at mainefarmersmarkets.org/market/machias -valley-farmers-market.

Lubec Market

On an empty lot on Water Street, Lubec (summer); inside Lubec Brewing Company (winter)

The Lubec Market is abuzz on Saturday morning when it is open. Usual hours are 9 a.m. to 11 a.m., from Memorial Day to October, and then 10 a.m. to 12 p.m. from November to Memorial Day on selected weeks. There are often up to fifteen vendors selling produce, meat, dairy, potted plants, artwork, and more. Live music is usually on hand as well. Find information at mainefarmersmarkets.org/market/ lubec-farmers-market.

Tide Mill Organic Farm Stand

Tide Mill Road, Edmunds

Tide Mill Organic Farm Stand sells their organic produce to stores up and down the Maine coast, but you can get it direct from the source on Saturday from 10 a.m. to 2 p.m., during the growing season. They offer their own organic raw milk, produce, various meats, eggs, and anything else the farm produces. Find information at tide millorganicfarm.com.

Denny's River Farmers' Market

15 King Street, Dennysville

The hours and day of this market are a bit of a moving target and may change during the course of a season, so check their Facebook page for up-to-date information. Locally made food, produce, meat, fiber arts, and crafts are all available here. Find information on Facebook at Denny's River Farmers' Market.

Eastport Farmers' Market

7 Washington Street, Eastport

The market is typically open on Saturday from 11 a.m. to 1 p.m., mid-June to mid-October. Selection varies but almost always includes a combination of produce, meat, dairy, herbs, artwork, and more. Find information at mainefarmersmarkets.org/ market/eastport-market-day.

Restaurants

On the surface, the restaurant choices in this region may look very homogenous, but look a little closer and you'll find some unique eateries that can keep you interested and well fed during your visit. If you want American food with a New England focus, you'll find that aplenty. The specialty is usually fried fish and/or fish chowder. Anyplace you go that offers these dishes is likely to do them well.

If you want to go beyond the typical American fare, there are quite a few options in the area, but they are dispersed all over the region, so do your research and plan ahead for your travels.

Vasquez Mexican Takeout

38 Main Street, Milbridge

Vasquez is a bit of a Down East phenomenon. From their roots cooking out of a converted RV for migrant laborers picking the blueberry crop, the Vasquez family has grown and invested in the business. They now have a permanent location on Route 1 in Milbridge with covered seating, though customers still order at a take-out window. At most mealtimes, expect a line, as locals and visitors alike call this the best Mexican food for many, many miles. All freshly cooked by family members, you can't really go wrong, so order the special or your favorite dish. The only drawback here is the prodigious quantity of Styrofoam that is wasted. Closes for the winter.

The Meadow's Takeout

1000 US Route 1, Steuben

Along Route 1 in Steuben, you'll find an understated takeout spot with a twist. The Meadow's specializes in Portuguese food with a decidedly homemade flair. The husband-and-wife team co-own and run the restaurant, and they take the quality of the food seriously, making all the marinades, mixes, and preparations by hand. If a *linguica* roll, *porco* dinner, or Portuguese fish cakes aren't your speed, they also serve the usual burgers with delicious hand-cut fries and a variety of other options. Closes for the winter.

Jo's World Famous Schnitzel Wagon

125 Dublin Street, Machias

The Schnitzel Wagon is just what it sounds like: an adorable wagon featuring authentic German schnitzel and brats. They also offer hand-cut french fries, deep-fried cheesecake, and other treats. Find more information at facebook.com/schnitzelwagon.

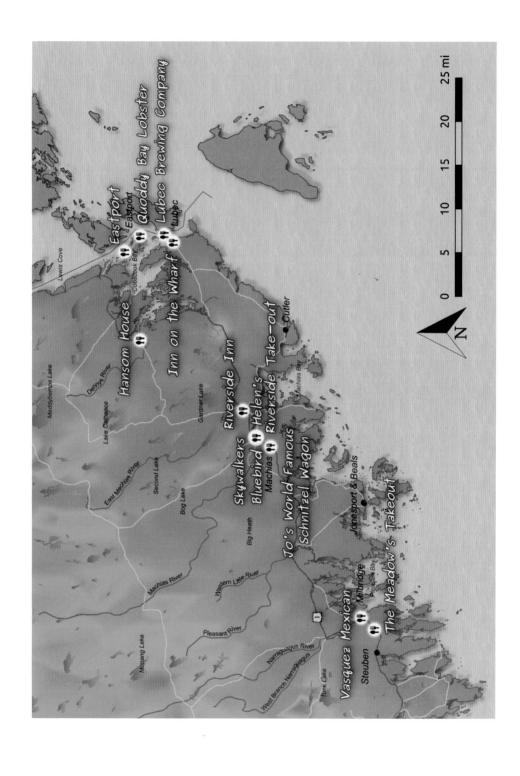

Helen's Restaurant

111 Main Street, Machias

and

Bluebird Ranch Family Restaurant

78 Main Street, Machias

I lumped these two popular eateries together because for most of the locals, there is a Coke/Pepsi aspect to choosing between them. If you sample the same dishes from the two, you'd be hard pressed to find a clear favorite on quality or taste. Nevertheless, most locals prefer one or the other and only reluctantly will agree to join a friend at the other. The big difference between them is atmosphere. Bluebird Ranch is pretty much as it has been for the fourteen years that I've been in the region. There is a diner-type room and a slightly more formal, though outdated, restaurant room. Helen's Restaurant burned down back in 2014, and the new building has a decidedly modern and slightly cold feel. The large windows offer a great view of the Machias River, or, on a warm day, you can sit outside on the deck watching gulls, eagles, and seals ply the water. On a cold day huddle close to the gas fireplace in the dining room. I will add that each restaurant has its specialty. I love the crab stew at the Bluebird, and Helen's pie is famous all over Maine and beyond.

The view from Helen's Restaurant overlooking the inner part of Machias Bay.

Skywalkers Bar and Grille

86 Main Street, Machias

Newly redecorated in rustic honky-tonk fashion, with a hand-carved map of the Machias River stretching the length of the bar, and corrugated aluminum on the walls, this is the perfect home for the Machias River Brewing Company. Enjoy a cocktail named after one of the Seven Deadly Sins or a beer brewed right on premises. The food menu tends toward Tex-Mex, but with lots of surprises and twists on the usual suspects. Frequent live music makes this the place to go for nightlife in Machias.

Riverside Take-Out

277 Main Street, Machias

On the way out of Machias headed toward Lubec and Eastport, you might want to stop in for a "Monster Haddock Burger" or their "420 Sampler." The menu options aren't necessarily different from most area takeouts, but you can't beat the size of the portions and their attention to the quality of their ingredients. Riverside has made moves recently to reduce waste and proudly proclaims their left-leaning politics with signs, posters, and donations to liberal causes. They are also very dog-friendly. Find them on Facebook at Riverside Take-Out or look for the rainbow flag.

Riverside Inn

622 Main Street, East Machias

Not to be confused with Riverside Take-Out or the variety of Riverside this or Riverview that, this is the only upscale dining option on my list. Ownership is in flux at the time of this writing, so I can't predict what changes will come, but the history of the Riverside is having small, intimate dinner service in the $30 to $50 range, with a view of the East Machias River. They also have a patio that is often open for afternoon drinks during the summer. The Inn has a number of rooms for overnight stays, including one suite with a deck overlooking the river.

Lubec Brewing Company

41 South Water Street, Lubec

When the Lubec Brewing Company opened several years ago, it filled a hole in the local economy that no one even knew was there. With excellent raw and unfiltered hand-crafted beer made with organic barley (at the easternmost brewery in the United States, I might add) and a menu of sourdough pizzas, fresh local soups, salads, and whatever else the cooks can find, along with live music several nights a week, this is one place not to miss if you are in Lubec in the evening. The friendly staff and owners have created the perfect atmosphere where locals and visitors mingle and even share tables as they watch locally popular musicians do their thing. Find information on Facebook at Lubec Brewing Company.

Hansom House

45 Main Street, Dennysville

After a full career owning a busy nightclub on Long Island, the "retired" owners of the Hansom House do not go out of their way to attract attention to their business. You kind of have to know about this place to know about it, if you know what I mean. Labeled "the most absurd bar in the world," the Hansom House needs to be seen to be believed. My description will inevitably fall short, so I'll just say that the atmosphere is warm and cozy, with plenty of distractions to keep you busy while you enjoy some live music or sit at the community table and meet someone new. (Hint—it's unlike anywhere you've ever been and mind-blowing that it is here.) The owners keep an excellent selection of wines on hand, or cocktails to order, and the food menu tends toward the simple. One year the only options were soup or a burger from the local organic farm, and it was all delicious. There is no online presence, but you can find pictures and reviews on Yelp or TripAdvisor.

Inn on the Wharf

69 Johnson Street, Lubec

The view from the restaurant at the Inn on the Wharf is worth choosing over many other typical American restaurants. Most tables have excellent views of the bay, and in

The Inn on the Wharf offers a restaurant, inn, whale watching, and bicycle rentals, and it has a store featuring local art.

warm weather there is deck seating available. Despite serving a fairly standard menu for the region, every dish is prepared with care and high-quality ingredients. The Inn on the Wharf also offers lodging, whale watching, a local arts shop, and other services (see page 111 for whale-watching information).

Quoddy Bay Lobster

Sea Street, Eastport

One of many places in the region to pick up a lobster roll or other local seafood favorites, Quoddy Bay Lobster generally stands above the rest for the size of the lobster roll (plus a whole claw on top!) and the view out to Passamaquoddy Bay from the picnic tables. Order from the window and enjoy the fresh breeze while you wait. Find information on Facebook at Quoddy Bay Lobster.

There are many restaurants to explore in Eastport, so I'll just recommend that you go and see for yourself. From fine dining and excellent baked goods to pub food and fried fish on the waterfront, there is something for everyone.

There is nothing like a lobster roll at the edge of the ocean.

Shopping

Shopping is no one's main reason for visiting the Down East region. Aside from food and cheap junk from the many chain discount stores, shopping is limited to a few key locations. Oddly, there is not a single clothing store in the entire region. A few stores have added a selection of work clothes or a few T-shirts sporting the name of a local town or lake. The hardware stores in some towns have an excellent variety of housewares, hunting and camping gear, pet supplies, and other departments outside the core home-repair options.

The shopping that is available other than the basic necessities already described tends toward locally made art that reflects the natural world. Pottery, paintings, and photography all evoke the rugged coast, deep forest, and summertime abundance that is Down East. Shopping may not draw someone to the region, but while you're here, take some time to check out the local art.

Columbia Falls General.

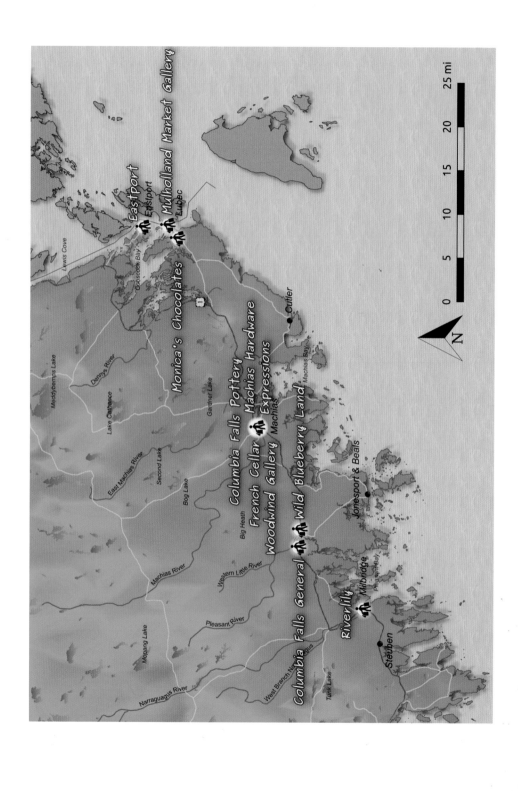

Wild Blueberry Land in Columbia Falls.

Riverlily in Milbridge.

Eastport has the most varied shopping in the region.

Riverlily

14 Main St., Milbridge

This is a shop that is unique in the Down East region but would be somewhat familiar to people who know Martha's Vineyard, Cape Cod, or even Bar Harbor. Here you'll find a busy assortment of beautiful, often nautical-themed decorations; handy and inventive kitchen gadgets; a carefully selected bookshelf with just the right combination of cookbooks, memoirs, and nature appreciation titles; greeting cards; and locally crafted jewelry. Riverlily definitely qualifies as the most "posh" shop outside Eastport.

Columbia Falls General

150 Main St., Columbia Falls

This shop opened in 2018 in a historic old building in the center of Columbia Falls, right next to the Ruggles House Museum and the Wreaths Across America Museum. The store carries an eclectic selection of food, locally made art, leather goods, and a few other items. The store itself is beautifully restored.

Wild Blueberry Land

1067 US Route 1, Columbia Falls

The big blue dome of Wild Blueberry Land is a regional landmark that is a draw for tourists and visitors. They offer handmade pies made with blueberries grown and harvested by the owners, as well as an assortment of blueberry-themed gifts and trinkets.

Columbia Falls Pottery

4 Main St., Machias

Despite the name, this shop is now located in downtown Machias. Pottery and statues crafted by the co-owners, April and Dana, feature local scenes, flowers, and other nature motifs. Their designs have been shipped all over the world, so you may see some familiar patterns at the shop.

The French Cellar

4 Colonial Way, Machias

The French Cellar is owned and operated by a chef who retired to the area and couldn't find anyplace to buy good wine and cheese. What else could she do but open the only wine and cheese shop in the region? They also have an excellent selection of craft beer. Wine tastings, from time to time, are a social event worth catching.

Expressions Arts and Gifts

11 Main St., Machias

Expressions is an art gallery that features works by local artists in all kinds of media, from oil paintings on canvas to photography to jewelry. You're likely to find some unique offerings here, since many of the artists' work isn't sold anywhere else and may reflect a lifetime of creating without a commercial outlet, until Expressions arrived in 2015.

Woodwind Custom Framers & Gallery

23 Main St., Machias

Woodwind Gallery is known for its collection of local paintings that often feature the natural world. They also sell art and framing supplies and do custom framing. The owner, Holly, is also an avid hiker who can give recommendations.

Machias Hardware

26 Main St., Machias

The hardware portion of this store was discontinued a few years ago, but the locally popular home goods and health food portion of the store remains. Known for the charming old feel, this is a place to find quality homesteading or kitchen supplies and unusual health foods. The owner, Michael, is a local history expert who can tell you about the region.

Monica's Chocolates

100 Route 189, Lubec

Monica's chocolates are divine and worth the stop. The shop is split between gourmet chocolates of all kinds and goods imported from Peru, where Monica grew up. Perfect as a gift for those back home or a treat for the adventurers in far eastern Maine.

Mulholland Market Gallery

50 Water St., Lubec

The gallery specializes in locally made art, including photography, paintings, fiber arts, sculpture, and other media.

Eastport

Rather than identify a specific art gallery or shop to check out in Eastport, I recommend that you spend some time walking the most lively downtown in the region. In the past decade or so, a plethora of new art galleries, cafes, restaurants, and bars have sprung up. The compact commercial district on Water Street is perfect for an afternoon exploration. Don't miss Raye's Mustard, which is at 83 Washington Street on the main route into the village of Eastport with tours of the last stone-ground mustard mill in the United States at posted times throughout the day.

Culture

Although the region doesn't have a lot of the entertainment that city people take for granted, there is actually quite a large selection of things to do. Here are a few ideas to get you started.

Music

Nightlife

Various Locations

Bars in the region offer a taste of nightlife with happy hours, open mic events, karaoke, and, especially, live music. Machias, Lubec, and Eastport each have a few options to choose from.

Summerkeys

Lubec

This is a very popular summertime series of concerts and arts workshops that take place all through the summer. Find information at summerkeys.com.

Machias Bay Chamber Concerts

Machias

A summertime series of chamber, classical, jazz, and orchestral music held in the beautiful Centre Street Congregational Church. Find information at machiasbay chamberconcerts.com.

Black Fly Ball

Machias

A one-night music festival in October featuring a variety of musical genres held on a series of stages in the Machias Valley Grange Hall and Bad Little Falls Park among the waterfalls. See page 66 for more information.

Machias Ukuleles

Various Locations

The Machias Ukuleles are one of the most popular and fun local music groups, featuring a loose-knit group of up to thirty ukulele players on stage together playing classic songs that you know by heart and will sing along to. Find information at facebook.com/machiasukuleles.

Contra Dances

Various Locations

Contra dances are held all around the region, typically at grange halls, churches, or the University of Maine at Machias. If contra dancing is something you love, or just want to see, try asking around at any of the local food vendors listed beginning on page 273. Local food and local music often go hand-in-hand.

Washington County Children's Chorus

Various Locations

The Children's Chorus plays a series of concerts across the region throughout the year. They also travel abroad to expose the young singers to other cultures and to bring some of Down East Maine to other cultures. Find information at washington countychildrenschorus.net.

Passamaquoddy Bay Symphony Orchestra

Various Locations

The orchestra plays a series of concerts around the region several times each year. Find information at facebook.com/pbsorchestra.

Balsam Valley Amphitheater

Columbia Falls

This is the only large music venue in the area that attracts touring bands for concerts throughout the summer. Find information at balsamvalley.com.

Milbridge Theater Outdoor Stage

There are events all summer long at the outdoor stage in the center of Milbridge. Find information at milbridgetheater.org.

Classes, Workshops, and Performances

Eagle Hill Institute

Steuben

A beautiful, forested campus that specializes in week-long in-depth science seminars on topics like salt-marsh ecosystems, fungi, lichens, spiders, and more. They also offer a selection of arts and humanities courses that are somehow tied to the natural world. Find information at eaglehill.us.

University of Maine at Machias

The university hosts a number of lectures, workshops, and other events throughout the year. The fitness center is the only full-service gym in the region, with an indoor swimming pool, weights, group exercise classes, stretching room, yoga classes, and more. Find information at machias.edu.

Cobscook Community Learning Center

Trescott Township

The Cobscook Community Learning Center has a busy schedule of continuing education and workshops, including topics like pottery, writing, photography, and more. The campus is also the home of a long-running Monday Night Music Circle that is open to everyone. Find information at thecclc.org.

Eastport Arts Center

Eastport

The Eastport Arts Center is the home of a variety of visual and performing arts groups that offer events throughout the year, including theater, film, music, art, and more. They have yoga classes and other educational workshops, too. Find information at eastportartscenter.org.

Artsipelago

Billed as "a cultural guide to the international Passamaquoddy region of Maine and New Brunswick," *Artsipelago* creates paper maps and online resources that list cultural and arts events in far eastern Maine and nearby New Brunswick. *Artsipelago* is published by the Tides Institute, a nonprofit promoting the arts in Eastport and the surrounding region. Find information at artsipelago.net and tidesinstitute.org.

Yoga, Tai Chi, and More Classes

Various Locations

There is yoga in just about every town, so look for local posters on bulletin boards. One school that holds yoga and tai chi classes in several towns is Bold Coast Yoga. They also offer yoga-teacher training. Find information at facebook.com/boldcoastyoga.

Museums

The Burnham Tavern

Machias

The Burnham Tavern is the place where Machias townspeople debated whether to revolt against the British in what became the first naval battle of the American Revolution (see Margaretta Days, page 54). The museum is owned and operated by the Daughters of the American Revolution–Hannah Weston chapter.

McCurdy's Smokehouse

Lubec

This collection of historical buildings in Lubec pays homage to the impact that the sardine industry had on the area.

McCurdy's Smokehouse is right in the middle of Lubec.

Beyond *Beyond Acadia*

While I feel like this area has everything someone would want for a week's or a month's or a year's stay, the following pages cover some ideas for ways to extend your vacation near the Bold Coast region.

Liberty Point, at the southern tip of Campobello Island.

Campobello Island

A full exploration of Campobello Island is outside the scope of this book, but visitors to the region should at least know that the option is available to cross the border into Canada and check out this quaint island village that is mostly known for Roosevelt Campobello International Park, which is jointly run by the US Park Service and Parks Canada. The focal point of the park is the cottage owned by Franklin Delano and Eleanor Roosevelt, now a museum. The park also has extensive gravel carriage roads open to bicycles and cars, as well as miles of hiking trails. Admission to the park is free. Finback and minke whales, along with porpoises, are often seen right from the shore at Liberty Point, which is the southern tip of the island. At the northern tip is East Quoddy Head Light, which is one of the most photographed and iconic lighthouses in New Brunswick. The lighthouse itself is only accessible for a few hours surrounding low tide and requires a walk across shifting and seaweed-covered rocks. The island is also rumored to harbor a wonderful treasure trove of worn sea glass on certain beaches at certain times of year.

Campobello Island is only connected to the US mainland by the Roosevelt International Bridge, but ferries connect the island with other Canadian islands in Passamaquoddy Bay and with the mainland. Note that a passport or passport card is required to enter Canada and to return to the United States. Find information at visitcampobello.com and fdr.net.

Acadia National Park

Acadia National Park is the most visited site in Maine, with upward of four million visitors in 2018. There is good reason for it to be this popular. The stunning beauty of the many mountains, streams, coves, rocky headlands, and even the carefully designed carriage trails are well worth the frustration of traffic and difficulty even parking at a trailhead. The campgrounds are well designed and inviting. The village of Bar Harbor has all the amenities you'd need, with plenty of shopping, dining, lodging, and services like banks and a hospital. Bar Harbor is also the most crowded town on Mount Desert Island, which is home to most of Acadia National Park.

To avoid many of the crowds, follow one or more of these recommendations: (1) Explore the Schoodic Peninsula, which is just across Frenchman Bay but takes more than an hour to drive to from Bar Harbor. A new campground recently opened, with hiking trails, carriage roads, and plenty of amazing views on the loop road. (2) Spend more time on "the quiet side," which is the western half of Mount Desert Island. Trails are just a little less crowded, traffic is a little less frenetic, and the quaint villages, like Southwest Harbor and Somesville, are a little less T-shirt shoppy. (3) Make your way to Isle au Haut, a large island that is part of the national park. You can take a ferry to the island to hike the trails for the day, or make reservations in advance for one of the remote campsites. Bar Harbor, the gateway to Acadia National Park, is less than two hours from Machias, and less than an hour from the western edge of the region covered by this book. Find information at nps.gov/acad/index.htm.

Baxter State Park

Mount Katahdin, Maine's highest peak and the northern terminus of the Appalachian Trail, is the primary attraction of Baxter State Park, but not the only one by any

The hike up Katahdin is a pilgrimage that most Mainers make at least once.

means. Thousands of people make the pilgrimage to the summit of the peak every summer, and it is an accomplishment to be proud of. There are, however, many other trails and remote campgrounds where you can really get away from it all without the pressure of peak-bagging. The drive to the park alone is an adventure. Baxter State Park is just under three hours from Machias. Find information at baxterstatepark.org.

Katahdin Woods and Waters National Monument

Founded in 2017, this new addition to the National Park Service's roster brings big attention to Maine's North Woods. The monument is some eighty-three thousand acres of forest, rivers, streams, lakes, and bogs, tucked up against Baxter State Park's eastern border. Camping is available for free on a first-come, first-served basis and the loop road is open for vehicles and mountain bikes. A variety of hiking trails are already available, with plans for more in the near future. It is a little more than three hours' drive to the monument entrance from Machias. Find more information at nps.gov/kaww/index.htm.

Fundy National Park

About a three hours' drive from Machias or Lubec is the jewel in the crown of the Bay of Fundy. The coast at Fundy National Park, in New Brunswick, has the highest tides in the world, with excellent sea kayaking and beach exploration. There are campgrounds, hiking and biking trails, and plenty of opportunities to learn about the ecology and cultural history of the region. Find more information at pc.gc.ca/en/pn-np/nb/fundy.

Acknowledgments

This book would not have been possible without my wife, Rebecca Baxter Bard. She encouraged me through years of knowing that this book was possible and was beside me at every step.

Of course, a book like this requires the help of many people. First and foremost, thank you, Bill Kitchen and Cat Cannon, for your friendship and hospitality as I made countless trips from Portland to Machias to do my research, and for your great advice and enthusiasm for the project.

My amazing former colleagues at the many conservation groups in Washington County deserve special recognition as well. Some provided input directly for this book, and all were tireless partners in creating the network of hiking trails that makes it possible for people to truly see and appreciate the spectacular beauty of the region. A partial list of these special people include Marty Anderson, Tom Boutureira, Alan Brooks, Ben Emory, Melissa Lee, Anne Marshall, John Marshall, Tom Schaeffer, Dwayne Shaw, Jacob Van de Sande, Patrick Watson, Deirdre Whitehead, Kyle Winslow, everyone else involved with Cobscook Trails, and the entire board of directors and staff of Downeast Coastal Conservancy. Washington County is truly lucky to have attracted this dream team to protect these remarkable natural treasures.

Thank you also to the many owners, managers, and staff of the businesses listed in this book, who were willing to talk with me about their business.

Apologies in advance for anyone I neglected to mention here. See you out on the trail!

Index

Sunrise Canoe and Kayak, 158, 160; Water's Edge Canoe & Kayak Rentals, 160

H
Hancock, 74, 94, 159
Hansom House, 281
Harrington, 35, 268
Helen's Restaurant, 44, 45, 144, 206, 279
hiking, 4, 37, 66, 76, 82, 124, 156–57, 161–260, 297; Birch Point Trail, 186–89; Black Mountain, 176–78; Caribou Mountain Loop, 178–82; Cobscook Bay State Park, 250–51; Cutler Coast Unit, 214–20; Eastern Knubble, 213–14; Great Wass Island Preserve, 197–201; Hamilton Cove, 227–30; Hollingsworth Trail, 183–86; Horan Head, 241–46; Ingersoll Point, 191–93; Klondike Mountain, 246–48; Long Point Preserve, 208–10; Machias River Preserve, 201–5; Middle River Park, 206–8; Moose Cove, 224–27; Moosehorn Wilderness Trail, 237–41; Mowry Beach, 248–50; Norse Pond, 220–24; Pigeon Hill, 189–91; Pleasant River Community Forest Trails, 193–96; Quoddy Head State Park, 230–33; Reversing Falls, 251–53; Schoodic Mountain, 175; Shackford Head, 258–60; Sipayik Trail, 255–57; Sipp Bay Preserve, 253–55; Timberdoodle Trail, 236–37; Tunk Mountain, 172–75
Hollingsworth Trail, 107, 183–86, 190
horseback riding, 122
hunting, 9, 23, 36, 37–38, 62, 64, 66, 159, 166, 283

I
Ice Age Trail, 2, 103–4
Independence Day, 60–62, 92

Ingersoll Point, 97, 191–93
Inn on the Wharf, 111, 160, 281–82

J
Jasper Beach, 80–81, 99, 109, 129
Jonesboro, 9, 95, 98, 122, 269
Jonesport, 10, 39, 43, 46, 61, 88, 95, 96, 197, 265, 269
Jo's World Famous Schnitzel Wagon, 277

K
Katahdin, 172, 174, 297–98
Klondike Mountain, 246–48

L
"Leave No Trace," 169
lighthouse, 46, 105–10; East Quoddy Head Light, 296; Libby Island Light, 109; Little River Light, 109; Lubec Channel Light, 91, 110, 248; Machias Seal Island Lighthouse, 219; Moose Peak Light, 108; Mulholland Light, 110; Narraguagus Light, 107; Nash Island Light, 107; Petit Manan Light, 107; Southwest Head Lighthouse, 219; West Quoddy Head Light, 82, 109–10, 230
light pollution, 5
lobster, 10, 11, 14–15, 46, 50, 61, 71, 99, 100, 108, 270, 282
logging, 9, 11
Long Cove Rest Area, 84, 103
Long Point Preserve, 208–10
Lost Fishermen's Memorial, 91
Lubec, 10, 29, 34, 39, 48–49, 60, 68, 82, 90–91, 99–101, 104, 110, 111, 114, 119, 123, 160, 211, 227, 229, 230, 234, 241, 246, 248, 260, 270, 288, 290, 294
Lubec Brewing Company, 280–81
Lubec Market, 276

Passamaquoddy Bay Symphony
  Orchestra, 291
Patrick Lake, 89
Penobscot (tribe), 4, 9
Pigeon Hill, 183, 189–91
Pinkham Bay Bridge, 86
Pleasant Bay, 183–96
Pleasant Point Reservation, 9, 62, 101,
  255
Pleasant River, 86, 87, 97, 158, 268
Pleasant River Community Forest Trails,
  193–96
Prospect Harbor, 86
Puckerbrush Primitive Gathering, 62
puffin, 31–33, 52, 54, 107

Q
Quoddy Bay Lobster, 68, 282
Quoddy Head State Park, 29, 48, 82, 101,
  109, 110, 118, 135, 211, 230–33

R
restaurants, 277–82
Reversing Falls, 82, 148, 251–53
Reynold's Marsh Overlook, 89–90, 156,
  157
Riverlily, 286
Riverside Inn, 280
Riverside Take-Out, 280
Rocky Lake, 119, 122, 135, 155, 266,
  269–70
Roque Bluffs State Park, 81–82, 125,
  128–29, 142
Ruggles House Museum Christmas Tea,
  71
running, 60, 61, 123–24

S
salmon, 26, 52, 60, 67, 77, 86, 88, 195,
  258, 260

scenic drive, 94–102; Centerville Road
  to Station Road, 98; Eastport/Sipayik
  on Route 190, 101–2; East Side Road
  to Basin Road, 97–98; Port Road/
  Route 192, 98–99; Route 187, 95–97;
  Route 191 through Cutler, 99–101
Schoodic Beach, 76, 125–27, 175, 178,
  181
Schoodic Mountain, 76, 125, 170, 175,
  178, 181, 182
Shackford Head State Park, 92–93, 102,
  135, 234, 258–60
shopping, 283–88
shorebirds, 33–35, 91
Sipayik, 62, 101–2, 120
Sipayik Indian Days, 62
Sipayik Trail, 101, 120, 255–57
Sipp Bay, 91, 234, 236, 253–55
Skywalkers Bar and Grille, 280
Smelt Fry & World Fish Migrations Day,
  52
spring, 7, 48, 52–55
Steuben, 35, 41, 86, 268, 273, 277, 292
summer, 7, 9, 31, 33, 56–63, 125, 129,
  152, 214
Summerkeys, 290
Sunrise Trail. *See* Down East Sunrise Trail
swimming, 125–30, 183, 252; Gardner
  Lake Dam, 130; Jasper Beach, 129;
  Machias River Heritage Trail, 128,
  204; Roque Bluffs State Park, 81, 82,
  128–29; Schoodic Beach, 76, 125–27,
  175; Tunk Lake, 127

T
tick, 18–19, 21, 25–26, 166
Tidal Falls Preserve, 74, 76, 82
Tide Mill Organic Farm Stand, 276
Tunk Lake, 94, 127, 172, 181, 268
Tunk Mountain, 94, 125, 170, 172–75, 182

U

About the Author

For fifteen years **Rich Bard** has been exploring and experiencing the best that the far reaches of the Maine coast has to offer by every means possible: on foot, snowshoes, and skis; by boat, kayak, and canoe; by snowmobile, ATV, pickup truck, and even small airplane. As a wildlife biologist with the Maine Department of Inland Fisheries and Wildlife for more than a decade, his territory included all of the Bold Coast and surrounding areas, and his work fostered a deep connection with the wild places of the region known as Down East Maine.

Rich is the executive director of Scarborough Land Trust and lives in Portland, Maine, where he loves to hike, bike, and search out the secret sweet spots with his wife Rebecca and son Max. He also loves to visit with his stepdaughter Zoe and her two children.